THE EMERGENCE OF ISLAM:

THE EMERGENCE OF ISLAM:

Prophecy, Imamate, and Messianism in Perspective

MOSTAFA VAZIRI, PH.D.

Visiting Scholar
Center for Middle Eastern Studies
University of California, Berkeley
and Political Science lecturer at
California State University-Hayward

BP
192.4
.V38
1991

PARAGON HOUSE
New York

First edition, 1992
Published in the United States by
Paragon House
90 Fifth Avenue
New York, N.Y. 10011

Library of Congress Cataloging-in-Publication Data
Vaziri, Mostafa, 1956–
    The emergence of Islam : prophecy, imamate, and messianism in
  perspective / Mostafa Vaziri. — 1st ed.
      p.   cm.
  Includes bibliographical references and index.
  ISBN 1-55778-451-5
  1. Shī'ah—History. I. Title.
BP192.4V38   1991
297'.82'09—dc20   91-2999
                                     CIP

Manufactured in the United States of America
10 9 8 7 6 5 4 3 2 1

This book is dedicated to the courageous and innocent children in the Intifada movement.

Contents

Contents

Acknowledgments

I wish I could name all the individuals who contributed to the writing of this book and to whom I am indebted in one way or another. Above all, I must recognize the scholarly and practical suggestions and criticisms of Professor Michael G. Morony of UCLA, who patiently read and reread the various drafts and the completed manuscript. I am grateful to him not only for guiding me to think like a scholar but also for having encouraged me to think like a sensitive human being. Special thanks are also due to Professor Ira Lapidus, who offered me assistance and introduced me to a number of important sources and ideas. My thanks as well to Professors William Brinner, Richard Bulliet, and Michael Stone, who drew my attention to important points.

It is my pleasant duty to further express profound thanks to Dr. Laurance Michalak and Mr. Robert Barde, who granted me the opportunity to receive the support of the Center for Middle Eastern Studies at the University of California at Berkeley.

Many of the ideas developed in the course of this text reflect the thoughtful contributions of my longtime friend Asghar Feizi, whose critical mind searches out vivid answers. I must also thank him for listening to my repeated, extensive, and ongoing discussions of the subject of this book.

My many thanks also go to Evelyn Fazio, the executive editor of Paragon House who patiently and soundly made helpful suggestions to make this manuscript more consistent. I am, too, indebted beyond words to the generation of young intellectuals, scholars, and graduate students whose enthusiastic and intense discussion on the subject of Islam have been a learning process for me.

Finally, I would like to recognize those who offered their help and

Acknowledgments

expertise, among them my close friend Murle Mordy, Ramona Heiber, Petra Greiner, and Steve Grey.

It is important to note that I am solely responsible for the content and the shortcomings of this book.

—Berkeley, California, 1990

The Early Islamic Period (610-874)

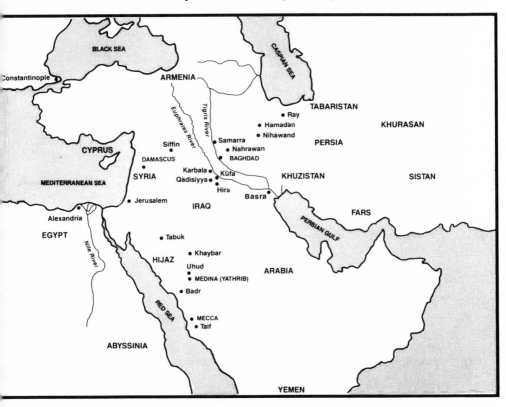

Preface

My interest in scrutinizing early Islamic episodes—the prophecy of Muhammad and the Shi'i development of a religious consciousness—began in my early youth in Iran and grew during my studies abroad, especially during my doctoral work in Paris in the early 1980s. What convinced me to pursue this research was my realization that Iranian beliefs that there is one God and that Muhammad is His messenger, that the holy infallible Imams are appointed by God to lead humanity, and that the twelfth Imam remains in occultation can be explained as phenomena rooted in Iran's cultural history and social consciousness.

These people only believe what other people believe. This may be so spontaneous that nothing ever causes them to question the foundation of the faith they have inherited from their ancestors. Further reinforcement of this faith is provided by social surroundings, traditions, and ceremonies such as religious meetings, songs (reading of the Koran or *rawda* [a mulla's retelling a religious event by singing]), and mourning for the past Imams—particularly Imam Husayn.

My curiosity about some of these religious beliefs became stronger as my understanding of what I read in the written history of Islam differed from what I had been exposed to in an orally transmitted Islamic culture. This discrepancy captured my attention, and eventually I decided to write this book as a means of reexamining old religious beliefs based on uncorroborated historical anecdotes handed down by the clergy. My aim was to investigate the established faith and contrast it with various ideas that reflect contradictory versions of Islamic religious documents. My intent is not to reject basic Islamic dogma but simply to replace old perspective with a new, critical approach.

Another reason for pursuing this project is that, while there have been fragmented critical studies of early Islam—particularly of the life of

Preface

Muhammad—there have been few such studies by Muslim-born scholars specifically on Shi'ism, early Islam, or a combination of the two. Many Islamic studies by Christian and Jewish scholars have been rejected by Muslim scholars as well as by those who are more sympathetic simply because they were not written by Muslims. Some of these scholars have been automatically identified with colonialism, Zionism, Westernism, or communism, each of which (according to the *ulama*) is shallow and/or carries an anti-Islamic bias. Also, there unfortunately have been few studies of the origins of Islam and Shi'ism by Muslim-born scholars interested in genuine self-examination rather than polemics.

Recently, Islam (and Shi'ism in particular) has begun to play an increasingly important role in the sociopolitical development of the Middle East; at the same time its political radicalism, with its antiforeign rhetoric, has obscured a set philosophical vision of the world. So far, any attempt to criticize this vision or the pronouncements and the viewpoint inherent in fundamentalist Shi'i interpretations has met a stone wall of religious defiance.

Any critical study of an established faith is likely to be treated with disdain precisely because the author is quickly embroiled in controversy with the psychospirituality of his fellow men, whose profound faith in divinity has been formed in a defined culture. At the same time, construction of a new paradigm to study the foundation of Islamic ideas requires a method of comparing the old perspective with the new. The angle of approach needed here is through historical sources, on the basis of which knowledgeable readers are able to make thoughtful comparisons that reflect their own level of knowledge and faith. This study is also intended to promote openness rather than opposition, awareness rather than polemics in the arena of Islamic scholarship.

I consider it necessary to survey the episodes of early Islam and the development of messianism in Shi'ism both because the Islamic masses are heavily influenced by the romantic vision of the past transmitted orally by the clergy and because the influences exerted by new scientific theories and modern education, by various interest groups, and by the changes brought about in the socioeconomic infrastructure of the local and world communities cannot be ignored simply for religious reasons. All of these things affect our everyday life, but the traditional approach continues to look unrealistically to the past for solutions to today's problems. It is crucial to scrutinize the oral tradition to detach it from romanticised notions and safely relate it to a new social understanding—particularly in the case of Shi'i Islam, which has been bound together with epics.

I must of course admit that a troubling feeling results from scrutinizing the faith and religious ideas of my own society. This is the most difficult aspect of my quest for transition through the trends of religious thought, but I am certain that a transition revolutionizing existing Islamic religiohistoric ideas is inevitable. In the past, such transitions have always worked against the powerful opposing forces of religious beliefs, but the reality and the indivisible forces of man's wisdom eventually determine the move toward new truth.

Introduction

Scholars have used various models for studying Islam but have always faced the danger that their work would be disputed—not on its merits but because of the inherent contradictions between the religious subject matter and the scholars' own value system. Pioneering orientalists provided a general structure of inquiry and valuable knowledge for subsequent scholars. Though as Edward Said suggests in his book *Orientalism* the methodology and evaluation of the many orientalists has to be inspected by freeing their studies from the western hostility toward Islam. Studies of Islamic theology, Sufism, and mysticism required the high level of technical precision that such authors as Louis Massignon, Reynold A. Nicholson, Ignaz Goldziher, and Henry Corbin provided. Intelligent studies of Muhammad include those by such great scholars as the Scottish Episcopalian W. M. Watt; the French sociologist and Islamicist Maxime Rodinson; the Englishman Sir Hamilton Gibb and other earlier orientalists whose work continues to have value; the Swede Tor Andrae; the Belgian Jesuit Henri Lammens; and the Italian prince Leone Caetani. Their work met criticism—again, not because of serious flaws in their remarkable accomplishments but because of inevitable disagreement and competition among the scholars themselves and because scholarly works must contend with the social and political consciousness of readers, for whom the period in which they live has a profound influence on their minds, their literary interests, and their morality.[1] Nor have scholars themselves been immune to the effects of ideology on their point of view.

---

[1] See J. Benda, "The Betrayal of the Intellectuals," *History of Western Civilization*, p. 82.

Introduction

Nevertheless, given constant change in political and social attitudes, new attempts should be made to bring fresh light to basic information, but (and more important) in terms of the emerging ideas, feelings, and attitudes of a new generation. Islam was systematically caricatured and attacked by medieval Christian polemicists—an enterprise spurred by many reactionary elements.[2] During the colonial period polemicists were more conciliatory, since achieving and maintaining domination over Islamic societies was the primary goal. Modern scholarship has tried to move away from religious or national bias and has attempted to engage in more objective research on Islam. The central deficiency in current academic research is its exclusiveness and the lack of impact of such works on learning and mass psychology.

Many Islamic traditions were recorded by early Muslim historians and many more were produced and recorded by subsequent generations of *ulama* in Arabic and Persian. These were commonly taken at face value by many traditional orientalists who read Persian or Arabic. Often, significant contradictions between the written material (which in turn contained many contradictory versions, especially in Islamic history) and the popular oral version have been ignored by such scholars.

My intention here is not to restudy in depth Islamic issues on which technical and detailed studies have already been undertaken by eminent orientalists and Muslim scholars; rather, I mean to fill in the gaps by presenting an argument based on early written history about the prophecy of Muhammad, the emergence of Shi'ism, and the occultation of the twelfth Imam, with the aim of systematically rectifying, adjusting, and (when necessary) confronting the unspecific and unwarranted religious versions the common folk know through oral transmission, notably in Shi'i Iranian society. I also attempt (both from the popular point of view and in light of the Western scholarly spectrum) to study certain injunctions, narratives, ideas, and events related to the prophecy of Muhammad and of the Shi'i Imams that people have taught their children and fought for. This study is thus devoted to clarifying what written history reports about early Islamic episodes, compared to what is "known" from mythological anecdotes by ordinary and zealous people among whom illiteracy is dominant. What is being done here is not difficult to understand:

---

[2] Maxime Rodinson, *Europe and the Mystique of Islam*, pp. 3–83. See also Edward Said, *Orientalism*, Chapters 1 and 2.

The dogma and the myths developed and maintained through the centuries, by Muslims in general and by Shi'i Muslims in particular, are being challenged by a more reliable version of history.

I also try in this work to clarify the influences of non-Islamic, non-Arab elements on the Islamic sociopolitical and religiodogmatic world and to trace the development that led to the formation of Islam itself and its Shi'i sects, particularly Ithna Ashari Shi'ism. Such clarification inevitably undermines the appearance of divine organization and preconception that is often loudly proclaimed and assiduously cultivated by the institution under scrutiny. The common religious distortions are many. It is my hope to expose and excise the flaws and to reconstruct the historical circumstances in order to produce an accurate portrayal of the foundation of the Islamic religion.

In addition, I offer some thoughts of my own on these subjects as well as the fruits of research of some prominent scholars of Islam who adopted a sociological approach. I approach these matters neither in defense of nor in opposition to particular issues of Islamic doctrine. My goal is to explain that recorded history and the consistent train of human events feed our logic and intellect better than predigested, undocumented, mythological ideas. As Maxime Rodinson says: "Nobody is exempt from the risk of making a mistake in his choice of materials or his reasoning. But one can at least strive to the best of one's ability to be well informed and rigorous in argument."

The task of rationalizing the old religious doctrine in its dogmatic and unquestionable form has proved extremely difficult, if not impossible. Neither the clergy nor the fundamentalists have ever been advocates of a new and critical approach to reconsidering the origin of their path. Indeed, they have often belittled or misunderstood those who have made such attempts. This inhibition of inquiry has prolonged the deprivation of those who seek new interpretations of old doctrine. Meanwhile, those people, affected by new scientific theories, new ideologies, the products of a modern world, and existing immense economic disparities, have developed a level of consciousness that can no longer be satisfied with old religious fables. The spiritual and philosophical torment of those who live in a semi-industrial society does not translate into a disbelief in God, but such people simply cannot continue to have faith that the old supernatural fables hold the cure to the socioeconomic ills they face.

For these and other sociological reasons, a cautious attempt to analyze the political and social conflicts of the early days of Islam is crucial. Understanding the episodes of Muhammad's prophecy in Arabia, the emergence of Shi'ism in Iraq, and the messianic development in Shi'ism would permit one, if not to change one's vision, at least to have less fanciful expectations from these sources. It has long been contended that Muhammad and the Shi'i Imams possessed supernatural powers and worked miraculous cures; their miracles are even believed to affect men today, centuries later. Apart from that, fundamentalists praise them as being role models—especially with reference to Ali's excellence, Husayn's bravery, and their martyrdom, which for centuries have encouraged extreme emulation among the Shi'ites. Husayn's martyrdom, as retold again and again by the zealots, had a profound psychological effect on the behavior of the Shi'ites. Many of the radical zealots carry intense feelings of guilt and blame for the death of Husayn and thus are driven to the point of suicide or else seek voluntary martyrdom through physical confrontation in a given situation rather than attempt religious persuasion. The eight-year war along the Iran–Iraq border during the 1980s was a notable example of such behavior among zealous believers; according to their religious reasoning, a violent death was preferable to peaceful reconciliation.

These remarkable cultural phenomena are connected to religious antecedents that reflect a highly romanticized vision of the past. These antecedents are the synthesis of the oral transmission of early Islamic episodes (sometimes inaccurate), along with the collective interpretations promulgated by the Shi'i *ulama*. Such antecedents enormously contributed to the sense of spiritual dependency and to the resignation of choice among Shi'i Muslims on a larger scale, since the word *Islam* means submission. But submission as a religious doctrine sometimes leaves no way out of trouble once historical events are set in motion. Because of this, much that is self-defeating is evident on the political, economic, and social scenes. History has demonstrated that dogmatic religious attitudes—whether based on accurate or on inaccurate historical accounts—offer very little room for inquisitive or progressive attitudes among believers with a rational bent.

It would be difficult to detect and examine all the religious exaggerations in Shi'i tradition. Veneration for the Imams (religious leaders) is the core of Shi'i belief: The Imams' alleged divine appointment, infallibility, perfection, and superhuman qualities found a deep religious expression that filtered down into a complex emotional, intuitive, legal, and theological culture during the centuries of the Shi'i existence difficult to harmonize with other early historical accounts and interpretations available to us. The historical careers of the Shi'i Imams are politically controversial. They were quietist toward the politics of the day; their followers wanted them to assert their rights as the true descendants and heirs of Muhammad. Their procrastination in planning for a military or a political confrontation with the Caliphate was, of course, justified by their weak military position but does not seem entirely in keeping with the superhuman powers and achievements attributed to them. Nonetheless, the flow of their politicomilitary incompetence was interrupted by the introduction of the dogmatic notion of *ghayba* (occultation, concealment). This idea became operative when the eleventh Imam apparently left no son as his heir, thus creating a circumstance suitable for the idea of a returning savior. Since that idea became the pretext for previous Imams' political failures, the expectation of the Imami Shi'ites for an immediate military expedition against the Caliphate was resolved and a strict limitation of the process and responsibility of the Imamate consequently determined after the occultation of the twelfth Imam. But the subsequent large gap in the leadership placed the handful of powerless Imami zealots into religious opposition against all who disbelieved their notion of the divine position of the Shi'i Imams. From this point forward, all acknowledgment of historical development and the emergence of new conditions was ignored, denied, and neglected, while the Imami Shi'ites fixed their vision on the past and concentrated on dogmatic hope for the future.

The Imams, despite their passive attitudes (except for Ali and Husayn), were considered the sole religiopolitical authorities, and as time passed their character and power were increasingly mythologized. Their biographies were reconstructed (in itself claimed to be the manifestation of superhuman abilities and thorough knowledge of the universe). Nevertheless, there appeared no concrete explanation of how these Imams came to be frustrated politically and their followers severely persecuted despite their limitless power. Eventually the Imami Shi'ites began asserting that the emergence of Shi'ism was divinely preordained and that the appointment of their Imams was first intended to be effective after the death of Muhammad, but sociopolitical circumstances changed the direction and probably the ideal result of this decision by God and His prophet (hence the Imams never made it to universal leadership).

Introduction

In primitive days it was considered no dishonor to the intellect if abstract metaphysical attributes were ascribed to the prophet or Imams; it was a legitimating antecedent of their existence as a sect, dissolving any worldly obstacles to its promotion. The passage of time has changed little of the Shi'ites' belief in the supernatural powers of the Imams and their descendants. In Islamic societies, the consciousness of people—in particular that of the more intellectual ones—for generations failed to generate a new interpretation of historical knowledge. According to Thomas Kuhn much of the sum of historical knowledge in many societies is probably an accumulation of misconceptions that has not yet led to formulation of new attitudes and personalities.[3]

Such religiohistorical views have created profound emotional disturbance accompanied by an irrational perspective on certain issues in life. Many of us have probably experienced these irrational feelings, the direct product of our understanding of the religious ideas of the past. Promoters of these irrational feelings have long seen the advantage of keeping the masses within the bounds of religious dogma rather than letting them experience the revolutionizing effect of the scientific approach, rational sociological concepts, and new structures in studying the religious past.

For example, we learn that Ali and Hasan were rather obscurely related to supernatural figures who happened to be members of the pre-Islamic Banu Hashim clan of Quraysh; they were known as the Caliph/Imam but the Imamate itself had developed out of the subsequent indefinite line of leadership. They were expected by their followers to stand firm against the Umayyad but instead accepted the truce with Mu'awiya (and Ali fought his former followers, the Khawarij). In all their behavior and knowledge, they never displayed any prescience or supernatural power of the sort subsequently ascribed to them by zealous Shi'ites. The rational study of history tells us that Ali and Hasan did not work any miracles whose impact affected the course of events in their time or thereafter.

Nothing disorderly would ensue in the world if these things were widely known. Instead, people would be encouraged to resist the influence of mythology in their daily activities, to update their concepts of the contemporary world, and to search fearlessly for answers to the mysteries of the universe on the basis of sane pedagogical instructions rather than

---

[3] See Thomas Kuhn, *The Structure of Scientific Revolution*, 2d ed.

through reliance on the supernatural. The Shi'i masses at large have demonstrated an incredible urge to submit to archaic beliefs derived from ancestral sources rather than entertain any cosmopolitan tendencies. The only tendency the Shi'i Muslims have exhibited in this century is to pick and choose various parts of existing ideas and institutions (including foreign ones) in support of their cause even as they eliminate the rest to promote their short-term advantage (as in the Persian Constitutional Revolution of 1906).

Many people ask how it was possible for generations of earlier Muslim societies to pursue innovations in science and philosophy in spite of the dogma of Islam. Similar questions in a different historical context could easily be asked about the European intellectual advances of the fifteenth and sixteenth centuries—a period during which Christian dogma governed the life of Europe. The answers in either case are complex and exceed the scope of this study. It nonetheless can be asserted that the flourishing of science and philosophy in medieval Islamic and Christian societies was not a product of religious dogma per se, but rather of specific sociohistorical conditions determined by existing intellectual forces as well as by the well-timed appearance of individual geniuses. At any rate, the dilemma of the struggle between dogma and logic in Islamic societies has been a familiar issue (as, for example, with Avicenna in the tenth century or Umar Khayam in the twelfth century) and one that lies close to the heart of the study of religious dogma through logical methods. Today, after centuries of struggle, the religious tendency toward dogmatic immobility has outweighed the impulse toward modern vision in Shi'i societies. As men and women search for a clear distinction between falsehood and truth, evil and excellence, they constantly confront the struggle of conscious against subconscious, logic against dogma, and reality against myth. Eventually, one finds himself running out of opportunity as his choices become limited in a given time and place. This book is an attempt to reason out the selected mythological faith that for a long time has found a secure place in the subconscious of Shi'i societies. Despite the suggestion of zealots, reason is not the enemy of faith; rather, it can offer strength to the spiritual self. As the Mahatma Gandhi said: "Faith is a function of the heart. It must be enforced by reason. The two are not antagonistic as some think. The more intense one's faith is, the more it whets one's reason. When faith becomes blind it dies."

A Note About Calendars

The Islamic and Arabic calendar is lunar and dates from the Higra (migration) of Muhammad from Mecca to Medina on July 14, A.D. 622. In this book, both Christian and Islamic dates are normally used. (In the bibliography, dates of the books published in Iran correspond to the Iranian civil calendar, which is solar.)

A Note About Terms and Transliteration

For the frequent transcription of Arabic and Persian names and terms, it was decided to use the standard scholarly transliteration system with the exception of certain words which still preserve the consistency in their pronunciations. Throughout the book the term "shi'a" or "shi'i" is constantly used. To clarify the difference and usage, it should be borne in mind that "shi'i" is an adjective, e.g., shi'i scholar, unlike "shi'a" which is used as a noun, e.g., an Iranian clergy is a shi'a; "shi'ites" is also a plural form of the word "shi'a." Shi'at Ali is used only as an Arabic term for the early followers of Ali who were subsequently called or known as shi'a or shi'ites (they were also the followers of Ali's descendants). In transcription of long Arabic names, the middle name "ibn" (which means son of) has often been changed to "b." in order to shorten it. For example, Muhammad ibn al-Hanafiya is changed to Muhammad b. al-Hanafiya; this rationale is customary.

PART I

The Emergence of Islam: Prophecy

CHAPTER 1
Muhammad in Mecca

The sacred stones were the poles of Arabian life. Polytheism, with a pantheon consisting of a hierarchy of manmade stone gods, was Arabia's prevalent religious philosophy. By the seventh century the Middle East, Central Asia, and the Mediterranean lands had already experienced the flowering of Greek mythology, Christian cultures in both Western and Eastern Roman empires, the Persian religious philosophies of Zoroastrianism and Manichaeism, and Buddhism in Central Asia. This thought-nourishing wisdom characterized an intellectual world that surrounded the Arabian Peninsula, where idolatry was a remnant of its earlier history, although in Central Arabia Judaism's religious rites were monotheistic and nonidolatrous.

Arabia lay in the middle of small colonies of the imperial states: Abyssinia, a Christian land allied with the Byzantine empire; the Ghassanid kingdom in Syria, organized under the Romans; Yemen to the south, subordinate to the Persians; and the Persian-organized Lakhmid kingdom centered in al-Hira in Iraq. Although Arabia was, in comparison, an unattractive land to rule, the empires nevertheless maintained footholds there, influencing tribal politics in an attempt to attract and recruit warrior monarchs. The seminomadic tribes openly expressed their joy or dismay whenever one empire defeated another (see Koran 30).

Arabia strengthened its common identity with trade treaties whereby Mecca became a commercial crossroads among the two subcontinents of Western Asia, East Africa, and the Mediterranean area, but internal warfare and tribal rivalries weakened its prospects of achieving collective and centralized political order. In modern terms, no central authority or regulations governed the Arabs, and the concept of binding law or higher authority did not extend beyond the limits of the tribe.[1] Bravmann notes that community procedures were instituted by certain individuals in pre-Islamic Arabia.[2] Bitterly antagonistic tribal factions fought to elevate themselves to the status of broader political groups, although at the cost of disunity. There were two kinds of political struggle in pre-Islamic Arabia:

1. Ongoing competition among tribal confederations that developed either around religious aristocracies or around nomadic warrior aristocracies
2. Larger-scale conflicts between powerful tribal confederations headed by warrior nomads and the surrounding states of northern and central Arabia.[3]

Tribal honor was based on the prestige of the tribe's commercial aristocracy, on the nomadic tradition of hospitality/generosity, and on the successes of its warriors. Dominant tribes collected taxes from tributary tribes and claimed various other privileges. A negative factor in the social life of Arabia was its stone-cult or idolatry: The Black Stone of Ka'ba had been an object of worship for centuries before Muhammad.

Foreign influences seem more political than religious, but foreign religious ideas must have been known practically everywhere[4]—in Mecca in particular, since it was a great market and transit point of caravans.

The idols were erected by the Arabs, yet worshiping them neither disconcerted nor embarrassed them in their cosmopolitan city.[5] Profit-making was the main concern of the Meccans, which hardly led them either to compete with or to establish themselves as practitioners of a new branch of world religious discipline. As time passed, the emptiness of their paganism forced dissatisfied believers to doubt their own religious beliefs rather than to seek a single god to worship. And those who wished to express spiritual longings of any kind had to fall back on alien notions

---

[1] Donner, *The Early Islamic Conquests*, p. 39.
[2] Bravmann, *The Spiritual Background of Early Islam*, pp. 123–194.
[3] Donner, *op. cit.*, p. 48.
[4] Von Grunebaum, *Medieval Islam*, p. 67.
[5] Mecca and its vicinity were the center of attraction and the place of important sanctuaries such as the Ka'ba.

and sentiments.[6] Four men, at a sacrificial feast the Quraysh (the most important tribe of Mecca, to which Muhammad belonged) held for one of the goddesses, separated themselves from their community by defying this ritual to seek a true faith based on the one that Abraham had found.[7]

The concept of monotheism was not widespread, but a community of *hanifs* (monotheists) had adopted this belief and had turned away from the pagan practices—especially in opposing bloody sacrifices (see Koran 2:130, 3:67–68). The absence of a satisfactory native doctrine led three of the four men to become Christians,[8] but the Meccans remained overwhelmingly pagan. Nevertheless, skepticism gradually spread among the newer generations, more and more tormented by religious doubt.

There were practically no scriptures for the Arabs to read; almost all were written in a foreign language. Christian monks and Jewish teachers made no attempt to translate their scripture into Arabic, in part because not very many Arabs could read.[9] Thus, for the *hanifs* and the dissatisfied, isolation from the ignorant masses and from public pagan ceremonies provided a nourishing environment for their hopes to obtain a clear vision of God.

Sixth-century economic activity in Mecca, aside from trade and pilgrimage benefits, remains unclear. Mecca and its vicinity supported no agriculture, and a virtual trade monopoly over slaves and local products had come to be exercised by the Quraysh tribe (notably the clans of Banu Umayya [Abd as-Shams] and Makhzum).[10] Consequently, how ordinary Meccans made a living remains a question. Probably some were engaged in work as artisans, others as semiskilled laborers, others as petty merchants, and the rest in irregular employment with meager pay. The gap between the mighty and the poverty-stricken was widening, and the hostile weather and occasional famines did not permit the poor to anticipate long and decent lives. The Arabian system could neither offer welfare or security in the face of tribal warfare nor provide

---

[6] Von Grunebaum, *op. cit.*, p. 69.
[7] Andrae, *Mohammed, The Man and His Faith*, pp. 110–111.
[8] *Ibid*; see also Cook, *Muhammad*, p. 14.
[9] Although it has been suggested that only seventeen people were literate in Mecca at the time of Muhammad (see al Baladhuri, *Futuh al-Buldan*, quoted by Dr. Issa Sadiq, *History of Education in Iran*, p. 101), this could not have been so, since Mecca was a trade and caravan center.
[10] Donner, *op. cit.*, p. 51.

meaningful spiritual and philosophical direction for the solace of its population.

In the latter part of the sixth century, around A.D. 570, Muhammad was born into a less important clan of the Quraysh known as the Banu Hashim. His early upbringing was disrupted by the sudden death of his parents; as a child he was fostered first at the house of his grandfather, Abd al-Mottalib, and later by his uncle, Abu Talib. He grew up as a shepherd and then became active in caravan trade working for a rich woman—the daughter of Khuld, Khadija. His profitable deals in business upgraded his position to that of a caravan operator. He seems to have been reflective as well as responsive to social issues, and he was renowned as an honest and promising young man. His honesty, youth, and charisma attracted Khadija to him, and Muhammad definitely recognized certain outstanding qualities in her. Thus, at the age of twenty-five, Muhammad married Khadija, who was forty. His religious motivations became more apparent in his mature years. Religious rituals played a large part in his life, even though these were in a paganized form, as Ibn Ishaq (the earliest biographer of Muhammad [d. 150/767]) reports: "The apostle would pray in seclusion on [Mount] Hira every year for a month and practice Tahannuth [religious devotion] as was the custom of Quraysh in heathen days."[11]

Muhammad's spiritual convictions seem to have been tied to deep Arab experience, but he developed certain ambivalent emotions toward his pagan community through the years. With regard to this ambiguity, one extensive study of an early tradition to determine whether Muhammad slaughtered or ate the meats sacrificed before the idols demonstrates that such authorities as al-Bukhari, Ibn Sa'd, Abd al-Barr, al-Bakri, Ibn Kathir, Ahmad b. Hanbal, Ibn Asakir, al-Dhaehabi, and al-Halabi concur that Muhammad offered meat to Zayd b. Amr b. Nufayl, one of the four men who became a *hanif*, but Zayd refused to eat flesh that had been sacrificed to idols.[12] As Zayd prayed at the Ka'ba, he said: "My God, if I knew what form of worship is most pleasing to thee, I would choose it, but I know it not."[13] Muhammad, in his years of prophecy, praised Zayd and said of him "on the last day Zayd will rise up, a community

---

[11] Ibn Ishaq, *The Life of Muhammad*, Sira, p. 105; see also Cook, *Muhammed*, p. 5.
[12] Kister, "A Bag of Meat," *Bulletin of the School of Oriental and African Studies* 33 (1970): 267–275.
[13] Andrae, *op. cit.*, p. 111.

in himself."[14] The main effort of Muslim scholars was and still is to argue that Muhammad was granted immunity from sin before he was honored with his apostleship. The ambiguity surrounding Muhammad's pagan life and his inner beliefs, influenced by various monotheistic factions, eventually resolved itself into the concept of monotheism, a concept that Jews and Christians already shared.

As time went by, he began to seek the truth more actively. Since he was tormented by the shallow religious beliefs of his community, he followed the example of other seekers of God in retreating to the solitude of the mountains near Mecca.[15] Muhammad experienced a religious crisis at the age of thirty (see Koran 10:18). After a long period of meditation in solitude, he began to embrace monotheism.[16]

At some stage he became a monotheistic believer like some *hanifs* in Mecca, but what else was on his mind? He made commerce more profitable in Mecca, respected the social and economic norms; what else was it, exactly, that Muhammad wanted, looked for, and did? No trustworthy text can tell us.[17] With regard to his claim to be a prophet, one general conclusion may be drawn: He could neither betray nor ignore his internal and spiritual development. But at what stage of his life did he feel the primary vibrations of change in his inner heart?[18] He never revealed this to anyone, and it remains an eternal secret.[19] Muhammad could have become a Christian or a Jew, but he chose not to do so. Perhaps his theological curiosity was satiated at the age of forty, and he sought other alternatives.

"The Arabs, a people without a Book and without a prophet, were, it is true, surrounded by peoples who did read sacred scriptures, but Muhammad must have learned, particularly from Christianity, that its unity was religious, not national."[20] Muhammad was aware of the Jewish expectation of the coming Messiah, and he also had learned (according to the Koran, at least) that Jesus had foretold the coming of a prophet named Ahmad (see Koran 61:6).

For Muhammad, the idea of religious unity became paramount, and

---

[14] *Ibid.*
[15] Von Grunebaum, *op. cit.*, p. 73.
[16] Lammens, *L'Islam, Croyances et Institutions*, p. 34.
[17] Rodinson, *Mahomet*, p. 75.
[18] Lammens, *op. cit.*, p. 35.
[19] Caetani, *Annali dell' Islam*, vol. I, p. 218.
[20] Andrae, *op. cit.*, p. 97.

he pressed for the abandonment of absurd religious practices and for the worship of one God. It is not clear that at this stage monotheism represented for him a simpler, more rational basis for theology than polytheism. But it does appear that Muhammad wished to change the image of God among the Arabs from a series of visible stone beings, each imbued with a particular dominant trait, to a more metaphysical representation of the Deity as unitary, invisible, and all-powerful. Necessarily, such a change attributed a more complicated character to God—as He was now said to possess all of the powers and tendencies once ascribed to different members of the pantheon—and it also invited deeper philosophical inquiry into the relationship between God and humanity.

It cannot now be determined whether Muhammad could really differentiate socioeconomic practices from spiritual convictions. At first, he criticized the religious practices of the Quraysh solely on the grounds of their worshiping idols, and he considered their socioeconomic practices to be peripheral. Only later did he recognize a positive link between religious and socioeconomic principles in Arab society. It was also later that circumstances allowed him to express his historical mission in a more precise form. But in the beginning, "the repression of messianism had reduced his mission to that of a monotheist preacher of rather ill-defined status."[21]

It has been said that, around A.D. 610, when he was about forty, Muhammad planted the seed of monotheistic belief, first among his family and then among the pagans of Mecca. His position as a preacher of a monotheistic faith became clear, and he began to preach the faith with borrowed terms and ideas—borrowed because Arabs had never assimilated such terms as *jahannam* (inferno), *Gabriel* (the name of an angel), and *nabi* (informer). Only through the Koran did these terms become part of the Arab vocabulary.

Muhammad's declaration of prophecy was based (as he put it) on divine revelation, and he gradually accustomed himself to this notion. He might have experienced an exclusive spiritual upheaval in his innermost being, which may have been accompanied by somatic phenomena.[22] Ibn Ishaq's account of the first phase of revelation from Muhammad's own experience is worth quoting:

---

[21] Crone and Cook, *Hagarism, The Making of the Islamic World*, p. 16.
[22] Van Ess and Kung, *Christianity and the World Religions*, p. 35.

"He [Gabriel] came to me," said the apostle of God, "while I was asleep, with a coverlet of brocade whereon was some writing and said 'Read' three times, so I read it and he departed from me. And I awoke from my sleep, and it was as though these words were written on my heart."[23]

The notion of revelation did not come to Muhammad in a vacuum and it was not accidental.[24] The doctrine of revelation already existed, and the assertion of hidden power had been utilized as a medium for religiophilosophical change in various times and places by talented and mystical individuals. According to the tenth-century scholar Biruni, Mani, a prophet and preacher, received a revelation from the king of paradise when he was twelve years old, and the Lord chose him to be His messenger at the age of twenty-four.[25] (Mani was crucified in A.D. 276 by the Persian king Bahram I at Gundishapur.[26]) Another advocate of the doctrine of revelation is the mystic prophet Elxai, who preached in the eastern part of Jordan. The Judeo-Christian doctrine of revelation also received considerable attention.[27] There were, however, thousands of prophets whose claims to revelation were based on anecdotes they purportedly received from God. Interestingly, three other prophets claimed to have received the revelation in Arabia immediately after Muhammad's mission was over. One of the three, Maslama, prescribed fasting, prohibited wine, and restricted sexual liberty. It has been suggested that, at one point, he had written to Muhammad to argue that God had given them a shared prophecy for Arabia. According to Abū Faraj Isfahāni (d. 356/967), shortly before Muhammad made his claim of prophecy, a famous poet of Taif, Abū Amr Umayya b. Ali al-Salt Thaqafi, asserted that he had received the call from God but that his attempt had been frustrated when Islam triumphed; in any case, he never converted to the new religion.[28]

After a long internal struggle, Muhammad became convinced that his

[23] Ibn Ishaq, op. cit., p. 106.
[24] Andrae, op. cit., pp. 94–113.
[25] Biruni, Athar al-Baqiya, p. 309.
[26] Ibid., p. 310.
[27] Recent and earlier studies provide fragmentary evidence (which is still controversial and perhaps not widely accepted within Christian scholarship) that Jesus' preaching was based on his travels and studies in central Asia; see Kersten, Jesus Lived in India.
[28] Shahrastani, Al Milal wal Nihal, vol. II, p. 400.

intercession between the Deity and the pagans was appropriate: "This idea struck deeper root in his soul than any other, that every people had their own prophet."[29] This is probably why he never gave a thought to the possibility of becoming a Christian.[30] However, unanswered questions about his thoughts remain. Did he honestly report that God spoke to him in Arabic through an angel? What did he experience? Was he sincere? No scientific grounds exist for tracing this peculiar phenomenon in our earthly experience. The concept of revelation has caused many difficulties in human logic; in speaking of it, otherwise persuasive historians and sociologists have made remarks that may sound immature to the common sense of an ordinary man. Ibn Khaldun (d. 808/406) emphasizes certain extraordinary experiences in the spiritual kingdom that only the prophets enjoy.[31]

Later accounts by Muslim historians about Muhammad's spiritual upheaval became more and more hyperbolic. The report of Mostaufi, a fourteenth-century historian/geographer, indicates that, for a period of six months, Muhammad was possessed with dreams and hallucinations.[32] Nishaburi (d. 506/1125), in his Rawdat al-Wa'izin, discusses the encounter of Muhammad with the angel Gabriel, their celestial journeys, and their earthly visits to a holy shrine—Jerusalem.[33]

The explanation by the twentieth-century French sociologist Maxime Rodinson of revelation is worth mentioning here. In his famous Mahomet he notes that the subconscious enables us to understand that individuals can receive auditory, visual, and intellectual messages from beyond without questioning their sincerity. Muhammad could have remembered the metaphysical phenomena Jews and Christians had described to him and could have associated his inner spirit with them.[34]

The many traditions that have attempted to describe Muhammad's visionary experience are inconsistent. How did this vision begin for Muhammad? Did he see the angel Gabriel in human form, or did he only hear him? Ibn Ishaq, the earliest authority, states that Muhammad saw Gabriel in human form on the horizon at Mount Hira (see Koran 53:6–10). However, it is certainly possible that, while contemplating at

---

[29] Andrae, op. cit., p. 107.
[30] Ibid.
[31] Ibn Khaldun, Discours sur l'Histoire Universelle, vol. I, p. 181.
[32] Mostaufi, Tarikh Guzideh, p. 135.
[33] Nishaburi, Rawdat al-Wa'izin, pp. 98–116.
[34] Rodinson, Mahomet, pp. 103–104.

Mount Hira, Muhammad suddenly sighted Halley's comet[35] (a spectacularly bright elliptically orbiting body in the solar system that passes near the earth every seventy-six years) when it approached the earth between March 607 and early 608,[36] and interpreted it as a divine sign, which may have been contemporaneous with his preparedness for revelation. Muhammad's record of his visionary experience (notwithstanding the way the Koranic verses have been interpreted) does not speak explicitly of his having seen the angel Gabriel; he rather mentions *hawa* (referring to *he* or a masculine object [not a star; Muhammad would have had no reason to misinterpret the form and the shape of a star]). He does not specifically refer to the angel Gabriel either. What he may have been referring to was an extraordinary thing on the horizon about whose nature he was unsure[37]—especially being "two bows' length" [distant]. The Koran reveals:

> One vigorous; and he grew clear to view when he was on the uppermost horizon. Then he drew nigh and came down till he was [distant] two bows' length or even nearer, and He revealed unto His slave that which He revealed. [53:6–10]

Interestingly, in 1528, various observers described the comet as like the "figure of a bent arm, holding in its hand a great sword, as if about

---

[35] According to the astronomy department at the University of California, Berkeley, Halley's comet was visible in both northern and southern hemispheres and on the Arabian peninsula in A.D. 607–608. See also Richard Stephenson and Kevin K. C. Yau, "Far Eastern Observations of Halley's Comet: 240 B.C. to A.D. 1368," *Journal of the British Interplanetary Society*, 28 (1985): 195–216.

[36] See Sagan and Druyan, *Comet*, p. 364; see also Nicholson, "Jupiter Stands Out," *Natural History*, Nov. 1985, pp. 98–102. The date of Muhammad's declaration of prophecy is estimated as being roughly around A.D. 610. Thus, the year 607–608 may be suggested as the date of the first visionary experience of Muhammad. Records show that many other bright comets were observed around the years between A.D. 602 and 614 in Byzantium, Arabia, Jerusalem, and elsewhere in the Middle East. See Ichiro Hasegawa, "Catalogue of Ancient and Naked-Eye Comets," *Vista in Astronomy*, 1980, pp. 59–71. There is also a claim that July 28, 610, corresponds to the "Night of Power," Lailat-ul-Qadr, usually believed to be the twenty-seventh day of Ramadan in that year. According to astronomer Hawkins, the calculation of the date of the sighting of the Ramadan moon is impossible (*Archeoastronomy Bulletin*, 1978, pp. 3, 6). (This report is from the January 1990 meeting of the American Astronomy Society in Washington, D.C.)

[37] For a picture of Halley's comet's position on the horizon at different times of night and early morning, see Nicholson, "Mars Is the One," *Natural History*, January 1986, p. 85.

11

to strike." This description is reminiscent of an account in the Bible: "And David lifted up his eyes, and saw the angel of the Lord stand between the Earth and the Heaven, having a drawn sword in his hand stretched out over Jerusalem." (I Chron. 21:16)[38]

Koranic verses corroborate the notion that Muhammad may have sighted Halley's comet again: "The heart lied not [in seeing] what it saw. Will ye then dispute with concerning what he seeth? And verily he saw him yet another time." [53:11–13][39]

Other reports suggest that Muhammad experienced this vision while inside a cave.[40] But it seems (except in this visionary description), at least from the process of revelation throughout his prophecy, that Muhammad's experience was basically auditory rather than visual. According to one tradition, Abdallah b. Umar asked the prophet, "Do you know when the revelation comes to you?" He replied, "I hear loud noises, and then it seems as if I am struck by a blow. I never receive a revelation without the consciousness that my soul is being taken away from me."[41]

In other words, Muhammad seems to have reported the visual experience only at the beginning of his career, perhaps in order to make his argument more effective. His experiences with wars, social matters, and individuals seem to have been concretely conscious decisions that grew into the idea of spontaneous divine inspiration.[42]

Muhammad had embarked upon a career in which disapproval of his pronouncements would have meant an intrigue against the abstract idea of creation and disputation of the world's mysteries, about which he claimed to have perfect insight. To assimilate this notion was probably as

---

[38] Oppenheimer and Haimson, "The Comet Syndrome," *Natural History*, December 1980, p. 56.

[39] Halley's comet can be observed when it passes nearest to the earth; it can also be seen on other occasions at a different angle when the nearer planets in the solar system are properly positioned and when the sun is not obscuring it. See the diagrams in Nicholson, "Jupiter Stands Out," *Natural History*, November 1985, p. 100, and Nicholson, "Games Planets Play," *Natural History*, February 1986, p. 80. Note that this is merely an attempt to scientifically explain what may have occurred and has no significance on the message of Muhammad.

[40] Andrae, *op. cit.*, pp. 42–52.

[41] *Ibid.*, pp. 49–51.

[42] *Ibid.*, p. 52.

painful and frightening for him as it was for his hearers in the beginning.

At any rate, Muhammad himself seemed to be frightened, shy, and confused in the face of this transcendental image. His many conversations with his wife, Khadija, and her cousin, Waraqā b. Naūfal (one of the four men who had become Christian and read the scriptures), freed him of his doubts and gave him the necessary support. He often said to his wife, "Woe is me, poet or possessed." Khadija's response was, "This cannot be, my dear. Perhaps you did see something."[43] At that time, the content of his message had no precise form; the only commitment Muhammad had made was not to be a polytheist. It is suggested that, prior to elaborating his ideas on the potentiality of the doctrine of revelation, he spent three years[44] with his household to become certain of his commitment to this daring enterprise. Members of his immediate family probably never knew in detail what his intentions were, but they took him seriously and continued their encouragement. As Ibn Khaldun asserts, Muhammad's character and behavior were the only proofs of his sincerity.[45]

During this private period he revealed verses that were short and simple, in marked contrast to later stages of his life when the verses and suras became longer and more complex (see Koran suras 96, 93, 74, 55, 51).[46] During the first stage of revelation, 22 suras containing 344 verses were revealed, in the course of which there were no signs or words calling him rasul or nabi, and no indication that the birth of a new religion was imminent. In the second stage, there were 26 suras with 849 verses; these, for the first time, vaguely mentioned the prophecy. Thus Muhammad shyly pronounced his mission without giving it precise form. In the third stage he referred the disbelievers to the Final Judgment.[47] There were no major religious innovations, no revolutionary ideas, and in general nothing shocking about his revelation. Consequently, there can be no doubt that "Muhammad never thought he had brought anything fundamentally new; he merely brought something new to his peo-

---

[43] Ibn Ishaq, op. cit., pp. 106–107.
[44] Most traditions indicate three years except Isfahani, Tarikhe Sini Muluk al-Ard wal-Anbia, p. 157, which states that it took the prophet six years to make his message public.
[45] Ibn Khaldun, I, p. 183.
[46] Ibid., p. 197; see also Rodinson, Mahomet, p. 101.
[47] Caetani, I, pp. 208–210.

ple."[48] Similarly, it is suggested that Muhammad's original accomplishment in his preliminary mission was in his teachings directed against the status quo.[49]

The monotheistic concept that formed the nucleus of Muhammad's teachings may have already been twenty-six-hundred years old at the time of Muhammad, since Abraham asserted the unity of God in the city of Ur. Arab society had been familiar with this concept until the accession to power of Amru b. Lahi, who abandoned the religion of Abraham and forced the populace to convert to idolatry.[50] Shahrastani (d. 548/1153), a twelfth-century historian, in his Al Milal wal-Nihal documents interesting traditions with respect to monotheism, resurrection, and certain specific rituals of pre-Islamic Arabia that were identical to those of the Islamic period.[51] The stirring of monotheism before Muhammad gave poets and soothsayers the opportunity to formulate previously unknown concepts; although frequently indifferent, the Arabs generally accepted this type of oratory. "When Muhammad was born, Allah was already known as the Lord of men, and it was realized that his writ went further than that of the idols. Allah enjoyed no cult. It may be that some Meccans held the opinion that the Ka'ba was Allah's Sanctuary."[52]

Quss b. Saedehe Ayadi, an Arab of the Jahiliya period (the Age of Ignorance—the pre-Islamic period), said about monotheism and resurrection: "Not at all, indeed, He is God, one God. He has not been born, nor does He beget. He made reappear and to Him, the return is tomorrow."[53]

Other pious individuals like Amr b. Zarb Adwani, Umayya b. Kana'ni, and Asam Tamimi (who later converted to Islam) abstained from drinking wine in the time before Islam.[54] Muhammad later forbade the practice of drinking alcohol in the third year of the higra (sixteen years after the declaration of his prophecy).[55] Aside from being opposed to drinking,

---

[48] Van Ess and Kung, op. cit., p. 13.
[49] Goldziher, Le Dogme et la Loi de l'Islam, p. 11.
[50] Isfahani, op. cit., p. 151; see also Shahrastani, II, p. 375.
[51] Shahrastani, II, pp. 373–416.
[52] Von Grunebaum, op. cit., p. 70.
[53] Shahrastani, II, p. 401.
[54] Ibid.
[55] Ya'qubi, History, vol. I, p. 409; Mostaufi, p. 144; C. Brockelmann, The History of Islamic Peoples, p. 25. Leone Caetani (Annali dell 'Islam, vol. I, p. 470) says that the interdiction of wine took place in the sixth year of Higra.

Afif b. Madi Karb proscribed adultery. Marriage of men to aunts, daughters, and mothers was also denounced. The customs of proclaiming divorce thrice to end a marriage, of washing after sexual intercourse, of *ghusl* (washing the cadaver before burial), and of the general cleaning of the body were all practiced in pre-Islamic Arabia. The Islamic ritual of pilgrimage, *hajj*, became identical to that of the preceding period. In one instance, according to Shahrastani, there is evidence that certain Arabs awaited the coming of a prophet.[56]

This awaited prophet was Muhammad, whose confirmation by the *hanifs* in particular became the basis for a zealot movement in Mecca— a movement that ardently championed Muhammad as prophet, promulgated monotheism (which certain surviving individuals still subscribed to), and expressed in metaphysical form the aspirations of the Arabs in Arabic. The Koran rejoices in this. "There are many passages in the *Koran* that appeal to this germ of national feeling and urge the people of Arabia to realize the privilege that had been granted them of a divine revelation in their own language and by the lips of one of their own countrymen."[57] (See Koran 26:192, 145; 43:2, 3; 42:7; 41:44; 39:28, 29; 14:97.) Other passages in the Koran repeatedly assert that nothing like it could ever be produced (see Koran 17:88; 2:23; 10:38; 11:13).

This Koranic picture can be ascribed to the backwardness of Arabian culture, which had failed to develop in literature (except for poetry) and in other areas of thought and artistic endeavor a level of excellence that had been achieved in the neighboring countries. The notion of the uniqueness of the Koran may have been an intentional challenge by Muhammad to his pagan opponents. In fact, the authoritative style of the Koran with rhyme, *saj*, had been produced by the *kahins* or *sha'irs* (poets) in form but not in essence, and not so consistently; these advantages guaranteed the superiority of Muhammad's position.[58]

Muhammad's public campaign to spread the message of monotheism from heaven did not greatly trouble the Qurayshites until, after three years of activity in Mecca, he directly attacked the pagan gods. The

---

[56] All instances from Shahrastani, II, pp. 399–416; see also Bravmann, *The Spiritual Background of Early Islam*, for further details of transmission of pre-Islamic rites and customs of Arabia into the Islamic period through the prophecy of Muhammad and the Koran.

[57] Arnold, *Preaching of Islam*, p. 2.

[58] Caetani, I, p. 210; Rodison, *Mahomet*, 109; Margoliouth, *Mohammed*, pp. 5–6.

rupture occurred when Muhammad began to proclaim to the people that their fathers died in unbelief. Muhammad's venture began to attract hostile opposition from individuals who disputed and questioned the genuineness of his revelation. Some subversive Meccans rejected his claim that he had been sent by God and asserted that they would prefer to have the Koran sent down by God or His angels visibly. So, in *sura* 6:8–10 of the Koran, Muhammad condemned those who ask to see an angel in order to believe His messenger. Ibn Ishaq's *Sira* reports that Muhammad was mocked by the people of the market:

> Whenever the apostle sat in an assembly and invited people to God, and recited the Koran and warned the Quraysh of what had happened to former peoples, al-Nadr b. al-Harith followed him when he got up and spoke to them about Rustam, the Hero, and Isfandiyar and the kings of Persia, saying, "By God, Muhammad cannot tell a better story than I, and his talk is only of old fables which he has copied."[59]

When Muhammad spoke of former peoples he was primarily addressing generations of other prophets (Noah's, in particular) that were punished by God in their earthly life as a prelude to the Final Judgment. This threat was meant to create an apprehension in the minds of unbelievers that God might impose a catastrophe, such as an earthquake or flood, on Mecca. He spoke of this last judgment in the present tense.[60] Muhammad himself would not have been surprised if it had happened. But the Meccan hearts by no means could be won. Frictions and arguments became the standard mode of communication between Muhammad and the Meccans, and for Muhammad the Koran was its vehicle. Members of the Banu Hashim clan habitually gathered around the prophet to protect him from attacks by his Meccan opponents. Nonetheless, verbal challenges to what he professed continued to be unleashed. One of his nine uncles,[61] Abu Lahab,[62] and his wife, Umm Jamil, the sister of Abu Sufyan, mocked and harassed him constantly. Muhammad revealed this *sura* about their fate: "The power of Abu Lahab will perish and he will

---

[59] Ibn Ishaq, *op. cit.*, p. 162.

[60] Andrae, *op. cit.*, p. 52.

[61] Abd al-Mottalib had ten sons (Abdallah, Abu Talib, Abu Lahab, etc.); see Emadzadeh, *Chehardah Ma'sum*, I, p. 42.

[62] Abu Lahab's freed slave Thowia was the first woman who nursed the infant Muhammad after the death of his mother Amina.

perish. His wealth and gains will not exempt him. He will be plunged into flaming fire, and his wife, the wood carrier, will have upon her neck a halter of palm fiber." (*sura* 111)

Sura 104 of the Koran refutes Umayya b. Khalaf, who, whenever he saw Muhammad, slandered and reviled him.[63] The Koran reserved the place for the verses about those who defied and agitated against Muhammad's claim.[64] It comes as no surprise that an estimated one-third of the 114 *suras* of the Koran stem from Muhammad's first ten years at Mecca.[65] The Meccans' provocation was that, in their view, Muhammad had slandered their fathers, divided the people, criticized their religion, and blasphemed their gods.[66]

His teaching provoked continued outpourings of contempt, and each time he turned to God for new verses to strengthen his prophecy.[67] The Meccans pressed to see Mohammad's God or His miracle so he could be believed. To the Meccan opponents, Muhammad has been more visible and tangible as God has been only a convenient theory.[68]

During the first five years of Muhammad's preaching in Mecca, the Qurayshites and the unscrupulous merchants of Mecca attacked his doctrine. It has been suggested that they were frightened that the new teachings would lead to a disrespect of Mecca and its sanctuary, and eventually lead to a decline in trade.[69] They also had a fundamental difficulty with some aspects of the new faith; specifically, they demanded a convincing description of the resurrection and the Last Judgment. They thought it was nonsense that one might be able to return to life again after one's bones had decomposed. Muhammad undoubtedly tried his best to illustrate the concept, but it was by no means hard evidence.

The days, months, and years were going by, and the Quraysh were waiting to see or hear something spectacular. Muhammad himself spent the days conversing with associates[70] and revealing verses to condemn those who annoyed him. The persecution of slaves and those who showed

[63] Ibn Ishaq, *op. cit.*, p. 162.
[64] Ibn Ishaq gives full account of these individuals, *ibid.*, pp. 161–181; see also Ibn Athir, *Al-Kamil*, vol. I, pp. 76–82.
[65] Goldziher, *op. cit.*, p. 6.
[66] Andrae, *op. cit.*, p. 125.
[67] Goldhizer, *op. cit.*, p. 23.
[68] Caetani, I, p. 212.
[69] Watt, *Muhammad: Prophet and Statesman*, p. 58.
[70] Caetani, I, pp. 325–326.

sympathy to Muhammad and his faith began to signal the determination of the Quraysh to end his troublesome preaching by force.

Thus the religious faith proclaimed by Muhammad led to a social conflict between his handful of faithful, predominantly undistinguished followers on one hand, and the distinguished merchants of the Quraysh (whose socioeconomic status was at stake) on the other. Muhammad was stirred by the fact that his monotheism might be crushed by the suppressive measures of certain Qurayshites. The number of converts had reached thirty-nine men and eleven women, and then Umar became the fortieth man.[71] Muhammad's quandary was temporarily eased by sending a group of emissaries to Abyssinia. This was assumed to be a hospitable land, monotheistic, with a tolerant Christian king, the Negus (Najashy). To send this emissary to Persia or to its colonies was out of the question, because Persia was a Mazdean land and had a full complement of Jewish, Nestorian, and Meccan allies.[72] Muhammad's decision to dispatch the mission to Abyssinia was taken in case the Qurayshites should decide to eradicate the converts.[73]

A group headed by Ja'far b. Abu Talib and including Muhammad's daughter Ruqiya and her husband Uthman b. Affan, departed across the Red Sea for Ethiopia. Muhammad remained in Mecca. He even went knocking from door to door or following people to preach his message,[74] but he saw no effect of his words upon the unbelieving hearts. He now appealed to God from the bottom of his grieving heart. Apparently it had been decided that nothing should be done but wait, and the Quraysh certainly had nothing to lose by doing so.

Muhammad's softened attitude, which found expression in such actions as occasionally inviting pagans to his home for food and drink, was conciliatory. However, his promise that any who followed him would become his brother, executor, and successor,[75] found no grounds for conversion among his clan, so he decided to seek other solutions. The accounts in some early traditions suggest that he came up with an extremely incautious plan to offer as a compromise. To please the Quraysh,

---

[71] Ibn Athir, I, p. 94; see also Mostaufi, p. 137.
[72] Rodinson, Mahomet, p. 145.
[73] Lewis, L'Islam d'hier a Aujourd'hui, p. 8.
[74] Ja'farian, Tarikhe Siyasi Islam, pp. 37–38.
[75] Ibn Ishaq, op. cit., p. 118.

he praised three of their goddesses (in lines known as satanic verses). This concession was a severe blow to his prophecy. Ibn Ishaq reports: "When the apostle saw that his people turned their backs on him and he was pained by their estrangement from what he brought them from God, he longed that there should come to him from God a message that should reconcile his people to him."[76]

Thus, verses 53:19–20 refer to the three female idols: al-Uzza, al-Manat, and al-Lat. As the Koran suggests, the Meccans regarded them as daughters of another male deity (to whom Muhammad referred as Allah).[77] Tabari (d. 310/923) a Sunni historian, indicates that, in the presence of worshipers, Muhammad added, "These are the exalted goddesses whose intercession with the Deity (Allah) is to be sought."[78]

Among his own followers, Muhammad was for a time suspect because of this "undivine" remark, but his message was nevertheless an attempt to bring him closer to his tribe. The attempt might have been an outgrowth of Muhammad's examination of the psychological aspects of compromise Ibn Ishaq reports: "When the Quraysh heard that, they were delighted and greatly pleased at the way in which he spoke of their gods, and they listened to him, while the believers were holding that what their prophet brought them from their Lord was true, not suspecting a mistake or a vain desire or a slip."[79]

The implications of this gesture caused many Christians and Jews to believe that the sect had renounced its monotheism and that Muhammad had reverted to his original polytheism.[80] "Muhammad temporarily yielded to the temptation to allow the pagan gods a place in his religion. The move was in human terms a dramatic success. But it was not monotheism."[81] The impulse to engage in such a compromising exercise proved unsuitable to his prophecy. He was aggrieved. Ibn Ishaq reports:

Then Gabriel came to the apostle and said, "What have you done, Muhammad? You have recited to these people something I did not bring you

[76] Ibid, p. 165.
[77] O'Leary, Arabia Before Muhammed, p. 198; see also Pickthall, The Meaning of the Glorious Koran (53:21), p. 377.
[78] Tabari, Tarikh, III, p. 881; see also Armavi (Mohades), Ta'liqat Naqz, vol. II, p. 1052.
[79] Ibn Ishaq, op. cit., p. 166.
[80] Rodinson, Mahomet, p. 136.
[81] Cook, Muhammad, p. 17.

from God and you have said what He did not say to you." Satan had intercepted something into his desires as he had on his tongue. So God annulled what Satan had suggested and God established His verses.[82]

"Are yours the males and His the females? That indeed were an unfair division! They are but names which ye have named, ye and your fathers, for which Allah hath revealed no warrant. They follow but a guess and that which themselves desire. And now the guidance from their Lord hath come unto them." [53:21-23]

The connotation of unfair division in verse 22 was that, in Arabia, the females were looked down upon, and yet the three goddesses were referred to as daughters of Allah, while the Qurayshites' elder children were males. Many Muslim scholars have attempted to disprove the authenticity of this event, in spite of transmitted isnad (early documents) from the earliest biographers of Muhammad—Ibn Ishaq, Ibn Sa'd, and so on. Montgomery Watt, a great scholar somewhat sympathetic toward the Islamic religion and critical of certain Western scholars who keep pounding away at the weak aspects of Islam, says: "It is unthinkable that anyone should have invented such a story and persuaded the vast body of Muslims to accept it."[83]

At any rate, the repentance of Muhammad created an ambiguity that magnified the previous controversy. The hostility increased and became irreconcilable in this religious feud. Meanwhile, news reached Abyssinia that the Meccans had compromised with Muhammad. Upon hearing this news the emigrants came back to Mecca, but by this time the Meccans had already broken away from Muhammad.

Mockery, cynicism, and boycott had characterized Quraysh relations with Muhammad and his followers. When the resistance of his compatriots to his message hardened into active opposition, he concluded that being disbelieved was the fate of every reformer and prophet, and he interpreted his sad experience as constituting one more proof of the validity of his mission.[84] Muhammad's subtle diplomacy began to alarm the Qurayshites when the second group of his emissaries to Abyssinia was received warmly. The Meccan delegation demanded their extradition; the king refused.

[82] Ibn Ishaq, op. cit., p. 166.
[83] Watt, Muhammad, Prophet and Statesman, p. 61.
[84] Von Grunebaum, op. cit., p. 75.

Now the Quraysh were frightened that a handful of Muhammad's disciples were preaching in Mecca and its surrounding area. Why such unrest among the Qurayshites? As one pagan of Mecca put it, "There is no reason why a man should not choose a religion for himself as he pleases."[85] But Muhammad's religious message embodied a socioeconomic as well as a political line, the repercussions of which had not yet been felt by the Arabs. The tenet of almsgiving (*zakat*), by which the rich man was morally obliged to help the poor with his surplus, represented a direct attack on a socioeconomic problem. On the other hand, Muhammad never directly attacked big business[86] or the institution of slavery; he seems to have considered slavery a natural institution and was content to preserve the status quo.[87] Nonetheless Muhammad's preaching provided a secure ground for the dissatisfied to oppose their oppressors under the divine protection.

> The changes in social structures in Arabia in the sixth and seventh centuries produced a state of dissatisfaction in certain strata of Arab society. These changes inclined the strata in question to pay attention to the preaching of a prophet whose thought was conditioned by his personal history, by the previously formed ideologies of which he had knowledge, and by the same social conditions that affected his hearers."[88]

It has been suggested that the first Muslims were progressively caught up in a wave of social discontent exacerbated by an increasing gap between the very wealthy and all others. They did not suddenly become social reformers but were encouraged over time to abandon fraudulent practices.[89] Increasingly the divine revelation was touching on economic and political issues, and these gradually but systematically were becoming part of Muhammad's mission. The formation of this religious movement received recurring impetus from the widely apprehended need to establish some sort of political authority combined with religious elements.[90]

---

[85] Cook, *op. cit.*, p. 16.

[86] The Koranic vision of the world "sees the world as a place where events are controlled by God, not by money and big business. This vision thus enables men to feel they were living significantly, although by the standards of money and big business, they were relative failures." Watt, *What Is Islam*, p. 96.

[87] See Petrushevsky, *Islam in Iran*, p. 13, and Van Ess and Kung, *op. cit.*, p. 9.

[88] Rodinson, *Islam and Capitalism*, p. 186.

[89] Watt, *What Is Islam?*, p. 96; see also Donner, *op. cit.*, p. 53.

[90] Gibb, *Muhammadanism*, p. 27.

This political wave, although slight, was considered dangerous by the oligarchy. In spite of a heterogeneous clan system, trade was prospering, slavery was common, and usury offered more than a few people the means for a good living. The lack of large-scale political organization in the central part of Arabia allowed each tribe to pursue its own policy. At the same time, Arabia had become an arena for two imperial neighbors, Byzantium and Persia. The Persians had gained a foothold in the region of Hijaz through the Lakhmid kingdom in Iraq, and their former control over Medina during the second part of the sixth century gave them additional reasons to attempt to cast their power over Mecca.[91] Tabari's chronicle of a war between the Persians and the Romans reports that the Qurayshite pagans were thrilled when they learned of the defeat of the Romans at the hands of the Persians; Muhammad and his companions, however, were not.[92] Sympathizing with the Christians, the biblical people, Muhammad revealed a *sura* in the Koran by the name of al Roum (or the Romans) in which he anticipated an imminent victory for the Romans: "The Romans have been defeated in the nearer land; and they, after their defeat, will be victorious." (30:2–3)

It seems that the political language of these verses was meant to weaken the Qurayshites psychologically on one hand and to appeal to the Romans and the Christians in general on the other. Aside from tactical considerations, Muhammad's high opinion of the Christians and the Romans was by and large based on Christianity's monotheism. This high opinion diminished in later years when Muhammad's army engaged in open warfare with the Roman army (the Muslims were defeated), and subsequent verses signaled the advent of bitter relations between Christians and the Muslims.

At this time, Muhammad's political and economic consciousness began to suggest to him new ways to pressure the Qurayshites in order to break down their resistance. His ingenuity vis-à-vis his contemporaries was becoming evident to him as well as to his opponents. He was no longer a marginal figure in Mecca. "The pagans showed great willingness to compromise; they offered to make him a king, or obtain suitable medical treatment for his psychic condition."[93] Muhammad's chances of

[91] Kister, "Al Hira: Some notes on its relations with Arabia", *Arabica* 15 (1968): 143–169.
[92] Tabari, II, pp. 737–739.
[93] Cook, *op. cit.*, p. 17.

success were good. If the Qurayshites had indeed offered to make him a king, his prospects could have become even brighter. But the prophecy of Muhammad was neither predictable nor systematic; and, impelled by the great economic, social, and psychological changes that had occurred in Arabia since the time of Abraham, the religion and legacy of mono-theism were taking him in a different direction. In the later stages of his prophecy, Muhammad formulated new alternatives that were alien to his predecessors'.

Muhammad's situation became critical with the sudden death of his uncle Abu Talib, who had always remained a polytheist.[94] Muhammad had enjoyed his protection (as head of the Banu Hashim clan) for over four decades.[95] Now he was no longer safe in Mecca. For the next three years, until his departure for Medina, his situation went from bad to worse. After Abu Talib's death, his brother Abu Lahab became head of the clan and Muhammad's protector. This protection was withdrawn, however, shortly after bitter disputes broke out between Muhammad on one side and Abu Lahab, Abu Jahl (another uncle), and their partisans on the other. On one occasion Abu Lahab asked Muhammad about whether his grandfather was in hell, and Muhammad had to say that he was.[96] This was the hardest thing for the Qurayshites to accept. Indeed, they regarded this type of belief a serious error and blasphemy.

The firmly rooted animosity between Abu Lahab and Muhammad led into an agonizing period of vulnerability. The Qurayshites now dared to throw a sheep's uterus at him while he was praying or to throw it into his mealpot.[97] To attempt any serious defense with his handful of converts against the Meccan community was unwise and, in practical terms, im-possible. Muhammad referred these demonic behaviors to God's anger and punishment in the next world. The hostile atmosphere in Mecca forced him to seek a safe place of refuge beyond the reach of the Qurayshites.

Resort to a relatively unimportant city, Taif, about sixty miles east of

---

[94] Tabari, III, pp. 861, 869–871; Cook, op. cit., p. 18; Ya'qubi's account (vol. I, p. 384) indicates Abu Talib's willingness to fight on the side of Muhammad, which many Muslims may have interpreted as his conversion to Islam. Allamah Tabatabai, Shi'ite Islam, p. 151, says that Abu Talib had embraced Islam but "he hid his faith from the people."
[95] Emadzadeh, Chehardah Ma'sum, vol. I, p. 43.
[96] Watt, Muhammed, Prophet and Statesman, p. 80.
[97] Ibn Ishaq, op. cit., p. 191.

Mecca, seemed a sensible strategy, since this city had a conflict of interest with the Qurayshites in Mecca, so Muhammad departed alone for Taif to seek protection.[98] But instead of being received with honor, as he had hoped, he was rejected, hooted at, and, immediately thereafter, expelled from the town and was lucky to escape alive.[99] It was in Nakhla that he met a group from Nashabin who had come to listen to his message. As the Koran records (see Koran, 46, 72), Muhammad was pleased to receive them as disciples, but the outlook for protection was meager. God made no suggestions to Muhammad other than advising him to wait.

About this time his beloved wife, Khadija, died. Shortly afterward he took another wife by the name of Sauda. Simultaneously he expressed affection for A'isha, who was six or nine years old.[100] The motivation for the latter marriage remains a matter of conjecture. Most of Muhammad's marriages, according to Muslim scholars, had political, social, and strategic importance; but the bond between A'isha, the young daughter of Abu Bakr, a longtime friend and close collaborator, could not have required such swift consummation. Further, "this relationship between a man of fifty-three and a girl of ten must have been a strange one, more like a father and daughter than husband and wife."[101] The purpose of this marriage in light of the age difference has still not been satisfactorily explained.

The crucial days, weeks, and months in Mecca spurred Muhammad to search desperately for refuge. The pilgrimage season had arrived, and the prophet met a group of six men from Yathrib (in later years called Medinat al-Nabi [the city of the Prophet]) in the north who had come to Mecca on the annual pilgrimage. This short meeting marked the beginning of a change in Muhammad's career. These men from Medina had understanding of and spiritual familiarity with the concept of monotheism due to their close contact with the Jews.[102] Five of the six men

---

[98] Ibn Ishaq, op. cit., p. 192. Mostaufi (p. 138) and W. Muir (p. 49) report that he left with Zayd.

[99] Watt, Muhammed, Prophet and Statesman, pp. 100–101.

[100] Tabari, IV, p. 1291, and Ibn Athir, I, p. 124, report that she was six years old; Mostaufi, p. 140, says nine years. (The marriage took place about three years later.)

[101] Watt, Muhammed, Prophet and Statesman, p. 102.

[102] Brockelmann, op. cit., p. 18; Margoliouth, op. cit., p. 121.

accepted Muhammad's doctrine,[103] but because of their own tribal feud in Medina, they made no commitment to collaborate with him. In any case, they agreed to meet again at the fair next year. During the next two consecutive years, they convened in Aqaba. This consultation was an unexpected source of ideas for Muhammad. It is argued that the apparent willingness of Medinans to work with Muhammad was a result of his opposition to the Meccan usurers.[104] This idea is parallel to another assessment: "Medina had sought him, not he, Medina."[105] Nevertheless, this by no means obscures Muhammad's charisma, which seemed to impress his followers at least as much as did his religious teachings. The hypocritical behavior of his tormented followers in later years provides evidence that Muhammad's powerful personality loomed larger than his unknowable divine message. The Koran (49:14) refers to this. Whatever the intentions of the Medinans, in the circumstances both Muhammad's life and his doctrine were at stake. The decision was finally made to join the two tribes of Aws and Khazraj.

At the last pledge at Aqaba, Muhammad was certain that his ideas would prevail, especially when he added an article to the agreement specifying that the Medinans were to obey him.[106] He was no longer shy and desperate. He had become sure of himself.[107] Although his fusion of doctrine had reached a stalemate with resisting forces in Mecca, later on certain geopolitical factors favorably served his cause.

Tribal strife, the lack of foreign domination, and cultural backwardness eventually became advantages enabling Muhammad to exert control over Arabian life in the years to come. His preaching in Mecca for thirteen years, with approximately ninety-two relatively short *suras*, had failed. He was now heading to Medina with only 150 Meccan converts to adopt a new method to actualize the dream of monotheism. This change of base for his operation was crucial. Otherwise, he would have gone under, as had many prophets before him.[108]

---

[103] Caetani, I, p. 314.
[104] Petrushevsky, *op. cit.*, p. 15.
[105] Gibb, *op. cit.*, p. 28.
[106] Le Bon, *Tamadon, Islam va Arab (Civilization Islamique)* p. 105. Ya'qubi, I, p. 399, indicates that Muhammad had gained confidence by having important men of Medina accept his faith.
[107] Caetani, I, p. 314.
[108] Van Ess and Kung, *op. cit.*, p. 11.

The Qurayshites had succeeded in luring some converts away from the movement and had persecuted others; now they plotted to kill Muhammad. The plot failed, however, and Muhammad revealed this verse:

And when those who disbelieve plot against thee, to wound thee fatally, or to kill thee or to drive thee forth; they plot, but Allah [also] plotteth; and Allah is the best of plotters." [8:30]

This verse aimed at disarming the Qurayshites psychologically, if not physically. But human events throughout the years at Mecca, which were absolutely unsatisfactory to God, gave the impression to the Qurayshites that, since God had not appeared to save His prophet and exact a bloody vengeance during this period, He might never appear at all.

Now Muhammad revealed that God had ordered him to fight back and had given him permission to shed blood, because God was prepared and quite able to help him.[109] But still the time had not come to fight the Meccans. This order was unlike previous counsel from God urging that Muhammad avoid the polytheists (15:94). It was not clear whether the prophet sensed this inner contradiction in the midst of his spiritual ecstasy. Whatever he conceived, for political reasons he had to change his attitude. Caetani, the eminent classical Italian scholar of Islam, regards Muhammad's ingenuity and success vis-à-vis his illiterate Arab contemporaries as the fruits of his personality more than of his ideas.[110]

To prepare properly for his emigration, a number of emissaries were sent to Medina to preach and report the situation to Muhammad in Mecca. At this time, the content of the Koran consisted of the unity of God and the resurrection but showed no vision of state authority. To the people of Medina, the relocation of Muhammad and his companions was a temporary relief until the situation eased in Mecca and they could all return home.[111] It was not a radical change, but such advancement was the best they could hope for at the time. The future would take care of itself. Muhammad promised them paradise, but that was the last thing on the minds of the Medinans. They desired something material, true, and tangible. They wanted peace and happiness in their own land, not

---

[109] Ibn Ishaq, op. cit., p. 212.
[110] Caetani, vol. I, p. 211.
[111] Ibn Ishaq, op. cit., p. 203.

a vague promise of bliss in another world of whose reality Muhammad could not offer the least guarantee.[112]

The sociopolitical channels were cleared for entering Medina, but one thought remained with Muhammad: How long could he trust the situation? Having lived in a commercial milieu with the knowledge of an Arab dominated by materialist perception, he knew that the truce could be broken at any time if his Medinan hosts could hope to profit from it. His bitter experiences at Mecca and the fiasco in Taif alarmed him. As long as he was defenseless, these scenarios might be repeated. Another theme that emerged in Muhammad's doctrine was based on the realization that reliance on preaching alone was futile in Arabia. He thus embraced the thesis that war and the use of force could be an embodiment of faith; Muhammad recognized clearly that a moral doctrine unallied to a powerful political authority would soon have died in Arabia.[113]

Muhammad's Meccan years ended in A.D. 622, to which point he had never concisely claimed to be the innovator of a new religion. He only aimed at restoring the ancient cult of Abraham, which the Jews and Christians already professed[114] but whose real substance had never reached the polytheists of Mecca. Muhammad attached Islam to Abraham, naming him as his religious ancestor. By proclaiming this patriarch the founder of Ka'ba, he allowed himself in the next few years to depaganize the old Meccan sanctuary and to devote it to the cult of Allah.[115] Muhammad left Mecca in July (Muharram) A.D. 622.[116] to adopt a vigorous relationship not only with the Meccans but also with those who disagreed with him. Consequently, Arabia and Islam became interrelated; Arabia told Islam what laws to formulate and Islam told Arabia what direction to take.

---

[112] Caetani, I, p. 337.
[113] Ibid., p. 325.
[114] O'Leary, op. cit., p. 23.
[115] Lammens, op. cit., p. 38.
[116] Isfahani, Tarikh Sini Muluk, p. 157, mentions Muhammad left two months after this date, but the year began in Muharram.

CHAPTER 2
The Higra:
Muhammad in Medina

His departure for Medina was a turning point both in the evolution of Muhammad's faith and in the creation of political authority in Arabia. As one contemporary Iranian scholar of Islam puts it, "Islam only began from the time when Muhammad was established in Medina."[1] In Medina, Muhammad's prophetic career shifted from preaching toward consolidation of power and exercise of temporal authority. During this period, he concentrated on previously ignored issues. In order to establish civil authority, he had to deal directly with socioeconomic issues; to pursue a political policy, he needed to build a strong fighting force. To support these secular interests, previously paramount religious issues were relegated to an accommodating background role. All of this was closely connected with Muhammad's new spirit and character.[2] The *higra* to Medina involved a series of calculations not unrelated to his own psychology, his political ambition, and the pressure of the Meccans.

How early Muhammad began to develop his political focus is not completely clear, but once, while he was still in Mecca, he said to Abu Talib, Tabari reports: "I want Arabs to unifiedly submit to my theory so that they can rule the Ajam [non-Arabs]."[3]

Here sociohistorical conditions, Muhammad's own plan, and his divine assignment were mixed together in his Prophetic career. Certain questions logically emerge about the role of free will and predestination in Islam. In the case of Muhammad, did God or circumstances bring him to Medina? Had he stayed in Mecca, would questions of army, state, and the like have been raised and handled as they were in Medina? Why

---

[1] Ja'farian, *op. cit.*, p. 147.
[2] Caetani, I, p. 211.
[3] Tabari, III, p. 869.

did Muhammad not stay in Mecca and die for his belief, as Jesus did in his time? Did Muhammad know precisely what the outcome of his activities would be? There were no answers to these questions when Muhammad emigrated to Medina following failure in Mecca and rejection elsewhere. Subsequent events suggest that free will and external circumstances lead man from stage to stage; Muhammad's prophetic career testifies how from a persecuted prophet he became a warrior. The narrow perspective widened when Medina offered him a temporary refuge. It seems that Muhammad as well as the subsequent Muslims were convinced that the turn of events was the divine will.

Whatever the secular demands of life in Medina, it also offered Muhammad opportunity to fulfill his urge to preach. But the change in his own situation brought an important change in the development of his faith as well. In Mecca, he considered himself to be acting in the tradition of the biblical prophets, who had saved men from deviation from the true path. In Medina, circumstances changed his goal.[4] The mockery and harm of the Qurayshites led him to use revelation and the verses of the Koran to curse them. The continuing hostile impasse inclined Muhammad to take measures other than the verses of revelation to retaliate, so his methods and responsibilities changed drastically.

Mecca had actively sought to destroy his faith. Medina, from Muhammad's point of view, had at least two important advantages: a great religious community—the Jews—already existed there, and the tribal aristocracy of Medina was preoccupied with internecine war. The feuding of the tribes served Muhammad's cause and paved the way toward unifying them under a central authority; on the other hand, the Jews later sharply criticized his prophetic position. In regard to Muhammad's statesmanship and prophecy in Medina, it is said that: "Muhammad's position as the head of state and his concern with legislation and administration naturally changed the subjects of his revelations to a considerable extent."[5]

During the early days after his arrival in Medina, Muhammad wrote a constitution of fifty clauses to govern relations among the *muhajirun* (emigrants), the *ansar* (helpers), and the Jews.[6] To encourage the Arabs to accept him as the prophet, he pressed on with his mission as the

---

[4] Goldziher, *op. cit.*, p. 8.
[5] Von Grunebaum, *op. cit.*, p. 79.
[6] Serjeant, "The Constitution of Medina," *Islamic Quarterly* 8 (1964): 3.

messenger of God and imposed a rule of absolute obedience such as the Arabs had never been subjected to (see the Koran, *suras* 8:20, 46; 33:33, 36; 48:17; 49:14; 4:59). Muhammad made emigration to Medina a divine duty, so all his followers had to comply. Closely oversight of the whole community (or, as he called it, *umma*) assured continuity and suggested solidarity; this Koranic passage implicitly rejects Muslims who did not emigrate:

> Lo! Those who believed and left their homes and strove with their wealth and their lives for the cause of Allah, and those who took them in and helped them: these are protecting friends one of another. And those who believed but did not leave their homes, ye have no duty to protect them till they leave their homes; but if they seek help from you in the matter of religion, then it is your duty to help [them] except against a folk between whom and you there is a treaty. Allah is seer of what ye do. [8:72]

Emigration thus became a prerequisite, and collaboration with the Medinan tribes on the basis of "Muhammad's constitution" created a sense of Muslimhood—a unity never seen before. This alliance inevitably conferred a certain degree of political authority and legitimacy on Muhammad as its architect. But economically, the emigrants could not have remained the welcome guests of sympathetic hosts in Medina indefinitely. Almsgiving was prescribed by Muhammad, but this kind of contribution could not fully satisfy the emigrants' needs. Then, suddenly, the productive solution of raiding Meccan caravans introduced a new source of support for the Muslim community and at the same time put an unexpected economic strain on the Meccan commercial empire. At this time the idea of *khums*, a fifth of the booty to be given to Muhammad for Allah, was introduced:

> And know that whatever ye take as spoils of war, lo! a fifth thereof is for Allah, and for the messenger and for the kinsmen and orphans and the needy and the wayfarer, if ye believe in Allah and that which we revealed unto our slave on the Day of Discrimination, the day when the two armies met. And Allah is able to do all things. (8:41)[7]

---

[7] During the battle of Badr a verse was revealed to pay a fifth to Muhammad for different purposes, the rest to be shared among the participants of war. (Only on one occasion did Muhammad spend the earnings that resulted from the surrender of the Banu Nadhir tribe for the needs of the emigrants [see the Koran, 59:7]. See Ejtehadi, *Vaze Mali va Malieh Muslemin*, p. 198.)

The policy of warfare inspired many more Arabs to join Muslim forces out of simple greed, a behavior that embodied a vague religious perception with which the Muslim community came to be closely identified. Such materialistic behavior became so conspicuous that a verse was revealed:

> Then will the believers say: Are these they who swore by Allah their most binding oaths that they were surely with you? Their works have failed, and they have become the losers. [5:53]

For certain bedouins Muhammad's monotheism was merely a theory. These nomads, conditioned by tribal desert life, were seeking worldly achievements. They preferred food over love, revenge over forgiveness, present life over future reward, and profitable slavery over freedom.

Muhammad's assessment of this tendency recalled his fruitless years in Mecca. He then had to take measures in Medina that satisfied his countrymen's material demands. Muhammad used the promise of material gain or the granting of a share of the booty or other gifts as an inducement to attract and hold many individuals who might then have occasion to think about their prosperity in this world and in the next.[8] He probably felt obliged to allow the people to maintain their materialistic norms while he concentrated his efforts on forcing them to follow his strict spiritual teachings. Muhammad preserved the status quo in the secular realm and attempted to consolidate power. The moral and spiritual level of those Arabs could not have been open to change as long as the quality of their material life was at stake. This became clear after the death of Muhammad, when many Muslims went back to their old polytheist life-style and refused to pay alms (zakat).[9]

In their conquest of Persia, the same Arabs, like any other secular army, pillaged with abandon and displayed virtually no respect for moral and humane values.[10] As a result of this Arab attitude Muhammad's teaching took a different direction both in form and—to a degree—in essence. Muhammad's enforcement of monotheism gradually led to his binding together of the religion of Abraham with worldly authority. Thus

---

[8] Donner, op. cit., p. 65.
[9] Ibn Tiqtaqa, Tarikh Fakhri, p. 100.
[10] Arab prosperity through greed and exploitation of their subjects became a justifying means to pursue Islamic goals. See Ibn Khaldun, I, p. 403.

Muhammad simultaneously promised a kingdom on earth fostered by himself and one in another world overseen directly by God.

From the eleven tribes of Medina Muhammad identified four essential elements: (1) helpers of Medina, (2) emigrants of Mecca, (3) hypocrites, and (4) Jews.[11] The helpers and emigrants in one camp and the hypocrites in the other continued their natural antipathy. The question of what role the Jews were to play was to be solved by Muhammad himself: "The apostle wrote a document concerning the emigrants and the helpers in which he made a friendly agreement with the Jews and established them in their religion and their property."[12]

In this document, the "constitution of Medina," Muhammad specifies that the Jews must pay *nafaqah* (alimony) along with the *mu'minun* (followers of Muhammad, as opposed to the Jews).[13] Based on this apparent friendship, several Jewish practices were adopted: fasting on the tenth day of the first month (Day of Atonement), facing Jerusalem in worship, and using the trumpet to call people to prayer. "At first the apostle thought of using a trumpet like that of the Jews, who use it to summon to prayer. Afterwards, he disliked the idea and ordered a clapper to be made, so it was duly fashioned to be beaten when the Muslims should pray."[14]

This practice changed when Abdullah b. Zayd suggested that a singing voice would be appropriate and Muhammad called Bilal to carry out this duty. The Jews continued to criticize Muhammad and his Koranic verses. They claimed that these contained errors and false statements, which—they said—proved that God had not authored them. The Jews as a group became a threat to the foundation of Muhammad's religious movement,[15] particularly when they detected his ignorance of the scriptures. Rejecting the conclusion that his message did not corroborate prior revelation, Muhammad could only support his position by asserting that the Jews and Christians had falsified their scriptures and that the Koran was the accurate record of revelation.[16]

---

[11] Muir, *op. cit.*, pp. 76–78. (The coming of the Jews to Arabia was in A.D. 71, when Jerusalem was destroyed; see *Iranshahr*, I, p. 584.)
[12] Ibn Ishaq, *op. cit.*, p. 231.
[13] Serjeant, *op. cit.*, p. 13.
[14] Ibn Ishaq, *op. cit.*, pp. 235–236.
[15] Watt, *What Is Islam?*, p. 102.
[16] Von Grunebaum, *op. cit.*, p. 78.

The Jewish rabbis annoyed Muhammad with questions so much that many Koranic verses of this period were revealed only in relation to the Jews. Ibn Ishaq states that the first hundred verses of the second *sura* of the Koran (the *sura* of the *cow*) allude to how to deal with Jews and hypocrites.[17]

Soon it became clear that Judaism and Muhammad's faith could not coexist. After approximately eighteen months[18] in Medina, Muhammad ordered a change of the *qibla* (the direction toward which Muslims face to say prayers) from Jerusalem to Mecca, to the Ka'ba. This was due to a statement by some Jews that "The apostle and his followers did not know the *qibla* until we showed them." So God revealed a verse to change the *qibla*.[19] Even so, the complete souring of relations with the Jews was yet to come.

Islam grew distinct from the doctrines of the Jews and the Christians. Because of the peculiar economic, social, and political situation of the Muslims, the gulf between Islam and other religions was widening. Muslims had to survive politically as well as financially, and consequently strings were pulled to redress their own particular grievances. What was once an Arab need thus became an Islamic one. Muhammad became the chief campaigner for Arab needs, and God played an auxiliary role in providing that need.[20] To carry on with life as Muslims, the Arabs could no longer remain passive monotheists in Medina. The socioeconomic circumstances included internal opposition and a poor economic situation forced upon them, but the prize was rich. Raiding caravans and waging warfare with divine justification satisfied their materialism and supplied them with a deeper spiritual drive.

In mid-624, a serious confrontation became a turning point in Muhammad's career; the event became known as the battle of Badr. This challenge represented the first important test of Islamic military maneuvers for the Meccans. The ensuing battle resulted in a victory for Muhammad, who considered it a divine punishment of the polytheists. The entire *sura Enfal* (Koran 8) relates the battle of Badr and links the victory

---

[17] Ibn Ishaq, *op. cit.*, pp. 239, 247.
[18] Tabari, III, p. 942, indicates sixteen months, Ibn Ishaq (*op. cit.*, p. 289) eighteen months.
[19] Tabari, III, p. 942.
[20] Caetani, I, p. 212.

to God and His will.[21] One verse states: "If you [Quraysh] cease, it is better for you, and if you return, we will return with a similar blow to that which we gave you on the day of Badr."

But the promise fell short. The Muslims were defeated in the next battle, at Uhud. The Qurayshites were disturbed when they lost at Badr, especially when some prominent figures and caravan owners were killed in the battle. Along with their dead companions, the Muslims took about fifty prisoners,[22] including the famous Abu Jahl. Some thought was given to putting all prisoners to death, although Abu Bakr pressed for mercy. Then a message was revealed, "leaving to Muhammad the choice of either slaying them or demanding a ransom."[23] Abu Jahl was beheaded; Muhammad said: "The head of His enemy is better to me than the best camel in all Arabia."[24] However, Muhammad also took Abu Jahl's famous camel and a sword known as Zul Fiqar[25] after taking a fifth of the booty as his share.[26] This victory had strengthened Muhammad's position as well as the confidence of his followers and marked the beginning of a career of uninterrupted warfare that included only rare setbacks.[27] Again, Muhammad was readjusting himself to accommodate new ideals.

The time came to raid the Jewish tribe of Banu Qaynuqa. One day Muhammad assembled the Jews in their market and urged them to accept him as the prophet of God, as they would find that action predicted in their scriptures. The Jews replied: "O, Muhammad, you seem to think we are your people. Do not deceive yourself because you encountered a people with no knowledge of war and got the better of them; for by God if we fight you, you will find that we are real men."[28] Then Muhammad revealed verses in *suras* 3 and 5 against them. This was followed by a blockade until the Jews surrendered. Muhammad had ordered their

---

[21] Ibn Ishaq, *op. cit.*, p. 321.
[22] Ya'qubi, I, p. 405, indicates seventy prisoners were taken, two were beheaded, the rest paid ransom. See also Ibn Athir, I, p. 152.
[23] Muir, *op. cit.*, p. 100.
[24] *Ibid.*, p. 98.
[25] Ibn Athir, I, p. 153; see also Qazvini Razi, *Naqz*, p. 527, where the version that the sword was brought down by Gabriel for Ali at the battle of Uhud, as is widely believed among traditional Shi'ites, is contested.
[26] Muir, *op. cit.*, p. 99.
[27] Margoliouth, *op. cit.*, p. 22.
[28] Ibn Ishaq, p. 363; Ibn Athir, I, p. 154.

death,[29] but they appealed for mercy. Subsequently they were exiled to the north; their removable assets were distributed among the army and their land confiscated. Tabari reports that Muhammad's fierce anger was followed in later years by an order: "Kill any Jew that falls into your power."[30]

> O ye who believe! Choose not for friends such of those who receive the Scripture before you, and of the disbelievers, as make a jest and sport of your religion. But keep your duty to Allah if ye are true believers. [5:57]

Muhammad's concern came to be for his own prophecy, not for monotheism, since both the Jews and the Christians believed in God but did not approve of Muhammad as the prophet of God. This discrimination led to the permanent message of Islam that the Jews and Christians have both corrupted the religion of God.

Almost a year after the battle of Badr the Meccans invaded the oasis of Medina with three thousand men, carrying the two goddesses al-Lat and al-Uzza with them. Muhammad's forces amounted to a thousand men.[31] To confront the Meccans, the Muslim forces were led to Uhud by Abu Khythama, who knew the road well enough to bypass the enemy.[32] There the two armies met. This expedition concluded with a severe defeat of the Muslims. Hamza b. Abdul-Muttalib, Muhammad's uncle, was slain. Muhammad himself came under attack in the hills, where his front teeth were broken and his face injured, and a good number of Muslims were killed. Before the Meccans returned home Abu Sufyan, the head of the Banu Umayya clan of the Quraysh at Mecca, said loudly to Muhammad: "This was in exchange for Badr."[33] Had God deserted His people? Muhammad immediately retorted, "But our dead will be in Paradise and yours in Hell." The most shocking moment for Muhammad was when he saw the mutilated body of his uncle Hamza. Then he said, "If God gives me victory over the Qurayshites in the future, I will mutilate

---

[29] Tabari, III, pp. 997–998.
[30] Ibid., IV, p. 1006; Ibn Ishaq, op. cit., p. 369. (See Brockelmann, op. cit., p. 26; (see Le Bon, op. cit., p. 107; see Watt, What Is Islam?, pp. 173–174).
[31] Mostaufi, p. 144.
[32] Ibn Ishaq, op. cit., p. 372.
[33] Ibn Athir, I, p. 178.

thirty of their men."[34] When the Muslims saw the prophet's grief and anger against those who had treated his uncle thus, they said, "By God, if God gives us victory over them in the future we will mutilate them as no Arab has ever mutilated anyone."[35]

Disappointment and a sense of uneasiness now prevailed among the Muslim forces. To restore their confidence, Muhammad revealed about sixty verses of the sura Umran (Koran 3). "Allah ordained this only as a message of good cheer for you, and that thereby your hearts might be at rest. Victory cometh only from Allah, the Mighty, the Wise" (3:126).

Other verses put the blame on some of the fighters who had abandoned their posts and their martyred comrades. God honored them as He willed:

> Allah verily made good His promise unto you when ye routed them by His leave, until when your courage failed you, and ye disagreed about the order and ye disobeyed, after He had shown you that for which ye long. Some of you desired the world and some of you desired the hereafter. Therefore He made you flee from them, that He might try you. Yet now He hath forgiven you. Allah is a Lord of Kindness to believers. [3:152]

It was reported, and the connotation of the verse indicates, that some Muslims had deserted their positions in order to collect valuable goods. The Arabs' materialistic drive obliged Muhammad to criticize this behavior in the Koran and blame it for the loss of the battle.

Some of Muhammad's followers complained about his absolutism and insisted that their opinions should have weight in the formulation of policy; they took the battle of Uhud as the basis of their complaint.

> They had no say in the direction of affairs, and alleged that if they had been allowed some lives would not have been lost. Although the Koran replies that the direction belongs solely to Allah, and that men who are destined to die at a certain time will die in any case, some attention is paid to these complaints, as later on in the revelation the prophet is told to consult them.[36]

---

[34] The Arabs' habit of revenge was usually based on one to one.
[35] Ibn Ishaq, op. cit., p. 387.
[36] Margoliouth, op. cit., p. 98.

As before the battle of Uhud, raids and military expeditions were directed repeatedly against neighboring tribes by the Muslims, to subdue and dispossess them. Simultaneously, arms and men were being gathered, spies were sent to Mecca, and preparations were made to confront the Meccans. Meanwhile, the Qurayshites decided that the time had come to crush Muhammad's forces as well as his faith with a fatal blow dealt by a force of ten thousand fighting men. The peril of annihilation alarmed Muhammad with his inferior army. On the advice of Salman Farsi, Muhammad ordered the entrenchment of Medina.[37] When the Quraysh came close to Medina, the digging had almost been completed. The Meccans never foresaw such a strategy. They simply could not cross the trench, although the ensuing skirmishes caused a few deaths. The abortive attempts of the Quraysh to engage the Muslims in general battle caused them great frustration. This encounter is known as the battle of Khandaq.

Not too long after Khandaq, the raiding expeditions resumed. This type of nourishment for a prospering economy was pleasing for the Muslims but painful for the victims of the attacks. Compelled to accept conversion, the neighboring clans also had to pay ransom. Justice was defined to suit the interests of those who imposed it. In the later stages of Islam, however, these judgments became the foundation of theology and shari'a (laws). One incident is illustrative. A few Muslims just outside Medina absconded with a herd of camels. Muhammad sent horsemen to bring them back. They were sentenced to have both their legs and their arms cut off and their eyes put out. After the sentence was carried out, Muhammad felt he had been excessive. Then he revealed a verse that limited punishment,[38] but it seems that this punishment embodied the harshness of desert life in Arabia and—whatever Muhammad's regrets may have been—it became an everlasting law of Islam.

Let us now turn to the story of A'isha, the wife of the prophet. The Muslim community was not occupied all of the time with warfare, and once allegations were made that A'isha might have had an affair. Once she was left behind the caravan, and the next day she was accompanied to Medina by a young man. She had satisfactorily explained the circumstances to her family, but upon Muhammad's arrival home from a journey

---

[37] Ya'qubi, I, p. 409; Ibn Athir, I, p. 203.
[38] Muir, op. cit., p. 141; the verse limited punishment to cutting off of the hands.

he heard some mischievous words and inquiries were made within the family. Waqidi (d. 207/823) suggests that Abu Bakr, A'isha's father, became extremely concerned about his family's reputation and said "What we are charged with today in Islam, we never experienced in the days of ignorance when we worshipped idols, and I know no Arab family with such grief."[39] A'isha pleaded innocent. Muhammad's cousin Ali said: "Women are plentiful, and you can easily change one for another." He told the prophet, "Ask the slave girl, for she will tell you the truth."[40] Muhammad fell into a trance and revealed verses; mention is made in them of calling forth four witnesses. If this number of witnesses cannot be found, those who made slanderous remarks are considered liars and are subject to punishment. The individuals who spread the words did not escape the lashes meant for them. At this time Muhammad adopted Jewish practice for dealing with adultery: stoning the adulterers to death. A verse was revealed specifically for Muhammad's own wives,[41] stating that they were not like the others. If they wronged him, their punishment would be doubled:

> O wives of the prophet! Whosoever of you commiteth manifest lewdness, the punishment for her will be doubled, and that is easy for Allah. [33:30]

After this scandal, apparently A'isha held a grudge because of Ali's doubt—"a slander which had a powerful effect on the future history of Islam".[42]

Another episode in which a woman played a key role involved Zaynab, the wife of Zayd b. Haritha, Muhammad's adopted son. Zayd, a Christian slave Khadija had given to Muhammad, was often called Zayd b. Muhammad because the Arabs referred to people by their adopted father's name. Zaynab, a thirty-five-year-old woman, was reputedly quite attractive, considering her age and compared to most women the same age at the time in Arabia.

---

[39] Waqidi, Al-Moqazi, vol. II, p. 323.
[40] Ibn Ishaq, op. cit., p. 496; Waqidi, II, p. 321; Ibn Athir, I, p. 227.
[41] Muhammad took four wives in one single year and fifteen in all. See Le Bon, op. cit., pp. 122–123; Yaqubi, vol. I, p. 452, indicates that the prophet took 21 or 23 wives; he divorced a few and he did not sleep with all of them.
[42] Sheikh Mufid, Kitab ul-Jamal, p. 92; Rodinson, Mahomet, pp. 235–236; Margoliouth, op. cit., p. 82.

Muhammad, in search of Zayd, went to his home. Zaynab, according to Ibn Athir (d. 630/1233), was naked and Muhammad saw her from behind a thin curtain and was attracted to her.[43] She went to get properly dressed, but meanwhile could hear Muhammad murmuring a few words. She only heard the words "Gracious Allah, good Lord who turns the heart." Zaynab, boastful of her charm, told the story to her husband, Zayd. Zayd went to Muhammad and agreed to divorce his wife for him. "Keep your wife and fear God," Muhammad replied. His refusal to marry Zaynab prevented scandalous allegations from being made by the Arabs. The prophet could not have married his adopted son's wife. Thereupon, however, Allah intervened to reveal new verses through Muhammad. After the trance and the new revelation about the new episode, Muhammad smiled and asked A'isha "Who would tell Zaynab that Allah had married us?" (see Koran, 33:36–40).

And when thou saidst unto him on whom Allah hath conferred favor and thou hast conferred favor: Keep thy wife to thyself, and fear Allah. And thou didst hide in thy mind that which Allah was to bring to light, and thou didst fear mankind whereas Allah had a better right that thou shouldst fear Him. So when Zayd had performed the necessary formality [of divorce] from her, we have given her unto thee in marriage, so that [henceforth] there may be no sin for believers in respect of wives of their adopted sons, when the latter have performed the necessary formality from them. The commandment of Allah must be fulfilled. [33:37]

Muhammad is not the father of any among you, but he is the messenger of Allah and the seal of the prophets; and Allah is aware of all things. [33:40]

This incident involving Muhammad's personal life shows him relying on revelation to suppress any doubt about his worldly desires or any suspicion of possible error in his private conduct. On the other hand, Zaynab boasted that her matchmaker was Allah himself, whereas Muhammad's other wives were simply given to him by their families.[44]

---

[43] Ibn Athir, I, p. 200.
[44] Andrae, *op. cit.*, p. 154.

Muslims were disappointed about this marriage, but (thanks to Allah's intervention) they did not criticize it publicly.[45]

Over the centuries the question of what exactly interceded between Muhammad and his human passions has been clouded by obscure interpretations that have hardened into dogma. Sometimes the religious assertion is made that Muhammad himself did not truly receive pleasure out of these marriages, that they only served various religious or political purposes. But it is said that, when the Koranic verse about Zaynab was revealed, A'isha said to Muhammad, "Truly thy Lord makes haste to do thy pleasure."[46]

Some Muslim historians have insisted that the nature of this marriage was judicial and had as its primary purpose providing a code for adoption. As soon as the verse (33:40) was revealed, the Koran suggested that Zayd be called by the name of his real father, Haritha, rather than by that of his adopted father, Muhammad. But assuming that this marriage did establish a code for adoption, questions remain as to how urgent the need for this code could have been and why it was necessary for Muhammad to obtain a new wife as part of the codification process. Nonetheless, in those crucial days, romance, politics, and religion became closely interwoven. A marriage had the social effect of affiliating one clan to another. The pre-Islamic custom of men taking a limitless number of wives persisted even after Muhammad and served as a useful political and religious instrument for establishing ties with other clans. However, the sociopolitical aspects of such marriages never obscured the pleasure of having a harem. On the one hand, a man was able to have sexual intercourse with several women and provide a commercial benefit as well as receive pleasure. But on the other hand, if a woman were to have sexual relationships with several men, she was regarded as promiscuous and immoral. Ultimately, polygamy in Islam is a result of the sociopolitical tradition of seventh-century Arabia and the ability or desire of the man to maintain a harem.

Note should be taken of a Koranic verse whose meaning is agreed upon by a consensus of Muslim scholars and theologians. *Sura* Women (4:3) connotes that men are allowed to marry four wives. This has led to many questions and debate because, when this verse was revealed,

---

[45] Le Bon, *op. cit.*, pp. 121–122.
[46] Ahmad ibn Hanbal, *Musnad*, I, p. 63; quoted by Tor Andrae, p. 154.

many Muslims already had six or eight wives. Had the provision of this account (four wives) been intended as a strict limit, Muhammad probably would have forced all Muslims to divorce wives exceeding four. Indeed, he probably would not have taken more than four wives himself. (Several of his companions—notably Ali, after the death of Fatima—also took more than four wives.)[47] This inconsistency suggests that this Koranic verse was meant to encourage men with one or two wives to acquire more, not to set an upper boundary of four.[48]

> And if ye fear that ye will not deal fairly by the orphans, marry of the women, who seem good to you, two or three or four; and if ye fear that ye cannot do justice [to so many] then one [only] or [the captives] that your right hands possess. Thus it is more likely that ye will not do injustice. [4:3]

In the political and military spheres, as already mentioned, Muhammad was making important advances against Medina's neighboring clans. The decline of the Meccan commercial empire became more and more clear, and the Quraysh decided to attempt to enter into a peace pact with Muhammad. Thus Mecca sent Suhyl b. Amr to seek a compromise. The Muslims saw in this pact an opportunity to buy time. The agreement specified laying aside war for ten years, during which period Muhammad would be permitted to visit Mecca for a pilgrimage but would stay there only three nights, so the Arabs could not say he had made a forcible entry. After a long discussion, peace was made and nothing remained but to write an agreement. Umar jumped up and went to Abu Bakr, saying: "Is he not God's apostle, and are we not Muslims, and are they not polytheists?"[49] Regardless of this, the pact took effect and lasted until the fall of Mecca.

As Muhammad's confidence grew, his political perspective expanded and he wrote letters to the neighboring empires to invite them to embrace the new religion. This diplomacy did not convey threat because Muhammad simply was not in the military position to turn his proposal into a major confrontation. This was not the case in the internal affairs of

---

[47] Tabari, VI, pp. 2695–2697.
[48] Watt, *Muhammad, Prophet and Statesman*, pp. 151–152; see also Watt, *What Is Islam?*
[49] Ibn Ishaq, *op. cit.*, p. 504.

Arabia, where the weaker clans were threatened. In the sixth and seventh years of the *higra*, Muhammad uninterruptedly overpowered tribes and expanded his jurisdiction.

Among the places under attack before the conquest of Mecca were two important towns, Khaybar and Fadak. When Khaybar was invaded, the terms offered were that if the inhabitants evacuated and kept nothing secret from Muhammad, their blood would not be shed. But according to al-Baladhuri, a tenth-century Muslim historian, the people of Khaybar requested permission to stay on certain conditions: "We [residents of Khaybar] have special experience in the cultivation and planting of palm trees."[50] Muhammad granted their request and allowed them to keep half of the grain and fruit they produced. Then Muhammad said: "I shall keep you settled so long as Allah keeps you."[51]

Fadak then drew his attention. Fadak's chief, Yush b. Nun, a Jew, agreed to give up half the land's produce. This arrangement was also accepted. But Fadak became Muhammad's own property, because its land had not been attacked by horse or by camel.[52] (After Muhammad's death, his wives and his daughter Fatima demanded as an inheritance the towns of Khaybar and Fadak but Abu Bakr and A'isha denied their claims. The wives subsequently dropped their claims, but Fatima remained firm.)

Now Yemen, which had been under the rule of Sassanid Persians since A.D. 572,[53] suffered the collapse of its central government in about 629; thereafter Yemen turned to Muhammad for governance.[54] The resulting great increase in Muhammad's power contributed greatly to the vital victory, the conquest of Mecca.

The breach of treaty between Mecca and Muhammad occurred in mid-629, when a tribe allied with Muhammad was attacked near Mecca. After a careful assessment, preparations were made secretly. Medina provided ten thousand men to make their way to Mecca. The Muslim army quickly forced the city to surrender. As a consequence, the leading Meccan leaders, including Abu Sufyan and his family, accepted Islam. These individuals once were Muhammad's staunch enemies and had

---

[50] al-Baladhuri, *The Origins of Islamic State* (Futuh ul-Buldan), vol. I, p. 42.
[51] *Ibid.*
[52] Ibn Ishaq, *op. cit.*, p. 523; Ibn Athir, I, p. 263.
[53] Petrushevsky, *op. cit.*, p. 3.
[54] Watt, *What Is Islam?*, p. 107.

killed his closest companions and family members (as Abu Sufyan's son Mu'awiya and grandson Yazid would confront, respectively, Muhammad's cousin and son-in-law Ali and his grandson Husayn in later years), but Muhammad demonstrated mildness in his treatment.

Although Muhammad may have been aware of the insincerity of their conversion, he began to appoint a number of important Qurayshites, notably the Umayya, to important military and government positions: they were experienced and capable people. Also, given their previously active role in Arabian politics, their exclusion would have left them with a strong sense of hostility against the state, which they might be in a position to undermine and seriously endanger.[55] To this point, the helpers of Medina and the emigrants of Mecca had been the dominant groups in Arabian politics, but following the conquest of Mecca the Quraysh were eventually brought into a partnership of power in the ongoing political enterprise.[56] Nonetheless, the Quraysh loomed larger in politicoeconomic status than the helpers and the non-Qurayshite emigrants.[57]

After Mecca, the neighboring areas, including Taif, were raided and captured. Muhammad, the strong man of western Arabia, now set his sights on Tabuk. This alarmed the Byzantine Empire and southern Syria, since the new power was expanding. As Muhammad was preparing for a military expedition, the dreadful heat and a dislike of strenuous war caused certain Muslims to refuse to go. Muhammad then revealed verses concerning them:[58]

Those who stayed behind rejoiced at sitting still behind the messenger of Allah, and were adverse to striving with their wealth and their lives in Allah's way. And they said: Go not forth in the heat. Say: The heat of hell is more intense of heat, if they but understand. [9:81]

For those whose opinion differed from that of the new conqueror, God promised punishment. Since these raids to subdue Arabia were

---

[55] Donner, op. cit., p. 67.
[56] Ibid., p. 77.
[57] Ibid., p. 79.
[58] Ibn Ishaq, op. cit., p. 603; Waqidi, III, pp. 778–781; Ibn Athir, I, p. 337.

considered divinely commissioned and therefore had to be carried out quickly, there was room for no second opinion.

When Muhammad reached Tabuk, its governor Yuhana b. Ruba came to make a treaty and agreed to pay a non-Muslim tax, as the prophet wrote a document for them. Ejtehadi indicates that Tabuk was the first time the non-Muslim tax (*jizya*) was assigned. He adds that, besides paying the poll tax, non-Muslim subjects had to obey these twelve strictures:

1. No malicious talk about the Koran (though the Koran was not yet a compiled book)
2. No defaming of the prophet
3. No seeking after Muslim women
4. No intentional misleading or taking possessions of Muslims
5. No slanderous remarks about Islam
6. No assistance to the enemies of Muslims
7. The wearing of special clothing different from that of Muslims
8. No building of houses near a Muslim neighborhood
9. No sounding of church bells or reading of non-Islamic sacred books loudly in the presence of Muslims
10. No drinking of wine in public or taking pigs into the market
11. No praying for the dead, and burial of the dead away from the Muslim cemetery
12. No riding of horses or carrying of weapons[59]

During the decade in Medina, strict customs and laws developed and were vigorously imposed on those subjugated. In this period Muhammad learned that economic pressure reduced opposition, and many victories were achieved by this means. He even issued instructions for military expeditions in the last days of his fatal illness.[60] He seems to have become less flexible toward those he defeated in later years, offering them the choice of either Islam or subjugation. This naturally led to conversion on a vast scale.[61]

The conquests of Mecca, Tabuk, and other important corners of Arabia made clear that Muhammad's formidable army would crush any nearby

---

[59] Ejtehadi, *op. cit.*, p. 189.
[60] Rodinson, *Mahomet*, p. 323.
[61] Margoliouth, *op. cit.*, p. 66.

resistance. By sending him deputations from all directions, the neighboring Arabs clearly demonstrated that they were more impressed by and
apprehensive of him and his army than of his religion and the prospect
of Hell.[62] Ibn Ishaq's account corroborates this argument as to why the
Arabs surrendered:

> In deciding their attitude to Islam the Arabs were only waiting to see
> what happened to this clan of Quraysh and the apostle . . . and when
> Mecca was occupied and the Quraysh became subject to him and he
> subdued it to Islam, and the Arabs knew that they could not fight the
> apostle or display enmity towards him they entered into God's religion in
> batches.[63]

At this point the tribes were no longer concerned with which idols to
worship; they were worrying about who was going to rule Arabia.[64] One
reaches a similar conclusion about the Arab surrender: It was not the
result of spiritual or religious awakening but rather achieved under political pressure.[65]

Finally, in the tenth year of the *higra*, the entire Arabian peninsula
had fallen under an ideological umbrella unknown in its history. The
clan system, although not completely crushed, was firmly subordinated
beneath a religious unity.[66] This unprecedented and uncharacteristic
unification of Arabia became effective through military victory rather
than through religious persuasion. Moreover, the military expeditions
were possible because of antecedent Arab experience in desert warfare
and because of widely shared avarice for wealth and power. The Arabs'
remarkable endurance in the heat and their body conditioning as a result
of bloody tribal conflicts contributed tremendously to Muhammad's
cause. The result was an almost unbroken string of triumphs through
eighty military operations,[67] fulfilling the aspirations of the Arabs ma-
terially and spiritually.

Three themes can be discerned in Muhammad's rise to power:

---

[62] Caetani, II, p. 432.
[63] Ibn Ishaq, *op. cit.*, p. 628; see also Ibn Athir, I, p. 349.
[64] Caetani, I, p. 212.
[65] Arnold, *op. cit.*, p. 41.
[66] *Ibid.*, p. 32.
[67] Ja'farian, *op. cit.*, p. 52.

1. He firmly established himself in Medina against the opposition of various powerful groups and tribes.

2. He initiated his career as a military commander, beginning with the plunder of Meccan caravans, followed by an early victory over the Meccans at the battle of Badr and building up to the eventual conquest of Mecca, which induced the Quraysh to collaborate with Muhammad. Once the Quraysh threw their full force into the effort to expand the Islamic state, the rate of this expansion in the final few years of Muhammad's life was spectacular.

3. He began the social unification of the Arabs, starting with consolidation of other nomadic groups in the vicinity of Medina, then (as his power grew) extending this process to other areas of Arabia.[68]

As to the emergence of the Islamic state and religion, resistance and opposition to Muhammad in Mecca and Medina led him from being a monotheistic preacher to becoming the prophet of a new religion, which led to the final formation of a distinctive faith and institution.[69]

The new religion that, in its earliest stages, sought merely to introduce monotheism to the Arabs became a mechanism to carry out military expeditions and to conquer lands. Thus, Muhammad's teaching concluded (11/632) with a sword, unlike his predecessors'. As Van Ess says: "Jesus came to grief in his earthly existence, but Muhammad was a success."[70]

A Final Comment

To reveal the day-to-day basis of Muhammad's mission, one must scrutinize the events that followed his prophetic career. For the claimed divine intervention that punctuated the daily life of Muhammad there is no intellectually satisfying proof. It seems most probable that Muhammad provoked and gave direction to the revelations himself rather than vice versa. After devoting thirteen years to proselytizing at Mecca, urging

---

[68] Donner, *op. cit.*, pp. 62–63.
[69] Gibb, *op. cit.*, pp. 25–26.
[70] Van Ess, Kung, *op. cit.*, p. 7.

acceptance of his evidently unappealing type of already known monotheism, in Medina he moved toward the creation of a system with a more definite yet still peculiar structure.

In Mecca he was not taken seriously because he lacked divine proof. He was considered a Judeo-Christian agent, and in part because of this only 150 people there converted to the monotheism he preached. In Medina, swords reinforced his words to the extent of making him simultaneously God's vicar and the head of an army of ten thousand men. History shows that Muhammad's theology did not have any spectacular intellectual repercussions on traditional Arabian society, either then or later; it was other lands' savants who gave an intellectual dimension to Islam. However, Muhammad's movement had an immense impact on the social and political status of the Arabs, one that dwarfed the impact it had on their religious beliefs.[71]

In Medina, as Muhammad gained confidence in his generalship, his sole desire became to make Arabia surrender to God through military conquest. The use of force was divinely approved for the purpose of creating the "government of God" with a mortal ruler at its head. Historical circumstances made it possible for Abrahamian monotheism to combine with Arab particularism to create an inseparable connection between state and religion.

Muhammad's personal life also became the basis for various formulations of the laws of Islam. "The codes of Islam grew out of the circumstances of the prophet's life, concrete, rather than framed upon abstract considerations."[72] Moreover, a certain parochialism is reflected in the implicit assumption that tribal politics and the norms of seventh-century Arabia had universal applicability, with no time limitation. It is not clear whether this idea was conceived by Muhammad himself during his trances or by later Muslims who developed a more sophisticated theology. If Muhammad's movement had been shaped in Rome, would the laws and jurisprudence he formulated have been based on Roman life or would Muhammad have sensed a necessity to create a Muslim state in the already advanced and centralized system of Rome?

It seems likely that the sociohistorical circumstances of the land where he preached would in any case have become a determining factor in the

---

[71] Caetani, II, p. 432.
[72] Muir, *op. cit.*, p. 140.

final form of his religion, given how closely interrelated Arabia and Islam became. Furthermore, it was in the first stage of his prophecy that the stormy town of Mecca drove him out and turned him from a passive preacher into a fighter and a prophet at the same time.

The move from Mecca to Medina brought about a practical swing in Muhammad's dealing with issues and individuals. This swing altered the nature of his diplomacy, evidenced by actions ranging from signing a peace pact with his Meccan opponents to decimating the Jews and denying the Christian faith (Koran 9:31). Whichever of these served his immediate goals became the policy and attitude of the Islamic community in general, since they were fitted forthwith into the putatively divine framework. The attitude zealous Muslims have staunchly held toward their prophet and his behavior for centuries is well expressed in this assessment: "Every historical consideration which can be applied to the situation bears out the rightness of his view."[73]

Notable among Muhammad's political readjustments was the one involving his relationship with the Jews, whom he first referred to as true believers in Abraham's monotheism but later turned against with bitter hostility—a change of position that gradually became a fixed animosity toward an entire religious community. Whatever the nature of the controversy between Muhammad and the Jews at that time, it should have been solved then. But the unalterable statements in the Koran denouncing the Jews and, to some extent the Christians, leave Muslims in a puzzling situation in dealing with these groups after an essential transformation in history. Muhammad's personal experience with the local community of Medinan Jews became the standard frame of reference to be upheld by later Muslims. In the course of Muhammad's long persecution of the Jews, he made his decisive final message clear to his community: "Let not two religions be left in the Arabian peninsula."[74]

The policy readjustments became a characteristic element in his prophetic career, as he moved away from his stagnant and unsuccessful position in Mecca that failed to attract people. A close comparison of the Meccan and Medinan verses discloses a comparable readjustment in the language of the Koran as well. The Meccan verses attempted a supplicatory persuasion to the faith; the verses revealed in Medina prescribed severe and violent penalties for unbelievers. In other words, humility and a degree

---

[73] Gibb, *op. cit.*, p. 30.
[74] Ibn Ishaq, *op. cit.*, p. 689.

of ecumenism marked his preaching in Mecca, whereas intolerance was the hallmark of his ministry in Medina.

> So have patience! Allah's promise is the very truth, and let not those who have no certainty make thee impatient. [30:60, revealed in Mecca]

> And fight them until persecution is no more, and religion is all for Allah. But if they cease, then lo! Allah is seer of what they do. [8:39, revealed in Medina]

For Muhammad, departing from Mecca was a means to save himself and his faith, but this move also gradually changed his cause. The Koranic verses in Medina contained a significant new element: its legislative language. Of course, the Meccan situation would not have allowed Muhammad to make a legislative declaration while his cause of monotheism itself was at stake. Later, however, to enforce his monotheism, he resorted to force, formed an army, promulgated necessary regulations, and in other respects functioned as the head of an army and a state. Thus a factual review of his prophetic career demonstrates that Muhammad's central cause was to establish monotheism among the Meccans but that peculiar circumstances compelled him to raid the caravans, prescribe *khums*, respond to the needs of his army, and amend and consolidate archaic Arab customs as statutes of his new religion.

Events such as the battles of Badr and Uhud, the affairs of A'isha and Zaynab, the exegetical challenge of the Jews, and the humiliating mockery of Muhammad by the Qurayshites became the occasions for revelations constituting a major part of the Koran. Consequently, these personal experiences and episodes out of a distinctly premodern Arab milieu deeply color and in some cases obscure the eternal decree of God for all mankind.

The quantity and volume of the verses in themselves raise questions. One may assert that the compiled book contains both too much and too little. Too much, because indeed many verses are repeated with slight variation; many of these verses could have been reduced strongly. Too little, because the passages are far too small to have been the record of twenty-three years of communication.[75]

Given the repetitiveness and the frequently speculative content of

---

[75] Margoliouth, *op. cit.*, pp. 8–9.

whole paragraphs of the Koran, in their controversial book Crone and Cook argue as a plausible explanation that "the book is the product of the belated and imperfect editing of materials from a plurality of traditions."[76] One can argue that repetition of the verses in worship can be an advantage. Aside from the Koran's repetitiveness, Muhammad never revealed a book; rather, he revealed only short injunctions, short visions, and parables.[77] Freezing certain doctrinal and statutory paragraphs into canonical form without including the imaginative ideas and the fables would naturally have led to major controversies among the Muslims. In the editorial sense, Muhammad probably never meant to have political directions, legal provisions, historical legends, and response to the polemics of the unbelievers all in one *sura* of the Koran.[78]

Furthermore, experts on the Koran have noticed that the chronology of the pre-Islamic prophecies is lacking.[79] In addition, it is believed that one of the reasons the Jews of Medina became critical of Muhammad was the confused chronology in his verses.[80]

After Muhammad's death the insufficiency of the Koran as a statutory basis for theocratic rule became a dilemma for the Muslims. Since the Koran dealt with the primitive conditions of seventh-century Arabia, new circumstances encountered in the conquered lands not only inclined the conquerors to borrow ideas from their subjects but also gave rise to the science of *hadith* (sayings of the Prophet). *Hadith* therefore became a supplementary authority in the development of both law and theology. The misuse and fabrication of *hadith* were repeatedly used to justify vicious policies favored by various factions within the Muslim community. Out of some two hundred thousand *hadiths*, not counting additional thousands that he rejected without examination, al-Bukhari (d. 256/870), the eminent scholar of *hadith*, selected only 7,300 *hadiths* as authentic.[81] Even so, many of these *hadiths* were repeated. At last, they boiled down to 2,762 in all.[82]

---

[76] Crone and Cook, *Hagarism*, p. 18.
[77] Von Grunebaum, *op. cit.*, p. 80.
[78] *Ibid.*, p. 81.
[79] Watt, *What Is Islam?*, p. 80; see also Van Ess and Kung, *op. cit.*, p. 10.
[80] *Ibid.*
[81] al-Bukhari's work contains 97 books divided by the subject of interest into 3,450 chapters.
[82] Gibb, *op. cit.*, p. 79.

The reliability of many of the *hadiths* approved by al-Bukhari, which were transmitted by 309 different people in total,[83] should be scrutinized in future studies. Nonetheless, as a means to enable the Arabs to constitute states, the *hadith* furnished an invaluable flexibility to fill the gaps, since the Koran by itself was inadequate.

Further insight into Koranic and Islamic laws is possible by focusing on tenets derived from foreign sources—notably from Christians, Romans, and Jews. These antecedents often circulated from culture to culture. For example, the Jewish rituals contained many variations, including elements of Roman law[84] and Greco-Roman material that must have passed into Islam through the Jewish medium.[85]

Patricia Crone argues that Roman influences on Islamic law are probably not as decisive as Jewish ones.[86] As previously noted, Muhammad adopted certain Jewish practices upon his arrival in Medina, and some Koranic verses match those of the Christian Gospel.[87] (This is probably why the Qurayshites thought he was simply repeating the old fables.)

And they say: fables of the men of old which he hath had written down so that they are dictated to him morn and evening. [25:5]

Who, when thou readst unto him our revelations, saith: [Mere] fables of the men of old. [83:13]

To explain how collections of these outside elements were mixed with themes from Arab life, remember that a series of anecdotes about persons and cultures was allusively shared among the Arabs. It has been said that Muhammad lived in a culture where the Hellenistic and Persian cultures were fairly though probably inaccurately known.[88] It is also asserted that his new religion included antecedents of pre-Islamic cultural life of Ara-

---

[83] Arberry, "The Teachers of al-Bukhari," *Islamic Quarterly* II (1967): 34–39.
[84] The Jews lived under Roman rule until A.D. 71, when Jerusalem was destroyed; then some Jews came to Arabia, but many remained in Roman and Byzantine Palestine.
[85] O'Leary, *op. cit.*, p. 171; see also Goldziher, *op. cit.*, p. 3; and Lewis, *Islam in History*, p. 240.
[86] Crone, *Roman, Provincial and Islamic Law*, p. 16.
[87] Margoliouth, *op. cit.*, pp. 134–148.
[88] O'Leary, *op. cit.*, p. 23.

bia, the survivals of ancient Babylonian culture, and elements from the stone age.[89]

But to deny any possibility that Muhammad's own knowledge and ideas may have influenced his revelations, the idea was adduced (probably by later Muslims) that he was illiterate and unaware of those elements. "This notion closed the door on any suggestion that the message of the Koran might be traced back through the history of religions."[90] Undocumented versions asserting that Muhammad maintained close contact with various literate men and that he journeyed to advanced cities may be rejected by the Muslims.[91] A late Shi'i source, Nishaburi's *Rawdat al-Wa'izin*, reports that Muhammad, in deep discussion with a Meccan, said: "Have you not the knowledge of previous books?,"[92] implying that he had learned the content of those books himself. It is possible, of course, that he himself had learned of their contents through discussion with others. The Koran (29:48, revealed at Mecca) indicates that Muhammad was not a reader or a writer of any scripture (Kitab). This verse may be a response by Muhammad to the accusation that he was merely plagiarizing the Christian and Jewish scriptures written in Hebrew and Aramaic or Greek; the passage thus may not necessarily refer to Muhammad's literacy in Arabic. "And thou [Muhammad] was not a reader of any scripture before it, nor didst thou write it with thy right hand, for then might those have doubted, who follow falsehood" (29:48).

Furthermore, Muhammad came from a prestigious tribe, and illiteracy would have disqualified him from operating a caravan. Other reports indicate that whenever the forces of Muhammad captured Meccan war prisoners, they were required either to pay or to teach Muhammad's followers in Medina how to read and write in return for their freedom. This suggests that Meccans—particularly those from advantaged backgrounds—were relatively more literate than their Medinan counterparts. It is far-fetched to conceive Muhammad as illiterate in such circumstances.

The writings of historians also corroborate the literacy of Muhammad,

---

[89] *Ibid.*, p. 193.
[90] Van Ess; Kung, *op. cit.*, p. 17.
[91] Muhammad had traveled with his uncle Abu Talib to Syria, where he learned the Torah from the local rabbis (see Le Bon, *op. cit.*, p. 101).
[92] Nishaburi, p. 142.

especially when he lived in Medina. Tabari, Ibn Ishaq, Ibn Khaldun, and Bukhari's references[93] indicate that Muhammad could write. For example, there is a *hadith* in which Muhammad asks for ink and paper in order to write his will.[94] Many other indications testify to the fact that Muhammad could write. Ayatollah Motahari, a modern Shi'i theologian, both confirms the literacy of Muhammad and clarifies the word *umi*, which was long used by staunch Muslims to connote the inability to read and write.[95]

We must take into account the body of facts that in sum are presented here in order better to understand the doctrine of Islam. Muhammad's personal and spiritual force instigated a movement and stirred the Meccan community; his monotheistic belief, although not original, blazed in his soul to such a degree that he became an outspoken preacher in Mecca. Later Muslims considered this a miracle, especially his assertions of having seen supernatural beings and having communicated with God in Arabic. In his thirteen fruitless years in Mecca, there was no sign of an impending miracle designed to save his prophecy until Medina sought him. However, it was the concept of miracles that gave his Islam a zealous and confident expression from which Muslims drew much of their courage and tranquility of soul. Rumi, the Persian poet and Sufi, eloquently describes the impact of miracle on the soul:

معجزاتی و کراماتی خفی   بر زند بر دل ، ز پیران صفی

که درونشان صد قیامت نقد هست   کمترین آنك شود همسایه مست

معجزه، کان بر جمادی زد اثر   یا عصا یا بحر یا شق القمر

گر اثر بر جان زند، بی واسطه   متصل گردد ، به پنهان رابطه

Secret miracles and graces emanating from the Pir transform the heart of the disciple. For within the saints there are spiritual resurrections innumerable, of which the least is this, that all nigh unto them become intoxicated with God.

If evidentiary miracles, like the Prophet's splitting of the moon, produce

---

[93] In addition to these early sources, see Ayatollah Morteza Motahari, "Payambar Umi," *Muhammad Khatam Payambaran*, pp. 560–562.

[94] Ibn Khaldun, I, p. 419.

[95] Motahari, *op. cit.*, pp. 565–572.

an immediate effect upon the soul, 'tis because the soul is brought into touch with the producer of the effect by means of a hidden link.[96]

Beyond proclaiming himself the messenger, was there anything to set Muhammad apart from his fellow men? Did he have unlimited knowledge of the unknown? Was he infallible? There are no signs that could prove strictly by sober logic that he acted other than as a historical figure who stood in defense of his belief. Sometimes Western scholarship has ascribed Muhammad's presentation of his prophetic revelation to hypnotic states or has attempted to apply some superficial scientific theories relating all types of semiconscious, trancelike, and inspired states in medical psychology to pathological or epileptic causes.[97] In the eyes of the medieval Christian polemicists, he brought forth a false religion and therefore was a false prophet. They gave Muhammad a name, Mahound—which meant The Prince of Darkness. Later polemics, such as Dante's *Inferno*, accused Muhammad of intriguing in a false religion and depicted him as suffering in Hell. Voltaire equally attacks the position of Muhammad, "a camel dealer," of claiming to have seen and conversed with Gabriel, for which he murdered men and took women into slavery in order to force them to believe that he was the apostle of Allah.[98] Similar attacks have been made by others whose sense of logic was disturbed by the question of why the Creator, with the whole world and all history to choose from, had selected Muhammad to guide his community, though it was limited in numbers, was of little significance, and was populated by folk who worshiped idols.

These polemics and questions, whether correct or incorrect, do not accord sufficient recognition to the position of Muhammad in seventh-century Arabia. His moral standards, his understanding of the world, his treatment of women, his sexual ethics, his views of slavery and economic issues were all conditioned in an environment he himself found utterly familiar. Muhammad would not have given much thought to how a man of the twentieth century, with its complex moral and social standards, would judge him. He must have seen some truth in the religious ideas to which he devoted himself. The objective of Muhammad to worship

[96] Translated by Reynold A. Nicholson.
[97] Andrae, *op. cit.*, p. 51.
[98] *Ibid.*, pp. 174–175.

the supernatural and the relations of man to the transcendent were echoes of more ancient ideas that he had assimilated. Based on this, his psychology, cultural milieu, and value system constituted a version of the truth for him.[99] The generations before him and after him created new religious ideas in accordance with their own sense of reality and tradition. It is wrong to say that Islam was original, miraculous, and the highest achievement of God. From the standpoint of the Koran, the final decree of God (especially in the early verses) dealt only with the pagan life of Mecca rather than with the fundamental sufferings of mankind throughout the world though it may be argued that the Koran's content is merely symbolic. Muhammad was conditioned by his familiarity with a very limited space and time, and he had no power to work miracles. He also shared the view that the message of God comes at different times for different people, and he saw absolutely no dishonor to his character and his people to proclaim himself a prophet.

What in fact became more problematic with the religion of Muhammad was not whether he was sincere or not but whether under it the struggle to preserve and encourage the flourishing new ideas and interests of different societies would be successful. Somehow, it has been easier for archaic religious elements to survive in communities through history, up to the present day, than for new ideas to survive in religious societies. Maybe the rigid interpretations of the orthodox in the face of a changing society have distorted our common sense by making man feel empty in his lonely soul in a wild world.

To conclude, Muhammad's prophecy and the ritual of his religion were decisively based on conditioned Arab particularism of the seventh century and on the universal dogmas of resurrection and monotheism. Muhammad tried to elaborate other positions between these two in an attempt to establish a consistent religious system. One of the basic causes that stabilized his prophecy among his contemporaries was that "he taught the lesson that a community under God was more meaningful and thus of a greater political promise than a community under tribal law."[100] Nevertheless, he used force to teach his people religious ideas. His religious passion in Mecca did not become the basis of his power in the way his sword did in Medina. As to whether he spoke of the truth, the

---

[99] See Watt, *Truth in the Religions.*
[100] Von Grunebaum, *op. cit.*, p. 72.

continuing path of knowledge and human progress will provide the ultimate answer to this. Rumi says this about the power of knowledge:

جمله عالم صورت و جان است علم   خاتم ملك سليمان است علم
خلق دریاها و خلق کوه و دشت   آدمی را زین هنر ، بیچاره گشت
زور نهنگ بحر ، در صفرا و جوش   زور پلنگ و شیر، ترسان همچو موش
هر یکی در جای پنهان ، جا گرفت   زور پری و دیو، ساحلها گرفت
آدمی با حذر عاقل کیست   آدمی را دشمن پنهان بسیست
میزند بر دل، هر دم کوبشان   خلق پنهان ، زشتشان و خوبشان
از هزاران کس بود نی یك کسه   خار ، خار وحیها و وسوسه
تا بینیشان و مشکل حل شود   باش تا حسهای تو مبدل شود
تا کیان را سرور خود کرده ای   تا سخنهای کیان رد کرده ای

Knowledge is the seal of the kingdom of Solomon; the whole world is form, and knowledge is its spirit.

Because of this virtue, the creatures of the seas and those of hill and plain are helpless before man.

Of him the pard and the lion are afraid; the crocodile of the great river trembles.

From him Peri and Demon take refuge; each lurks in some hiding place.

Man hath many a secret enemy; the cautious man is wise.

There are hidden beings, evil and good: at every moment their blows are falling on the heart.

The pricks of angelic inspiration and satanic temptation come from thousands, not only from one.

Wait for your senses to be transmuted, so that you may discern these occult presences.

And see whose words you have rejected and whom you have as your captain. [101]

---

[101] Translated by Reynold A. Nicholson.

PART II

The Emergence of Shi'ism

CHAPTER 3
The Succession Debate and Shi'at Ali

Conflict in Islamic society led to a major upheaval within the Muslim community not long after Muhammad's death in A.D. 632. The historical background of the newly converted Muslims, social alignments, and doctrinal drives made upheavals and cleavages inevitable. The rise of Shi'ism as a sect was a product of the clash of sociohistorical forces that we must now explore.

In order to investigate the Shi'i sect, we must examine the historical controversy about the succession from Muhammad to Ali. The subsequent development of Shi'ism likewise demonstrates the effect of such sociohistorical forces on the final formation of the sect; Islam was not the single determining force. To understand this thesis, we must put the emergence of the Shi'i sect in perspective so that we can see the links among the formative forces.

The Shi'i sects of Islam emerged from a complex tribal, social, doctrinal, political, and economic background. Shi'ism—in particular Ithna Ashari Shi'ism in the form subsequent theologians (*ulama*) feel it always held—is a sect and doctrine believers feel was entirely preordained by God. The Prophet and the Shi'i Imams had clear visions about its directions, its whereabouts, and even the ultimate number of its twelve Imams. This belief, along with the assertion that Ali was the legitimate successor designated by Muhammad, has occupied the works of Islamic historians and sociologists endeavoring to sort out which events actually took place and which were interpolated into or altered in the works of later Shi'ites. Such an investigation obliges us to consider with care sociohistorical conditions, ethnic composition, religious consciousness, political and economic ambitions, and psychological factors.

Whether Shi'ism in the form we know today was perfectly conceived in the past or was simply the product of a sequence of fortuitous events depends on the viewer's perspective. From a religious standpoint, the doctrinal belief of Shi'ism is considered to have begun with Muhammad's knowledge imparted to him by God. This knowledge, along with the Prophet's enlightened politicoreligious consciousness, was then transmitted through *akhbar* (reported traditions) and *hadiths* to the descendants of Ali and eventually to the *ulama*. This thesis is buttressed by the argument that, since God has perfect and complete knowledge, He willed Shi'ism to take the direction it took in history. From sociological and historical standpoints, the analysis of Shi'ism as both sect and doctrine involves evaluating and comparing the early historical reports (Shi'i and Sunni traditions), including the Koran and Ali's compiled sayings—both *Nahj ul Balagha* (compiled by Sayyid Razi of Baghdad [d. 406/1016]) and the later versions (compiled by later theologians) that appeared after Shi'ism had taken a more definite shape. This approach also requires us to regard the development of Shi'ism in a broad historical context rather than from a strictly religious point of view.

The followers of Ali were called Shi'at Ali, just as the followers of Uthman were called Shi'at Uthman (Uthmaniya) and the followers of the Banu Abbas were called Shi'at Banu Abbas. In this analysis, the word *Shi'a* (follower) will be used to refer to the followers of Ali and his many descendants. To explore the development of Ithna Ashari Shi'ism this study discusses each of the Shi'i Imams in his historical context; this will highlight how their behavior was influenced by their individual situations and will trace the way events played out.

Ali and the Succession Issue

Two serious problems followed Muhammad's rather unexpected death. First, confusion immediately arose about succession, about which subsequent generations of Muslims have continued to argue to the present day. Second, Muhammad left Muslims with no mechanism for developing theology and no canonical statutes for dealing with situations and issues that might appear within societies other than seventh-century Arabia.

Muhammad's prophecy had not outlasted the first generation of converts (who retained many characteristics of pre-Islamic life) when all were faced with serious stress in the recently established kingdom. Controversy enveloped the prominent companions of Muhammad as tensions grew between the emerging elites and the old tribal aristocracies of Arabia. Prestige was measured by criteria that included religious piety, charisma, genealogy, year of conversion, and leadership qualities.

The succession debate centered on selecting a leader whose abilities and charisma would match those of Muhammad himself. The procedures and considerations that governed the successor's selection are not recorded in sufficient detail for us to know clearly what words were exchanged and what compromises were made in order to save the new Muslim hegemony. The initial conflict seems to have been between the *muhajirun* (the Meccan emigrants to Medina) and the *ansar* (the Medinan helpers hospitable to the new faith). This controversy, however, was not only a competition between the elites of the two cities but also a continuation of pre-Islamic intratribal rivalries—Aws and Khazraj in Medina, the two competing clans of the Quraysh in Mecca (Banu Umayya and Banu Hashim), and sundry minor tribes in the vicinity.

The towns, tribes, and clans as a heterogeneous system recently conquered by the Prophet probably had little sympathy toward Islam and one-man leadership. An example of this hostility occurred after the death of Muhammad when some members of various tribes refused to pay alms (*zakat*) and went back to their polytheistic life-style.[1] Their refusal to pay homage to the new faith was equally a refusal to recognize the new leadership. It was ultimately decided that this leadership would remain in the elite circle of powerful converts. The clan system and tribal politics (norms of pre-Islamic life) were now to be subordinated under a formidable united system having one ruler—a system under which the Arabs had never lived. A key question was which tribe's powerful representative would emerge as the leader. Certainly the selection would not fall to some obscure minor tribe or clan in a remote area of the Arabian peninsula.

Tabari illustrates the rivalry for leadership between the Aws and Khazraj tribes in Medina. Banu Khazraj introduced its candidate, Sa'd b. Ubada, and Banu Aws responded by allying itself with the Meccan emigrants simply to prevent the emergence of Banu Khazraj as the leading tribe.[2] The role of the Meccans in this affair is significant in view of their economic and political strength and, more important, their claim

---

[1] Ibn Tiqtaqa, *Tarikh Fakhri*, p. 100.
[2] Tabari, IV, pp. 1347–1348.

to have a Meccan prophet. The subsequent Caliphs (Abu Bakr, Umar, Uthman, Ali, the Umayyad and Abbasid Caliphs) were all Meccans and, above all, Qurayshites.[3] The Quraysh tribe of Mecca gained its authority and significance through two competing clans and families within the tribe: the house of Hashim and the house of Abd as-Shams. The pre-Islamic term for the leading family of Quraysh clan was *Ahl al-Bayt* (members of the house), which in later Islamic terminology referred specifically to the descendants of Muhammad.[4]

The enmity and rivalry between the two households began in the time of Abd Manaf (the father of Hashim and Abd as-Shams and the leading figure in Mecca), when Hashim emerged as more able than his brother, Abd as-Shams, in controlling the affairs of Mecca. The power of the family of Banu Hashim later declined, and eventually his other brother Mottalib and his nephew Abd al-Mottalib succeeded him. Meanwhile Banu Abd as-Sham's successors—his son Umayya and his descendants —ensured the prosperity of the family. Abu Sufyan was the head of the Banu Umayya (Abd as-Shams) when the prophetic career of Muhammad b. Abdallah b. Abd al-Mottalib restored power and prestige to the Banu Hashim clan. Nawbakhti (d. 299–309/912–922) indicates in his *Kitab Firaq al-Shi'a* that the animosity between Abu Sufyan and Muhammad, between the Shi'a and Banu Umayya (Umayyads), and between Banu Abbas (Abbasids) and Banu Umayya can be traced back to the conflict between Banu Hashim and Banu Abd as-Shams in the pre-Islamic *jahiliya* period.[5]

The Meccan emigrants proved to have the upper hand in selecting a successor to Muhammad. The most powerful converts were considered as the prospective leader of the *umma*, the Muslim community. Some individuals, (such as Abu Sufyan and his collaborators)—regardless of their significance in Arabian tribal politics, were out of the question. This was less because Abu Sufyan's clan was a rival of Muhammad's than because he was at first a staunch enemy of Islam and only became a convert when his native city fell into Muslim hands. Another factor that may have excluded him and his clan in the minds of the Prophet's

---

[3] Nawbakhti, *Firaq al-Shi'a*, pp. 35, 44.
[4] Morony, *Iraq After the Muslim Conquest*, p. 492; Jafri, *The Origins and Early Development of Shi'a Islam*, p. 7.
[5] Nawbakhti, p. 32.

companions was that the clan of Umayya already had preeminent socioeconomic status. Had political power been turned over to the Umayya,
the clan would have become the absolute ruler of the community with
no way to turn back. On the other hand, completely excluding the Banu
Umayya from the elite circle would have endangered the community's
prospects of remaining a successful political enterprise. It fell to the clan
of Banu Hashim, another prominent clan in the ongoing elite aristocracy,
to deal with the honor of having had the Prophet come from it. One of
the important male representatives of this clan was Ali ibn Abi Talib,
Muhammad's cousin, who was then in his early thirties.

Apart from candidates promoted out of clan and tribal considerations,
candidates whose succession claims were based on early conversion (sabiqa), age, and notable service to Islam, included Abu Bakr, Umar, and
other companions of the Prophet. This is not to say that Ali or other
close companions from various tribes were less pious or rendered less
service to Islam. But the general feeling among the companions who did
not have a strong tribal affiliation or who belonged to minor clans was
for suppressing the tribal maneuver for supremacy. Both Abu Bakr and
Umar were from lesser clans of the Quraysh tribe, whose ancestor Ka'b
was common to all clans within the Quraysh, including Banu Hashim.
Had there been a rivalry between Banu Hashim and the clans of Abu
Bakr and Umar, it could not have reached the same degree of intensity
as did the one between Banu Umayya and Banu Hashim.

The idea of assigning the leadership to one of the already-leading clans
may have been quite unpopular, a possibility supported by Umar's statement to Ibn Abbas: "The people do not like having the Prophethood
and Caliphate combined in the Banu Hashim."[6]

As understood by those masses whose fate and future status depended
upon its outcome, the decision was between bringing to power an important tribal figure and bringing to power a man whose seniority and
religious piety outweighed his background in the tribal and family aristocracy. Abu Bakr loomed large as a candidate in view of his age, his
bounty in freeing slaves, his services to Islam, his close companionship
to Muhammad, and his willingness not to prefer his family or clan over
others—a characteristic demonstrated when he appointed Umar, not a

---

[6] Tabari, I, p. 2769, cited by Jafri, op. cit., p. 13.

family member, to succeed him. (Of course, Umar did not appoint any family members either when he appointed the council of six to decide his successor.[7])

Nonetheless, the entire matter of candidacy for leadership was filtered through tribal interests in one way or another. It may very well be that some factions even considered that no centralized leadership was necessary. In any case, Abu Bakr was given the oath of allegiance through Umar's promotion and in reaction to the hasty move of the *ansar*, in the prevailing climate of political ambiguity in which one tribe was allied against another. Ya'qubi (d. 260/897), a Shi'i historian, assesses the feud as the usual kind—mainly politicotribal.[8]

Such arbitration in selecting a leader was quite new and shocking to certain tribes—particularly those of southern Arabia who practiced hereditary succession; the northern tribes were accustomed to electing a leader.[9] Despite these conflicting customs, the religiopolitical mood did not allow for any interpretation of various tribal practices in such a way as to satisfy them all during the crucial period immediately following Muhammad's death.

The influence of such social and tribal structures in subsequent Arabian politics, as well as the hidden ambitions of various factions, had not yet been accounted for. Caetani indicates that Muhammad's infant son Ibrahim, had he survived, might have been considered the leader and the prophet of the Muslims, and all of the stages that actually occurred might have been bypassed.[10]

With regard to the selection of Abu Bakr, the contemporary scholar Seyed Husain Jafri asserts that his succession was realized neither through free election nor through the free choice of the community.[11] This may be so, but was this not also the case with the selection of the subsequent Caliphs—Umar, Uthman, and Ali himself?

The trend toward having the eminent elites or the entourage of the potential candidate give the oath of allegiance became something of a pattern that the ruling Caliphs followed, as did those who unsuccessfully

---

[7] Jafri, op. cit., p. 81.
[8] Ya'qubi, II, pp. 2–4.
[9] Jafri, op. cit., p. 12; Watt, The Formative Period of Islamic Thought, p. 43.
[10] Caetani, Annali, II, p. 311 (see notes).
[11] Jafri, op. cit., p. 49.

sought the Caliphate. The question arises as to whether or not Abu Bakr was recognized as the legitimate leader of the community. The way Muhammad consolidated power through military means seems to have been matched by his successor, who appears to have borne in mind that the tribes and clans preferred having their own representative in power to having no access to the central leadership. Such factions as Banu Umayya, Banu Hashim, and various tribes among the *ansar* saw in this avenue a hope of gaining power in the future.

Before we discuss the position of Ali concerning the selection of the Caliph, we should take note of certain movements that took shape under the prophetic assertions of various individuals throughout the peninsula during the Caliphate of Abu Bakr.

The emerging prophets might have genuinely felt that they had received the call from God, though their enterprise may also have been triggered by a desire to gain independence from the dominant local religions. Fred Donner observes: "None of these movements seemed to have involved an outright rejection of Muhammad's prophetic mission . . . but they did oppose the extension of the political control of the Islamic state."[12]

Although the notion of revelation worked successfully for many Arabian prophets (including Muhammad), it created problems for those who already found themselves in conflict with the interest of a powerful state apparatus. In the eleventh year of the Higra, Aswad b. Ka'b Ansi asserted that he had received the call; his religious communion was short, as he fell victim to a Muslim attack.[13] Taliha was another individual who invited people to a new faith during the Caliphate of Abu Bakr.[14]

Muhammad b. Ali b. Tabataba, known as Ibn Tiqtaqa (709/1310) relates in his *Tarikh Fakhri*[15] the interesting story of the two other important prophets who also claimed to have received revelations from God—Maslama and a woman called Sajah—suggesting that Maslama's call was more substantial than that of other short-lived prophets since he prescribed fasting, prohibited wine, and restricted sexual liberty, as

---

[12] Donner, *The Early Islamic Conquest*, p. 85.
[13] Shahrastani, II, p. 400.
[14] Ya'qubi, II, p. 4; Mostaufi, p. 168.
[15] Ibn Tiqtaqa, pp. 101–102. See also Ya'qubi, II, pp. 4–9; Tabari, IV, pp. 1311–1314.

well as preaching the oneness of God and the Day of Judgment. "The style of the few sayings of his that have come down to us is strongly reminiscent of, but appears somewhat inferior to that of the Koran."[16] Maslama reportedly asserted that the prophecy was shared between him and Muhammad prior to the death of the Qurayshite prophet, Muhammad.[17] Both Maslama and Sajah seem to have attracted a great number of disciples on their own, and it is reported that they went into open confrontation against each other before they were married. Their gigantic rival, however, was the Muslim community, whose army suppressed their religious movement and eventually killed Maslama.[18]

Many of the emerging forces both inside and outside the community were tamed by the Muslim forces, as though Arabia were intent upon adopting the centralized form of government its neighbors had long practiced.

As head of the Islamic community, Abu Bakr now tried to consolidate power, planning to unify the tribal aristocracy under an Islamic religio-political umbrella. The procedure for succession to the leadership by which Abu Bakr was selected was ambiguous but it amounted to acclamation and, as such, did set a useful precedent. Nonetheless, the method by which Umar, Uthman, Ali, and in later years the Umayya succeeded to power as vicars was subsequently given a title, the Caliphate, and the ruler was called Caliph.

The Caliphate itself developed into a unique institution that in later years legitimated its own authority by claiming various divine characteristics.[19] The selection of Abu Bakr as the ruler of the Muslim community met with mild defiance from various individuals who apparently wished to reserve certain privileged interests for their household or tribe. Abu Sufyan, the powerful leader of the Quraysh, was among those who opposed the selection of Abu Bakr on grounds that he came from a lesser clan of the Quraysh. Abu Sufyan, doubtless aware of his own weak religious credentials, he urged Ali, as a shrewd Hashemite, to defend the prestige of the Quraysh, offering Ali allegiance and full-scale support

---

[16] Von Grunebaum, op. cit., p. 71.
[17] Donner, op. cit., p. 78; see also Tabari, IV, pp. 1311–1314.
[18] Ibn Tiqtaqa, pp. 101–102; Mas'udi, Muruj ul-Dhahab, I, p. 660; Ya'qubi, II, p. 4.
[19] Watt, "God's Caliph: Quranic Interpretations and Umayyad's Claim," Iran and Islam, ed. C. E. Bosworth. See also Crone and Hinds, God's Caliph.

if he would denounce Abu Bakr.[20] But Ali knew well that, if he did so, he would have to resign himself to being the puppet of Abu Sufyan and the clan of Umayya. According to the Shi'i account of Nawbakhti, however, a number of *ansar* and members of the Banu Hashim clan gathered in the house of Ali and Fatima and refused to swear allegiance to Abu Bakr, as they wished to have Ali designated as leader. But following Umar's harsh argument with them, they all gave a prompt oath of allegiance to Abu Bakr. Still Ali seems to have pressed his candidacy. Umar and Abu Ubayda b. al-Jarah advised him that he was not far from becoming a leader, but that this must take place in due time, as he was a bit young. Ali replied, "O *muhajirun* [emigrants], do not remove the Kingdom of Muhammad from his family."[21]

The Banu Hashim clan's only success (at least until the Fatimid Caliphate [260/873]) was to be realized through Ali, but circumstances were unfavorable at this time and there was nothing to do but to wait. This fact signified for the first-generation converts of Banu Hashim (whose minds were conditioned in the pre-Islamic era of tribal politics) another blow to the fortunes of the clan. Ali and his clan may have felt uneasy; they probably expected to be considered and treated more respectfully than to be displaced during the debate over the succession. Mas'udi (d. 345/956), an early Shi'i historian, reports in this regard that Ali said to Abu Bakr, "You did not consult with us, and you ignored our rights." Abu Bakr is said to have replied, "Yes! But I was frightened by the threat of chaos when the *ansar* and *muhajirun* were intensely arguing, while the *ansar* appointed their leader."[22]

From this and other dialogues, and from the general attitude of the participants, it appears that Ali and the Banu Hashim expected the leadership to remain within the clan of the prophet, and apparently Ali was the sole male heir (*warith*) and guardian (*wasi*) of the Ahl al-Bayt of the Banu Hashim. Nawbakhti indicates that, during his dialogue with Ali, Abu Bakr said in a fatherly tone, "If you wish not to recognize me, I will not insist upon it."[23] According to the same tradition, Abu Bakr

---

[20] Tabari, IV, pp. 1335–1337 (the dialogue between Abu Sufyan and Ali took place when Ali was planning to swear allegiance to Abu Bakr). See also Mostaufi, p. 168; *Nahj ul Balagha*, V, p. 29; Nawbakhti, *op. cit.*, p. 39; Ya'qubi, I, p. 526.

[21] Nawbakhti, p. 40.

[22] Mas'udi, I, p. 657.

[23] Nawbakhti, p. 40.

even suggested revoking his designation as a successor if Ali and others objected. The sources are contradictory in their reports of the time of Ali's recognition of Abu Bakr, but Ali finally resolved his doubts and decided to give his oath of allegiance. Apparently the obstacle causing Ali's delay had been Fatima, his wife and the daughter of the Prophet.[24] Fatima's main concern reportedly was that her father's heritage, prosperity, and title must be restored to the family and simply could not be turned over to somebody else. Fatima's claim to the private property of her father—especially Fadak—turned into a continuing controversy with Abu Bakr, who refused to give it to her. We will return to the Fadak affair later; now it will suffice to mention that Fatima's claim as the inheritor of her father's wealth was somewhat different (as regards dealing with Abu Bakr) from Ali's claim as the male representative and guarantor of the interests of the house of Banu Hashim, his Ahl al-Bayt. Some sources assert that Ali recognized Abu Bakr instantly; others report that he delayed recognition at Fatima's insistence.[25]

The property of Fadak, which Muhammad had made his own private property after its expropriation by the Muslim forces, became the focus of controversy between Muhammad's successor, Abu Bakr, and his legal heir, Fatima. Fatima asserted that this land was promised to her by her father. Abu Bakr, as the new leader of the Muslim community, refused to turn it over to her; instead, it was decided that the income from Fadak would be used for the public treasury. In this regard A'isha said to Fatima, "The prophet said to me, 'What we leave as *sadaqa* cannot be inherited.' "[26] Abu Bakr said, "And I shall abide by this."[27] But upon reconsidering the case, Abu Bakr told Fatima, "No evidence can be accepted unless it is rendered by two men or a man and two women." Abu Bakr's revised pronouncement resulted from the insistent pressure of Fatima. In this case, Ali and a woman (Umm-Ayiman) had testified in favor of Fatima, but because the number of witnesses was insufficient under Abu Bakr's new standard, the claim was dismissed.[28] Not until about two hundred years later did the Abbasid Caliph al-Ma'mun order Fadak to be delivered to the descendants of Fatima.[29]

---

[24] *Ibid.*, pp. 41, 42; Mas'udi, I, p. 659.
[25] Nawbakhti, p. 41; Mas'udi, I, p. 659. See also Jafri, *op. cit.*, p. 51.
[26] Al-Baladhuri, I, pp. 50–51. See also Ya'qubi, II, p. 1.
[27] Tabari, IV, p. 1335.
[28] Al-Baladhuri, I, p. 52.
[29] *Ibid.*, p. 54. See also Ibn Athir, I, p. 264.

The Fadak affair and the shaky status of the Banu Hashim clan on the eve of the emergence of a new Muslim government had annoyed the Ahl al-Bayt. Ali intimates this in his sayings compiled in *Nahj ul-Balagha*.[30] Due to the displeasure with which Abu Bakr viewed them, the Banu Hashim began to wonder what rights and privileges they would enjoy in subsequent political stages. They knew that, by lineage, their clan had better claims to rule Arabia under the leadership of Ali. However, the prevailing sociopolitical atmosphere inclined them to reconcile now in order to be in a position to better themselves in the future rather than isolate themselves and create a hostile and poisonous atmosphere. Thus Ali—whether before or after the death of Fatima (the sources are contradictory)—stepped forward to recognize Abu Bakr, and so did the Banu Hashim family and friends of Ali (Salman Farsi, az-Zubayr, al-Miqdad, Abu Dharr, and others). Neither Shi'i nor Sunni sources suggest that, during the controversy over designating a successor to Muhammad, Ali was proclaimed successor by the Prophet at a place called Ghadir Khum.[31] This raises the whole question of the legitimacy of assertions by subsequent followers of Ali about the authenticity of a controversial *hadith* revealed at Ghadir Khum in support of Ali's claim to succession that justified the functioning and emergence of their sect of Shi'at Ali or Shi'ism.

Exactly when this *hadith* (which became a pivotal text condemning the ruling Caliphs on the one hand and praising Ali and his descendants on the other) emerged cannot easily be determined. This *hadith*, "Those for whom I am *mawla* [master, friend?] should also accept Ali as such," is attributed to Muhammad, who reportedly declared it at a place called Ghadir Khum during his last pilgrimage. If we accept the validity of this *hadith* and the reality of the event, various ramifications should be noted regarding succession after the Prophet.

This *hadith* must be interpreted in terms of the underlying reasoning: why Muhammad said it and what he meant by it. The Sunnis have argued that ill feelings and attitudes had arisen among numbers of Muhammad's followers toward Ali for various reasons.[32] According to this theory, Muhammad's praise for Ali was impelled by a desire to combat malaise and to restore respect for him. Supporting this interpretation is

---

[30] *Nahj ul Balagha*, CCII, p. 565.
[31] Nawbakhti, p. 43.
[32] Jafri, *op. cit.*, p. 21.

the ambiguity of the word *mawla*, which can mean either "friend" or "leader." The Shi'ites prefer to read this *hadith* as testamentary. To them, Muhammad had found the time suitable to appoint his successor, and he intended *mawla* to mean "leader." Shi'ites further claim that some Koranic verses that made Ali's special status explicit were altered or eliminated by Uthman (the third Caliph), during whose time the Koran was compiled as it is known today.[33]

In addition, the Shi'i accounts of the Ghadir Khum *hadith* emphasize an ambiguous Koranic verse[34] that supposedly was revealed to Muhammad to announce the appointment of Ali as his successor: "O Messenger! Make known that which hath been revealed unto thee from thy Lord, for if thou do it not, thou will not have conveyed His message. Allah will protect thee from mankind. Lo! Allah guideth not the disbelieving folk" (5:67).

There is also a general consensus among both Shi'i and Sunni scholars and historians that this Koranic verse was revealed especially about Ali: "Your friend can only be Allah; and His messenger and those who believe; who establish worship and pay the poor due and bow down" (5:55).

The Shi'i assertion that Ali was the only legitimate successor to Muhammad has been supplemented by various traditions and interpretation of events and sayings reported by Shi'i scholars and theologians. Although all of these assertions provide certain ammunition for the argument, the real problem lies in speculative rather than concrete interpretations of these traditions. The shadowy interpretations of the Koranic verses mentioned above vary from one source to another. For example, verse 5:67 carries in its language the same general imperative pattern that the Koran employs all along, but the Shi'ites claim that this verse was followed by a declaration that Muhammad put into the form of the Ghadir Khum *hadith*.

Obscurity and confusion would probably have been avoided if Muhammad had established his news about his successor in Koranic form rather than in *hadith* form, since the latter not only invites skepticism about the transmitters of the *hadith* but also encourages disagreement as to its interpretation. Ibn Khaldun, a fourteenth-century Tunisian his-

---

[33] Lammens, *L'Islam*, p. 50. See also Momen, *An Introduction to Shi'a Islam*, p. 81.
[34] Allamah Amini in volumes I and II of his *Al-Ghadir* incorrectly mentions verse 70 of Sura 5 instead of verse 67 of Sura 5.

torian and sociologist, responds to the claim of the appointment of Ali and his descendants as Imams in a way that is shrewd but reasonable: "If the appointment of vicar (Imam) was to be one of the pillars of the faith, such as prayer, Muhammad would have prescribed it."[35]

With regard to the purported alteration and suppression of the Koranic verses favorable to Ali and his descendants by their enemies, it must be noted that Ali himself is widely believed to have been one of the memorizers of the revelation. It is hard to imagine that, during the compilation of the revelation, such alteration could take place without Ali's objection or detection. Moreover, Ali's right to succession as allegedly stipulated in the original verses would have been understood clearly during the crucial days of designating a successor and would have enabled Ali to voice a stronger opinion about his rights based on the eternal decree of the Koran.

The eminent twentieth-century Shi'i scholar Allamah Amini, in his voluminous work al-Ghadir,[36] provides a summary of the traditions regarding the validity of the Ghadir Khum hadith and then attempts to interpret it to the satisfaction of the Shi'i believers. His work is among the most authoritative of its kind, and he is certainly a scholar whose views and arguments are regularly used by the ulama to give a more intellectual tone to their religious assertions. Sheikh Amini has tried to scrutinize and interpret the word mawla, which is at the heart of the controversy, in order to determine whether Muhammad used this word to designate Ali or simply to praise him. He provides eight different definitions.[37] In one judgmental instance, he states that the word mawla was meant to signify "master" or "great leadership" when employed by the Prophet, but that the Arabs were intolerant and refused to admit its real meaning.[38] This proclamation by Amini about the Arabs contemporary to Muhammad would only have been true, however, if the Arabs had refused the leadership of Abu Bakr, Umar, Uthman, and Ali in the subsequent stages.

The internal opposition that arose during the reigns of Muhammad's successors had nothing to do with any refusal to admit the meaning of

---

[35] Ibn Khaldun, I, p. 420.
[36] Amini, Al-Ghadir, translated into Persian, vols. I–XXII (1340/1961–1365/1986).
[37] Ibid., II, p. 314.
[38] Ibid., pp. 294–295.

mawla. All four Caliphs in their turn established their leadership, and the Arabs became subordinated accordingly. Thus, for example, an organized army and leadership made Arab expansion possible, as well as Abu Bakr's wars of apostasy, Umar's conquest of Persia, and Uthman's and Ali's various expeditions throughout the emerging Islamic Arab empire. Thus the Arab expansion was made possible by the Arabs' not refusing the concept of leadership. In another instance, Amini argues that the word *mawla* must mean "Imam" and "the First" (referring to Ali as the first Shi'i Imam and the first legitimate leader—necessarily by disregarding other Caliphs).

Amini emphasizes that these meanings are approved by Arabic-speaking scholars.[39] But there is no structural frame of reference through which the argument could become effective behind these indecisive speculations and interpretations. It seems that the stalemate in the argument over the designation of Ali by Muhammad remains in a propagandist stage in which partisans single out materials favorable to their cause and then provide approximate interpretations for them.

The extended works of the Shi'i authors and theologians have also developed significantly in such a manner. For instance, a present-day theologian, Husayn Kashif al-Qita Najafi, raises a question that he also answers: Why did the companions of the Prophet ignore Muhammad's instructions in the Ghadir Khum and (purportedly) other *hadiths* that confirmed Ali's right to succession? "Perhaps the entourage of the Prophet either had not heard such *hadiths* or, if they had heard them, had never understood their true meaning."[40] Kashif al-'Qita and Allamah Tabatabai add that, being aware of his rights, Ali swore allegiance to and collaborated with the Caliphs who preceded him because he observed the splendor of Islamic expansion under them and recognized their effort to rule without any absolutism.[41]

Amini's next comment on the supporting *hadiths* that supplement the Ghadir Khum *hadith* is that al-Bukhari (d. 258/870) and al-Muslim (d. 263/875), the two authoritative scholars of *hadiths*, failed to report a complete account of many viable *hadiths* in their *Sahih** works. Amini

---

[39] *Ibid.*, pp. 297–304.
[40] Kashif al-Qita Najafi, *In Ast A'ieen Ma* (This Is Our Faith), pp. 137–138.
[41] Najafi, *op. cit.*, pp. 142–143; Allamah Tabatabai, *Shi'ite Islam*, p. 44.
* *Sahih* is a book title that refers to the validity of the *hadith*. Literally, *sahih* means "correct ones."

suggests that various *hadiths* apparently favorable to the Shi'i doctrine but rejected by al-Bukhari and al-Muslim are reported by another *hadith* scholar by the name of Hakim Nishaburi. In addition, Amini provides the list of medieval Muslim historians (among them a few mentioned in this study such as Tabari, Ibn Khaldun, and Shahrastani who inherently are not sympathetic to the Shi'i cause and only mention the story or the *hadith* of Ghadir Khum to refer to the Shi'i belief and not necessarily to give certain validity to it) as well as the names of the companions of the Prophet and other *Ulamas* in order to prove the reality and importance of the *hadith*.[42]

One contemporary expert on the *hadith* suggests that, for *hadiths* to be accepted as a source of legal ordinance, they must satisfy five criteria: continuity of the chain of transmitters (*ittisal asanad*); integrity (*adalah*) of the transmitters; soundness of the memory of the transmitters; conformity of the *hadiths*; and absence of defects (*illah*) in the *hadith*.[43]

With regard to rejection or acceptance of any transmitted *hadiths*, applying these rules leads to the conclusion that the pro-Ali *hadiths* could easily have been based on religious partisanship in the course of the ongoing controversy between the Shi'i and Sunni sects. In fact, *hadith* fabrication for propaganda purposes was a by-product of the political hostilities between the Umawi and Abbasi Caliphates and the opposition (the emerging Shi'i sects). Thus the grounds for carefully verifying the validity of the transmitted *hadiths* depends significantly on the reviewer's own religious and ideological orientation. Ignaz Goldziher, in his *Muhammedanische Studien* (1890), shows how the *hadiths* have been affected by political and sectional interests, as it is evident that there is a lack of systematic transmission and a serious shortage of coherence and objectivity in the sayings and actions of the religious leaders to whom the *hadiths* are attributed.[44]

For practical purposes, it is important to note a few points about Ali's right to succession. First, there is no evidence that Ali or the other companions of the Prophet brought up any relevant *hadiths* at the time of selection of the first successor. Ali himself, as shown in the *Nahj ul Balagha*, made no explicit or implicit reference to the existence and

---

[42] Amini, *op. cit.*, II, p. 251; vol. I, pp. 22–241.
[43] Azami, "Hadith: Rules for Acceptance and Transmission," *The Place of Hadith in Islam*, pp. 19–21.
[44] Watt, *Formative Period*, p. 64, quoting Goldziher.

significance of such *hadiths*. In Shi'i doctrine, the explanation is that there has been a conspiracy of silence about this gap in the historical record—presumably imposed by the same authorities who edited the original evidence.

Second, in light of what has been said about the *hadiths* relating to Ali's right to succeed the Prophet, it is reasonable to raise another point. Assuming that Muhammad did indeed make many references to his appointment of Ali to be his heir, it seems odd that he never suggested reconfirmation and transcription of this message—especially considering that it contained such a crucial declaration for the future of the Muslim community. Muhammad was a shrewd preacher and warrior; he pursued his religious ideas from a meager situation in Mecca to an established state religion in Arabia and rarely left room for any approximation of his message. So far as the validity of this *hadith* is concerned, it may very well be assumed that Muhammad never wished his companions to be deprived of evidence of his bounty or his compliments. Indeed, it is not far-fetched to believe accounts that Muhammad greatly enjoyed his relationships with his faithful companions. For example, apart from his companionship with Uthman, Muhammad married two of his daughters, Umm-Kulthoum and Ruqiya. Abu Bakr, who arranged Muhammad's flight from Mecca to Medina, also gave his young daughter A'isha to Muhammad in marriage. Umar was father and son-in-law of the Prophet, and Talha and Zubayr fought for Muhammad with distinction. All of these facts and many others must have filled Muhammad's mind with undeniably fond memories, to which he always addressed his benediction. It is true that Ali was Muhammad's cousin, son-in-law, faithful companion, and (above all) clansman. But Muhammad could not have favored Ali above the others out of simple family favoritism if his religious and sociopolitical policies were to be based on divine law.

Third, any effort by Muhammad to appoint Ali would have run counter to the clan and tribal customs of the northern Arabs that prescribed leaving the nomination of the leader to the people. Because of such customs, the Arabs of pre-Islamic Mecca never had a monarchic king, and indeed during the crisis they balloted to elect a leader.[45] In contrast, the tribes of southern Arabia (the Yemenites) had been gov-

---

[45] Jafri, *op. cit.*, p. 22.

erned for hundreds of years (until the early sixth century) by hereditary kings to whom were attributed superhuman qualities.[46]

A tribal explanation from which the ruling Caliphs and the Alids (Shi'a) equally drew legitimacy was that Muhammad had specified that the governorship was to remain within the Quraysh tribe. Sheikh Amini reports a *hadith* that corroborates this assertion: "People must obey the Quraysh, and the Qurayshites are the leaders of the Arabs."[47]

This *hadith* certainly served the cause of the Qurayshite supremacists (such as the Umayyad and Abbasid) vis-à-vis other ambitious but less established tribes. Nevertheless, the clan of Banu Hashim of the Quraysh was not left empty-handed, and through favorable use of this *hadith* prevented clan annihilation and promoted their religiopolitical ideas in later stages when they became a minority within a multiethnic Islamic community.

To validate the Shi'i argument about Ali's special position, some commentators focus on the marriage of Fatima, the Prophet's daughter, to Ali, which was seen as tribally significant as both were Hashimite. (This is especially important as Muhammad's lineage continued through this marriage, even though it also continued through other marriages, because this marriage was more significant and consequential for the Shi'ites). Of course, this concept became crucial when the critical years under Umayyad rule affected the followers of Ali. But Ali married twelve other wives after Fatima, taking a total of 395 mates (*azwaj*). He is also said to have had seventeen sons and nineteen daughters after those borne by Fatima.[48] Thus it may be argued that his marriage to Fatima at the same time Uthman married two of Muhammad's daughters had no particular spiritual significance in a polygamous society.[49]

As to the appointment of Ali by the prophet Zayd, the son of Zayn al-Abidin (the fourth Shi'i Imam after Ali) is said to have denied such a designation.[50] Ibn Khaldun and Ibn Ishaq indicate that Ali himself

---

[46] Watt, *Formative Period*, p. 43, quoting Ryckmans, *L'institution monarchique en Arabie avant l'Islam*, Luvain, 1951, p. 329.
[47] Amini, *op. cit.*, II, p. 9.
[48] Donaldson, *The Shi'ite Religion*, p. 15.
[49] Lewis, *L'Islam d'hier*, p. 13.
[50] See Ibn Hazm's discussion in Friedlander, "The Heterodoxies of the Shi'ites in the Presentation of Ibn Hazm," *Journal of American Oriental Society* XXVII (1907): 74, quoted by Jafri, *op. cit.*, p. 290.

knew too well that Muhammad had not composed a will and had not selected a successor.[51] In a review of various texts and books that the Shi'i writers used as references, Ibn Khaldun regards the origin and the transmitters of these texts as unknown.[52]

It is well known that, after the renewal of opposition in Iraq failed to elevate the children of Ali to the Caliphate, the issue of the Ghadir Khum *hadith* became central. Thereafter, polemical literature began to emerge in support of Ali's claim until at last, in the tenth century, the Buyids (a Shi'i dynasty) came to power in Iran, giving fresh confidence to Shi'ism. The accession to power of the Safavids in sixteenth-century Iran resulted in the suppression of Sunnism and paved the way for the development of Shi'i propaganda in its monolithic form. To authenticate their religiopolitical case, the Shi'ites discarded and ignored many sources and ideas, and Maryam Mir Ahmadi suggests that this was responsible for the decline of intellectualism during that period.[53] The rise of the school of Isfahan in the Safavid period and the establishment of the school of Qum during the rise of Reza Khan in the twentieth century were milestones in the development and promotion of Shi'ism and fostered the production of massive volumes of Shi'i literature and religious materials.

How Ali himself reacted to and evaluated the situation from the time Abu Bakr succeeded Muhammad as the first leader to the time of his own appointment as the fourth successor to the Prophet may provide some clarification of the reliability of the reported version of Ali's designation by the Prophet.

Ali and His Politics

Ali may have been aware that his youth put him at a disadvantage to become successor to the Prophet. Ali was perhaps thirty-three, while Abu Bakr was in his early sixties. Some sources report that Ali subordinated himself to the central authority of the three succeeding Caliphs (Abu Bakr, Umar, and Uthman) and played the role of important coun-

---

[51] Ibn Khaldun, I, p. 420.; see also Ibn Ishaq, *Sira*, p. 682.
[52] *Ibid.*, p. 386.
[53] Mir Ahmadi, *Din va Madhab dar Asre Safavi*, pp. 76–77.

selor to the Caliphs. Having been passed over for Caliph and having previously worked with each of the first three Caliphs during the prophecy of Muhammad, Ali evidently deemed it appropriate to work toward constructing a cohesive and strong Islamic community under their leadership. Shi'i sources prefer not to mention that Ali recognized the work and legitimacy of his three immediate predecessors as Caliph, tending instead to attribute such cooperation (as Jafri suggests) to Ali's heroic character and sense of sacrifice for the faith, which also helped save the Caliphs from committing serious errors.[54] It is true that Ali disagreed with the Caliphs on certain issues, but these instances did not profoundly diminish the positive relationship that they had built. Thus Ali cherished and complimented Umar in the *Nahj ul Balagha*.[55] After Umar was assassinated and while his body was lying for burial, Ali observed "There is no name on earth dearer to me than the one God has inscribed on his ledger for this man under the cover."[56]

Umar had also regarded Ali with high respect. Before his death he appointed a commission of six to decide on his successor; Ali was one of the six. The fact that Ali named his subsequent sons Abu Bakr, Umar, and Uthman[57] offers another indication of his affection and respect for the three ruling Caliphs. Ali had on a few occasions saved Uthman's life. Just before Uthman's assassination, as Mas'udi reports, Ali sent his sons Hasan and Husayn along with others to defend and protect Uthman. Hasan was injured in the skirmishes as the assassins forcibly entered Uthman's house, where they killed him. Upon receiving the news, Ali rushed to the scene and reacted to it with anger, slapping Hasan, pounding Husayn's chest, and damning others for their inability to save the Caliph.[58] Following this assassination, Ali was accused by his rivals of having conspired in the murder in order to succeed Uthman himself. Ali was also accused of not having punished the assassins, who afterward proclaimed him the successor to Uthman. Among the participants in the assassination, as al-Baladhuri reports, were two hundred Kufans led

[54] Jafri, *op. cit.*, pp. 60–61.
[55] *Nahj ul Balagha*, CCXXVIII, p. 625.
[56] Ibn Sa'd, *Tabaqat*, III, i, p. 102; *Rauzat us Safa*, II, p. 219, cited by Donaldson, *op. cit.*, p. 20.
[57] Tabari, VI, pp. 2695–2696.
[58] Mas'udi, I, pp. 701–702; Ibn Tiqtaqa, pp. 116, 134 reports that Ali only sent Hasan. See also Nawbakhti, p. 53; Jafri, *op. cit.*, p. 87.

to Medina by Malik al-Ashtar,[59] the man who pressed for Ali's designation as Caliph.

Although Ali did not take an active role in politics across a wide spectrum, he did undertake official duties as a counselor and courtier in Medina. Tabari mentions that Ali served as Umar's official representative in Medina.[60] Yet subsequent followers of Ali tried to minimize his involvement with the Caliphates of Abu Bakr, Umar, and Uthman, because they belonged to an antagonistic tradition. According to the Shi'ites, the first three Caliphs deviated from the prophetic tradition to provide the basis of Sunni tradition. Ali was recognized as the symbol and innovator of Shi'ism. However, the development of this religiopolitical philosophy, to which Ali never overtly subscribed himself, has never been fully explained. Ali seems to have embodied the ideal of loyal protector of the Caliphate under the three Caliphs, although it has been asserted that Ali did not want to be bound to precedent when the Council (*shura*) met to select a successor to Umar. Allamah Tabatabai tries to explain this paradox, despite the fact that the Shi'a and Sunni were not yet distinct sects, but it is rather difficult for him to detach his explanation from the already rooted Shi'i fundamentalism. He timidly states: "Members of the Shi'ite community even fought hand in hand with the Sunni majority in holy wars (Jihad) and participated in public affairs. Ali himself guided the Sunni majority in the interest of the whole of Islam whenever such action was necessary."[61]

All of this raises the question of whether Ali was fundamentally opposed to or in favor of his predecessors. Ali, who had been inclined to cooperate with the rulership of the three Caliphs, could not completely have hidden his desire to safeguard his clan's interests. In his famous exposition of *as'Shaqshaqiyya* in *Nahj ul Balagha*, Ali expresses his grievances about the plundering of his heritage while the successors passed the Caliphate to each other from Abu Bakr to Umar. Throughout this period, Ali realized that his privileges and position could only be saved by patience.[62] On the other hand, he specifically praised Umar by saying "May God be with him, he straightened the crooked and cured the ills.

---

[59] al-Baladhuri, *Ansab*, V, p. 59, quoted by Morony, *Iraq*, p. 485.
[60] Tabari, IV, p. 1632.
[61] Tabatabai, *op. cit.*, p. 44, quoting Ya'qubi.
[62] *Nahj ul Balagha*, III, p. 20.

He performed the *sunna*. He left this world pure with little errors."[63]
Indeed, Ali is reported to have restored Umar's policies in Iraq.[64]

It also appears in some of the expositions of *Nahj ul Balagha* that Ali
at the same time had some hesitance about accepting the position of
Caliph.[65] Sunni sources assert that there was no opposition between Ali
and the first three Caliphs, but this is not entirely true: Ali, as the
inheritor of the Banu Hashim clan and the representative of the Ahl al-
Bayt, was supported by some of the Prophet's companions (among them
a number of Banu Umayya, Talha, and Zubayr who, at the time of Ali's
designation as Caliph, turned against him), although he was not so
popular in a wider context; thus he must have had a convincing reason
to feel that his authority should not have been ignored. The Shi'i interpretation is that Ali's quiescent attitude symbolized his opposition to the
first three Caliphs, and this idea convinced the vast majority of subsequent Shi'ites who could find no direct support in contemporaneous
sources for the divine appointment of Ali by Muhammad. Moojan
Momen observes: "Ali's retirement from active public life seems to
support the idea that he felt that he had received some specific designation by Muhammad. This is all that can be gleaned from the
sources."[66]

It would be far-fetched to believe that Ali whole-heartedly devoted
himself to service on behalf of the three Caliphs, and yet there is no
evidence in the most likely sources (such as the Koran and Ali's own
compiled sayings in *Nahj ul Balagha*) to defend explicitly the notion of
Ali's personal appointment by Muhammad. Nonetheless, Ali was fully
aware of the lack of any defined constitutional roles of succession. Abu
Bakr was selected under peculiar circumstances, Umar was appointed by
Abu Bakr, Uthman was designated by the council of six men, and Ali
was proclaimed by his entourage (Uthman's killers). Significantly, Ali
knew that the succession was not hereditary; and in fact he waited for
his turn to come. Later we will review evidence making it clear that Ali,
Hasan, and Husayn made no specific designation for their successors to
the position of Caliph; indeed, the hereditary notion was simultaneously

---

[63] *Ibid.*, CCXXVIII, p. 625.
[64] Morony, *Iraq*, p. 485.
[65] One example is *Nahj ul Balagha*, CCXXIX, p. 625.
[66] Momen, *op. cit.*, p. 62.

developed by both the Banu Umayya Caliphate after Ali and by his followers.

For the moment, it is essential to distinguish between, on the one hand, Ali's state of mind as reflected in his compiled sayings and in other early traditions and, on the other, the later religious convictions developed by the Shi'ites. It certainly sounds convincing to Shi'i ears when Amini quotes a Sunni source (Ali b. Ahmed Wahidi, who cites Abu Hurayreh) to the effect that Ali himself composed poems about his designation by Muhammad—an analogy comparable to that of Harun by Moses.[67] Such a poem carries a sufficiently important message that Ali must at least have acknowledged the idea of his appointment (if one existed) in order to prevent his future followers from going astray; yet an obscure Sunni source refers to it, while Ali himself does not mention it at all in his sayings in Nahj ul Balagha.

Adding another idea to our discussion may give a better picture of what Ali's position was during the twenty-five years of the three Caliphs' leadership. From both Sunni and Shi'i sources one can infer that Ali was shrewd, heroic, and harsh—especially when he felt that the prophetic order was being threatened. A few examples demonstrate Ali's suppressive dealings with those who did not favor Islamic orders. Ya'qubi reports that, during the bloodless fall of Mecca, Ali wanted to kill two of his own relatives who had gone into hiding but Muhammad dissuaded him from doing so.[68] Al-Baladhuri reports that, on another occasion when Ali's emissary to Sistan (a province in Persia) was killed by the natives of that land, Ali ordered in revenge the massacre of four thousand local people, although he was informed that their total population did not exceed five hundred.[69]

Ali's enthusiastic participation in battles while in the army, in a duel during the time of Muhammad, and again when he became the fourth Caliph provide convincing evidence that he was unafraid to confront opposition. Thus he was probably not deeply perturbed, at least in regard to the prophetic order at Ghadir Khum. Otherwise the violation of so crucial an order would have impelled Ali to take impetuous and severe measures to deny the legitimacy of the three succeeding Caliphs. Moreover, apart from his knowledge that he had not been designated Mu-

---

[67] Amini, op. cit., III, pp. 53–54.
[68] Ya'qubi, I, p. 419.
[69] al-Baladhuri, Futuh (section on Iran), p. 151.

hammad's successor, he may have thought that he simply did not have the necessary charisma and the requisite influence over the majority of Medinans to gain enough support. As it was, Ali's main support came from Iraqis, whose interest and purpose coincided with his own: "When Ali came to Iraq, the dissident elements there supported him to the extent that he supported their interest."[70]

For twenty-five years Ali not only did not oppose the expansion of Arab domination and the prosperity the Islamic community achieved through the governance of the three Caliphs, he also oriented his mind around what had been achieved within the empire. His heading of the expedition of new armies to Dailam in Persia to suppress the opposition[71] and his decision to send his sons Hasan and Husayn on a mission to occupy Tabaristan[72] demonstrate Ali's ultimate approval of and contribution to the policies of the Caliphs. Clearly, what Ali did and how he behaved is better understood by reading what he and the early sources say than by reading polemics written by partisans of subsequent factions such as Ali's followers who opposed the ruling Caliphs in later stages, who wanted to further a specific political agenda.

Ali, the Caliph, and the Succession Crisis

Political ambiguities were created by the way in which Ali received the sworn allegiance (35/656) of Malik al-Ashtar, who had led the Iraqi opposition to Uthman's policies, by the number of dissatisfied Iraqi *ashraf* who feared the growing power of Umayya in Damascus, and obviously by the support of the Banu Hashim. These ambiguities were to be cleared in the months and years to come.

Uthman, the third Caliph, was from the clan of Banu Umayya, and his clansmen of the Sufyani family were growing in strength politically, economically, and militarily in Syria. Al-Baladhuri indicates that Abu Sufyan owned land near Damascus even before the conquest.[73] Apart from the rivalry between the Banu Umayya and Banu Hashim clans, a

---

[70] Morony, *Iraq*, p. 485.
[71] al-Baladhuri, *Futuh* (section on Iran), p. 81.
[72] *Ibid.*, p. 92.
[73] al-Baladhuri, *Futuh*, p. 129, quoted by Donner, *op. cit.*, p. 96.

historical rivalry existed between the Syrians (Ghassanid kingdom under the Romans) and the Iraqis (Lakhmid kingdom under the Persians). The assassination of Uthman by an Iraqi mob and the designation of Ali as Caliph under such circumstances gave both the Banu Hashim and Iraqis an opportunity to even old scores with the Banu Umayya and Syria. The Iraqis who offered Ali their staunch support were opponents of Uthman in Iraq and did not necessarily have any religious basis for supporting Ali.[74] Other early supporters of Ali began to resist the reimposition of control by the Meccan elites, notably the Umayya.[75]

Some remained sympathetic to Uthman and his household. This group, called Uthmaniyya or Shi'at Uthman, were against the emergence of Ali as Caliph, even though they may have had a hand in the assassination plot against Uthman. Nonetheless, this group was not necessarily pro-Mu'awiya (the son of Abu Sufyan in Damascus), and only later did the Uthmaniyya merge with the forces of Mu'awiya. It should be emphasized that Uthman may have been vulnerable to criticism for his handling of religious and state affairs, but among his followers his aristocratic origins made up for his lack of personal abilities. Thus his influence over his supporters should not be ignored. Even in Muhammad's eyes, Uthman's prestigious family background outweighed his religious piety.[76]

Ali faced fierce opposition from the Uthmaniyya once he was designated Uthman's successor. At this point, various parties for multiple reasons joined to topple him. Among the factions of the Uthmani opposition, A'isha (the wife of the Prophet), Talha, and Zubayr were participants for their own personal reasons. A'isha's reasons stemmed from her longstanding dislike of Ali, especially her bitter experience with him when Ali slandered her by accusing her of having an affair with another man. Talha and Zubayr, who had already given their oath of allegiance to Ali,[77] probably saw that the situation suited their ambitions to emerge as contenders for the Caliphate. Ali, on the other hand, with

---

[74] Morony, *Iraq*, p. 485.
[75] *Ibid.*, p. 484.
[76] Brocklemann, *History of Islamic Peoples*, p. 63; see also Goldziher, *Le Dogme*, p. 159. Rodinson, *Mahomet*, p. 129, indicates that the apparent reason for Uthman to convert to Islam was his love for Ruqiya, the daughter of Muhammad.
[77] Sheikh Mufid, *Kitab ul-Jamal*, pp. 60–61, indicates that Talha and Zubayr had given Ali their allegiance out of fear and pressure, not voluntarily; thus they left Ali's party.

his meager popularity in Medina, found himself at the head of a massive army in Iraq. He flatly denied knowing about the assassination plot[78] (including the identities of those who plotted it), but in the end he never punished the assassins. The Iraqis urged Ali to fight back, but Ali was confusedly reluctant.[79] Finally, five months after his accession to the Caliphate in 35/656, he led an Iraqi army against the Uthmaniyya and others who opposed him and the Iraqis who had joined him.

The ensuing war was pressed by various factions under the banner of avenging the blood of Uthman. This was the first and bloodiest battle fought among Muslims themselves; Mas'udi reports more than thirteen thousand men from A'isha's army and five thousand from Ali's were killed.[80] In this battle, which became known as the battle of al-Jamal (Camel), Ali was victorious and thereupon forgave and released A'isha. Kurt Fischler proposes that the reason A'isha suddenly turned against Ali was that he, as the functioning Caliph, reduced A'isha's stipends by eighty thousand dirhams.[81] This may have been one of the impulses, but the real roots lie in the early family makeup in which A'isha, as a young wife of the Prophet, may have felt slighted by the reception she got from Muhammad's daughter Fatima, who could not easily have accepted this young girl as her stepmother.

A'isha came into opposition by contesting the right to the property at Fadak claimed by Fatima and Ali's side and out of dislike for both. Ali's dislike may be even more complex, since its bases were both personal (Ali's slanderous remark about A'isha) and political (Ali's competition for succession that ended in the designation of A'isha's father, Abu Bakr). It may be that A'isha despised the fact that the Banu Hashim favored its Ahl al-Bayt, where she felt out of place.

In any event, A'isha wrote to Mu'awiya b. Abu Sufyan, an Umayyad, asking him to oppose Ali and the accession of his clan to power.[82] Thus clan politics were instrumental in her conscious instigation of hostilities between the two rival clans of the Quraysh.

---

[78] See various expositions cited in the *Nahj ul Balagha*.
[79] For a brief detail of Ali's state of mind and affairs, see Mas'udi, *Muruj*, I, pp. 714–731; Ya'qubi, II, p. 80. See also Sheikh Mufid, *Kitab ul-Jamal*, p. 206.
[80] Mas'udi, I, p. 708; Tabari, VI, p. 2471, indicates that more than 10,000 people were killed.
[81] Fischler, *A'isha After the Prophet*, p. 416.
[82] See Fischler, *op. cit.*, pp. 423–442.

The battle of al-Jamal was the product of many hidden issues that surfaced after Uthman was murdered and Ali succeeded him as Caliph. In this period Mu'awiya, the eminent Umayyad representative, found circumstances favorable for extending his strength within the empire and casting his power over Iraq—not only to satisfy the Syrians, but also to topple Ali's Caliphate there. At the same time, Mu'awiya felt the danger that Ali as Caliph might order him replaced as governor in Syria. Mu'awiya shrewdly revived an old Arab tribal practice of blood revenge (which had a Koranic justification); since Uthman was an Umayyad, a member of his Ahl al-Bayt would be justified in declaring war against Ali. Julius Wellhausen says: "Revenge for Uthman was the title upon which Mu'awiya founded his right of inheritance."[83] Montgomery Watt similarly indicates that Mu'awiya's promotion of the idea of avenging Uthman's blood, in view of Ali's refusal to do it, gave him the necessary elements to make a grab for power.[84] About two decades later, when Ali's son Husayn was killed by the Umayya, the concept of revenge for the Ahl al-Bayt arose from the same Arabian background that had been brought to Iraq by the Arabs.[85] As previously mentioned, Mu'awiya's supporters, Shi'at Mu'awiya, gradually merged into the Shi'at Uthmaniyya to confront the dissidents of Iraq and challenge Ali's Caliphate.

Ali's present supporters included those who were his earlier supporters from Medina; anti-Uthmani factions motivated predominantly by economic considerations; the Iraqi tribal aristocracy (ashraf), who were suspicious of the Umayyad expansion; and importantly, the Kufan population as a heterogenous tribal composition. All of these came together to organize a front called Shi'at Ali, the followers of Ali. As Jafri indicates, the term Shi'at Ali came to include everyone who supported Ali against A'isha, and from this point on the Shi'i group rather indiscriminately included groups who backed Ali for reasons that could not have had a religious basis.[86] Morony refers to Ali's own earliest protégés, who began to resist the reimposition of control by the Meccan merchant elite, who were the late converts (specifically the Umayyad).[87] These intertwined

---

[83] Wellhausen, Arab Kingdom and Its Fall, p. 135.
[84] Watt, Formative Period, p. 83.
[85] Morony, Iraq, p. 492.
[86] Jafri, op. cit., p. 96.
[87] Morony, Iraq, p. 484.

reasons all promoted Ali to be the leader of Iraqi opposition to the Syrian yoke.[88] Such opposition by the Shi'at Ali established in Iraq was therefore not a religious sect but a political opposition.[89]

It is essential to understand that the Shi'i group only took on the character of a religious enterprise in subsequent years; initially it existed as a political and military organization, and its aim was to fight the Umayya of Syria. In this way A'isha, the Shi'at Uthman, and the Shi'at Mu'awiya provoked and united the Shi'at Ali. Again, the issue of Ghadir Khum was not the basis upon which the Banu Hashim and the Iraqis justified their defense against external opposition to Ali's designation as Caliph.

The battle between the forces of Mu'awiya and those of Ali took place at Siffin (north of Kufa and east of Damascus) in July 657. The split within the Muslim community was becoming more evident, but the nature of the conflict yet remained to be understood by both parties. The implication of seeking revenge for the death of Uthman led a number of parallel rivalries—the Iraqo-Syrian affair, the emerging elites versus the old elites, the pious individuals versus more secular tribal leaders (Khawarij versus Ali and his support from the tribal leaders), and Banu Hashim versus Banu Umayya—into the next stage of dispute over the newly formed Muslim empire. This battle, which left forty-five thousand Syrians and twenty-five thousand Iraqis dead,[90] introduced a new religiopolitical consciousness and new social movements aimed at reforming the Arab hierarchy and guaranteeing the privileges and prosperity of those belonging to the traditional tribal aristocracy.

Though the Arabs were the privileged group throughout the empire,[91] the internal conflict of interest eventually led to a violent revolution in 132 A.H. (A.D. 750), in which the Abbasids (the lineage of Banu Hashim) successfully overthrew and murdered the Banu Umayya.[92] Thus the two clans of the Quraysh tribe, as well as the Iraqis and Syrians, finally cleared their old accounts. The Medinan *ansar* (helpers), who never achieved the status of a ruling elite, tried to restore their faded fortunes by backing

---

[88] Wellhausen, *Religio-Political Factions in Early Islam*, p. 96.
[89] *Ibid.*
[90] al-Minqari, *Waq'at Siffin*, p. 773.
[91] Von Grunebaum, *op. cit.*, p. 199.
[92] Alid Shi'a pretenders defied Abbasid rule due to the political rivalry of two factions within the Banu Hashim. See Donner, *op. cit.*, p. 275.

THE EMERGENCE OF ISLAM

Ali against other factions of the Quraysh, but despite much effort they never succeeded.[93] Thus *ansar* remained and maintained their officialdom in Iraq.

Mu'awiya's challenge constituted the means he had selected to qualify himself for the Caliphate. His aristocratic background attracted many highborn men of Arabia and Syria, who were principally concerned with preserving their privileges rather than with avenging the blood of Uthman. Mu'awiya's options were limited, so he decided to march against Ali on the same grounds of avenging the blood of Uthman, meanwhile keeping his own ambitions well in the background.[94] Nasr ibn Muzahim al-Minqari (d. 212/828) reports in his book *Waq'at Siffin* on letters exchanged between Ali and Mu'awiya, in which Mu'awiya criticizes Ali for boasting about his early conversion and services to Islam, and states that he considers them insignificant in light of Ali's having provoked those assassins to kill the pious son-in-law of the Prophet, the Caliph Uthman.[95] It must have been a confusing period to make a political choice for Muslims caught in the middle.

The Kufan contingents, under the leadership of Malik al-Ashtar, had sworn him their allegiance. Ali had also made it possible for those who were not induced to support the Umayya to join him instead. The non-Arabs (*mawali*) of Kufa—mainly Persians who either had been brought to Kufa by the warriors of the battles of Qadisiya (15/636) and Nihawand (21/642) or had been among early merchant settlers—supported Ali as well.[96]

Ironically, some people believe that the Persians had a special religious attraction to the house of Ali (Ahl-al-Bayt), or in fact introduced the concept of hereditary succession into the doctrine of Shi'ism. But the hereditary issue suffers from lack of evidence, since as many Persians lived at Basra as at Kufa, yet those at Basra do not appear to have supported Ali's family claims, whereas they made significant contributions to the movements of the Khawarij.[97] Of course, the initiative to

---

[93] Donner, *op. cit.*, p. 274; see also al-Minqari, p. 130.
[94] Donaldson, *op. cit.*, p. 34.
[95] Al-Minqari, pp. 123–130.
[96] See Fischler, *op. cit.*, p. 428. (Ali had eight thousand *mawali* and slaves registered in the Kufan army; see Morony, *Iraq*, p. 244, quoting Tabari, I, p. 3372.)
[97] Morony, *Iraq*, p. 497.

support Ali was maintained by individual Arab elements of Arab background until A.D. 685.[98]

At any rate, the battle fought at Siffin defined opponents not by religious preference but by the political camps within the community. The term *Shi'a* was, as yet, used strictly in a political sense. Not surprisingly, many of those (such as the Khawarij) who supported Ali in the battles of al-Jamal and Siffin turned against him as the political climate shifted. Thus the Shi'at Ali did not necessarily have any interest in turning the tide of opinion in favor of Ali and his Ahl al-Bayt on the basis of some supposedly superior religious position. But, on the other hand, according to Shi'i sources, Ali is said to have been praised and given the titles of *wasi* and "the Inheritor" by his Medinan companions such as Abu Dharr,[99] as well as by the Banu Hashim clan. Moreover, apart from the rebellion against Uthmani rule and the Umayyad expansion in Iraq, religious dedication and the prospect of a religious (as opposed to a tribal) nobility must have represented a significant factor for certain Iraqis in their support for Ali against Mu'awiya.

Nonetheless, this problem of intentions surfaced when the battle at Siffin ended through arbitration with no definite military result. The negotiations took place between representatives of both sides, Amr ibn al-As from Mu'awiya's side and Abu Musa al-Ash'ari from Ali's side. Jafri reports that Abu Musa was the choice of the tribal leaders, who convinced Ali to accept him,[100] and asserts that "Abu Musa's record indicated that he had been in favor of the Meccans and of overall domination by the Quraysh."[101] The settlement between the two forces led to their truce, but this in turn made one group (the Khawarij) secede, saying, "Judgment belongs only to God."[102] These combatants refused to be bound by the treaty conditions and to accept the peace accord between the two factions of the Quraysh (Banu Hashim and Banu Umayya) and between other tribal interest groups in the midst of which the deprived pious masses were caught up. The political slogans of the Khawarij were directed toward the radical political consciousness of the historically unprivileged

---

[98] *Ibid.*, p. 492.
[99] *Ibid.*, p. 486.
[100] Jafri, *op. cit.*, p. 122.
[101] *Ibid.*
[102] Morony, *Iraq*, p. 469.

masses. Donner writes: "Those of groups outside of the elite that wished to gain access to it (notably the pious and the Khawarij) relied increasingly on the importance of virtuous, properly Islamic behavior as justifications for holding power."[103]

But the attitude of the Khawarij developed an increasingly religious orientation after the group seceded from Ali's army; as Morony observes, the group began its independent role in such a manner, but this gradually led to its political opposition in Iraq in later stages: "It became increasingly obvious that the Khawarij were less interested in the claims of either Ali or Mu'awiya than they were in providing a vehicle for protest and armed revolt against whoever happened to represent the establishment in Iraq."[104]

In such circumstance the new division in the supporters of Ali emerged, separating the Shi'at Ali and the Khawarij. The Khawarij's withdrawal from Ali's forces equally signified their disapproval of Ali's Caliphate as they had denounced the supremacy and monopoly of any tribe over another. Such defiance may also have had to do with opposition to the alleged *hadith* prescribing that the monopoly of rulership was to remain within the Quraysh tribe, the effect of which was to legitimate the claims of both Ali and Mu'awiya. The Khawarij in later stages began to preach and promote freedom of candidacy for the Caliphate, and they believed that the Caliphate should be open to anyone from an Ethiopian slave to a highborn man of Medina. As they migrated southward to Basra, they designated as their Caliph Abdollah b. Wahb Rasibi. This attitude upset the tribal leaders in Kufa, who urged Ali to take action against them before planning a new attack on Mu'awiya, simply because the Khawarij were a threat to their standing whereas Mu'awiya was not.[105]

Ali launched an attack on the Khawarij at Nahrawan (38/658), northeast of Kufa. In slaying them he weakened his position, creating even more enemies at a time many of his supporters among the tribal leaders at Kufa were making under-the-table deals with Mu'awiya.[106] Consequently, we may conclude that the Shi'i party of Ali was by and large a

---

[103] Donner, *op. cit.*, p. 275. In pre-Islamic aristocracy, *nasab* (nobility of descent) systematically validated their claims to authority or noble status.
[104] Morony, *Iraq*, p. 470.
[105] Jafri, *op. cit.*, p. 123.
[106] *Ibid.*

movement that historically matched the peculiar circumstances of anti-Uthmani movements in Iraq and actually had very little to do with Ali's divine claim to the succession to Muhammad, as the subsequent Shi'a would argue. Further, it seems that both the Shi'at Ali and Khawarij movements did not stem from the Muslims of Mecca and Medina but rather from among former nomads.[107] It is true that the small group of *ansar*, together with Ali's close friends and family members, relocated to Kufa, but this cannot be taken as evidence that the real reason was the emergence of Shi'ism in its religious form. The motives for backing Ali varied (as indeed was the case for those who followed the descendants of Ali in later years), but as a whole such motives became the basis for the development of religious sectarianism in Islam. Marshall Hodgson says with regard to the Shi'at Ali:

> The Shi'i began as a minority party whose leader was rejected by the other companions of the prophet . . . hated by Kharijites, resisted by the Syrians, unloved by the Hijazi supporters of Zubayr . . . and not well supported even by the Kufans to whom he could at least guarantee the presence of their treasury.[108]

After the battle of Nahrawan, certain Khawarij—whose religious and political aspirations were frustrated—decided to attempt the assassination of the three important leaders: Mu'awiya in Syria, Amr Ibn al-As in Egypt, and Ali in Iraq. The attempts were made, with various results. Mu'awiya was wounded but recovered. Amr Ibn al-As was not hit at all; the person who had substituted for him in a prayer meeting because he was ill was assassinated. For Ali, the blow was fatal (d. 40/661); Ibn Muljam, Ali's assassin had reportedly been promised marriage to a woman whose family members were slain at Nahrawan in return for the assassination of Ali.[109] However, the assassin never made it to his bride. He was first imprisoned and then killed just as he had killed his victim: Hasan executed him in accordance with the request of his father Ali.

The physical elimination of Ali had a number of unresolved political

---

[107] Watt, *Formative Period*, p. 42.
[108] Hodgson, "How Did the Early Shi'a Become Sectarian?" *Journal of American Oriental Society* 75 (1955): 2.
[109] Ibn Tiqtaqa, p. 139; Mostaufi, p. 196.

and religious implications, but his removal greatly strengthened Mu'awiya's position in the short term: "With Ali's death, the tide turned against Iraqis and they became part of the United Kingdom which Mu'awiya created."[110]

The Iraqis soon realized that their policies were inadequate to the task of dealing with the Syrians. Ali's naivete may have been reason for criticism, as may his antagonism to A'isha and her entourage, his ambiguous position vis-à-vis the Caliph Uthman, and his covert dealings with the Umayya, which led to a catastrophic compromise and eventually to the secession of the Khawarij. Some commentators note that Ali's political record was not too impressive.[111] And Muhammad, while acknowledging Ali's bravery, must have realized "that Ali had not the makings of a successful statesman."[112]

On the other hand, to some Ali was a political hero, a pious man whose memory was cherished. His death left a gap in the religiopolitical aspiration of certain Iraqis. It is even said that he was given the title Mahdi, "guided by God."[113] It was during the political turmoil following Ali's death that, among the heterogeneous population of Iraq, a minority was solidifying whose new religious consciousness was based on contemporaneous persons and events. Their souls blazed with the certainty that Ali was a real hero, and a popular heroic figure has certain distinctive characteristics:

> The naive desire to magnify one's hero by lifting him as far as possible out of the human sphere combined with age-old tradition that underlined the significance of the extraordinary personality by ascribing to him the cooperation or even the submission of the non-human cosmos.[114]

The impact of the events that took place during the short Caliphate of Ali in Iraq ultimately resolved into the formation of new religious thoughts and the attribution of superhuman and divine qualities to Ali (and subsequently to his descendants). The emergence of a group of

---

[110] Wellhausen, Religio-Political Factions in Early Islam, p. 96.
[111] Von Grunebaum, p. 186.
[112] Watt, Muhammad: Prophet and Statesman, p. 230.
[113] Snouck Hurgronge, Der Mahdi: Verspreide Geschriften, (Bonn, 1923). Quoted in Lewis, Origins of Ismailism, p. 25, and Sachedina, Islamic Messianism, p. 9.
[114] Von Grunebaum, p. 92.

ghulat (exaggerators) among the followers of Ali played an important role emotionally in creating the legend associated with him. The *ghuluww* (assertions and exaggerations) provided a bargaining position for reviling and slandering other parties, such as the Umayya and Khawarij. These unsystematic extreme attributions of perfection to Ali subsequently convinced many that Gabriel had made a mistake in presenting the Lord's message to Muhammad instead of to Ali.[115] In this connection, it is worth quoting a description of Ali's miraculous birth as formulated by certain extremists whose words and ideas passed from one generation to another. A modern Shi'i writer, Sayyid Muhammad Kazim al-Qazwini, first describes how the wall of the Ka'ba split to enable Fatima bint Asad, Ali's mother, to enter. There she gave birth to Ali, and then:

> Muhammad, who had not yet received God's revelation to preach Islam, went to see the newborn child. As he entered the house, the baby Ali smiled broadly and spoke, reciting from Quran 23:1–10, where God says, "Successful are those believers who humble themselves in their prayers . . . and they will be the heirs." Muhammad turned to Ali and said, "Surely the believers have become successful through you." This was Ali's first miracle: speaking in the cradle like Jesus and, through divine revelation, reciting a portion of Quran, even though God had not yet chosen Muhammad as His Messenger. Ali had the knowledge that the Quran existed eternally with God.[116]

However, the further elaboration of the initial superhuman qualities of Ali and the assurance of its transmission in this form took place in the post-Ali period, when the consistent followers of Ali (Shi'at Ali) had become a distinct party. From an anthropological and sociological standpoint, one may wonder why the majority of the Kufan people supported Ali zealously while others, especially the Basrans (such as the Khawarij), did not. In other words, why did the Kufans not desert Ali as the Khawarij had? Was it a reasoned choice, or the law of probability, or cause and effect, or reverse psychology, or an issue of preserving the advantages of one community against another?

---

[115] Goldziher, *Vorlesungen*, p. 219, quoted by von Grunebaum, p. 188.
[116] al-Qazwini, *Ali min al-Mahd ila al-Lahd*, 7th ed. (Beirut: Dar al-Turath al-Arabi, n.d.), pp. 18–25, quoted by Moosa, *Extremist Shiites*, pp. 66–67.

It cannot easily be shown that the motivation was religious, because such a conclusion would then lead us to believe that all those who initially gave support to Ali (including the future Khawarij) must have joined Ali, regardless of the political developments, for a specifically religious reason. It must be acknowledged, however, that the piety of Ali and of the future Khawarij must have been a common ground, apart from their shared political interests, in order for them to be absorbed into each other. Many seem to have supported Ali simply in return for his leadership, since there was no dominant figure in the tribal system of Iraq. The Khawarij guaranteed Ali support until the policy of compromise with the Umayya occurred; then they broke with Ali politically—not, as the subsequent Shi'i belief would have it, because they were against religion. The fact that after Ali's death the Khawarij turned to his son Hasan for cooperation in fighting against Mu'awiya[117] proves that they were seeking proper charismatic leadership, not a standard-bearer for a new Islamic sect.

The support of Kufa for Ali and his family may have had to do with the tribal composition of the city and with their distant past.[118] Kufa had been established as the garrison city after the battle of Qadisiya (15/636) with the Persians. The campaigners from Qadisiya and those from the following battle of Nahawand (21/642) were settled in Kufa. The initial settlers were twelve thousand Yemenites (southern Arab tribes), eight thousand Nizaris (northern Arab tribes), and some four thousand Persians.[119] The population multiplied and the new generation was in part the product of mixed parents over the next two decades when Ali came to Kufa, but the cultural and traditional attitude of the tribes about leadership was largely retained. The Yemenite tribes of southern Arabia (in contrast to the northern tribes) practiced and believed in the hereditary succession of a priestly king with superhuman qualities.[120] In addition to the Arab factor, the Persians' heritage of charismatic kingship probably contributed to the development and adoption of this notion of priestly or charismatic leadership. As already noted, the city of Basra also had a significant Persian population, but the people there were not

[117] Jafri, op. cit., p. 155.
[118] For information on the urban settlement of Kufa, see Morony, Iraq, pp. 239–245.
[119] Ibid., p. 108, quoting al-Baladhuri.
[120] Watt, Formative Period, p. 43; see also Jafri, op. cit., p. 117.

inclined to look upon the descendants of Ali as the only legitimate leaders.

In terms of tribal composition, with marginal differences Basra received the migration of the same tribes as did Kufa. Therefore, the influences, linkages, and similarities of the two political poles of the two cities differ merely in having Kufa support Shi'ism and Basra Khawrijism. There are other similarities and contrasts, perhaps connected to the contrast between Jewish and Christian influences or between the Nestorians and the Monophysites. However, there may be an independent similarity of certain ideas between the Khawarij and the Nestorians and between the Shi'a and the Monophysites.[121]

Further assessments may help provide answers as to why Kufa played a significant role in promoting and supporting Ali and his Ahl al-Bayt. Kufa must be seen in perspective as the capital of the Arab empire under Ali in the struggle to legitimate its standing against the imposing capital of Damascus under Mu'awiya. Mu'awiya's introduction of hereditary succession could have brought the Kufans into competition with the Syrians in their de facto capital under Ali's descendants. The treasury in Kufa as the capital, giving it a substantially more priority than Basra, may simply have split the common interests of the two communities. The other factor that gave priority to propaganda in favor of Ali's household by the Kufans was the relocation of the Banu Hashim clan and a number of the Prophet's companions along with Ali to Kufa, not to Basra. (A number of the Prophet's companions settled in Basra in later years.) The rivalry between the two clans of the Quraysh—the Banu Umayya, now in Damascus, and the Banu Hashim in Kufa (especially since the Prophet belonged to the Banu Hashim clan)—on the one hand and the image that the Basrans gave refuge to those who disagreed with Ali (the Khawarij) as a result of Ali's truce with Mu'awiya on the other combined to place the Kufans in a peculiar position to pursue a religio-political enterprise that suited its population, its goals, and its current debate with Damascus.

In light of the difficulties involved in analyzing the vision of these people then, given that various habits, practices, and rites of the pre-Islamic period were adopted and translated by different communities into

---

[121] Watt, *Formative Period*, p. 43.

Islamic customs, it could perhaps better be understood that certain governing historical conditions made them do what they did and think what they thought. As the historian Michael Morony observes:

> Every first-generation Muslim was a former pagan, Magian (Zoroastrian), Jew, or Christian. Because of the mixed composition of the Muslim population, it was inevitable that the ideas and attitudes brought by the converts from their former religious traditions would affect the way they dealt with religious issues as Muslims.[122]

The shaping of parties and the emergence of sects after the death of Ali became dominant in Iraqi tradition for the next three hundred years. The movement continued unabated in Kufa; it only searched for a leader, which brings us to discuss the events surrounding the careers of Hasan and Husayn, Ali's sons, and the subsequent development of Shi'i formation.

---

[122] Morony, *Iraq*, p. 431.

CHAPTER 4
After Ali: The Formation
of Shi'ism

Hasan

After Ali's death forty thousand Kufans gave allegiance to his elder son Hasan. The Kufans' choice of Hasan as successor was consistent with their interest in a continuation of the policies Ali had undertaken. There is no evidence that the designation of Hasan was by Ali's special appointment or recommendation; it was simply a logical decision by the Kufans to select Hasan, although not all the supporters shared the same feelings or aims.[1]

The move by the Iraqis to introduce Hasan as the head of the Islamic community was based on various complex reasons, among which was the desire to prevent the old Meccan elite—the Umayya—from gaining power to the extent of subjugating Iraq as well as the Banu Hashim.

The designation of Hasan also meant maintaining a Caliph for the whole empire in the capital city of Kufa, as had previously been the case in Medina for Ali's predecessors; and such an arrangement would have guaranteed that the treasury, along with the Caliph, would remain in Kufa. In accordance with tribal custom, Hasan, as the eldest male descendant in the line of Abu Talib (Ali's father) and as the grandson of Muhammad, was the guarantor of the interests of the Banu Hashim clan. This also carried a religious overtone, since having the Prophet come from it gave the Banu Hashim clan the prestige to loom large and secure a wide range of powers in tribal politics.

For the Banu Umayya, allowing the Caliphate to remain within the Banu Hashim after Ali would have meant relinquishing its own superior

---

[1] Jafri, *op. cit.*, p. 132.

position within the Quraysh's traditional clan competition. Hasan's designation was surely based both on his degree of piety and the congruent interests of various groups and on the direction of political events. Which factor weighed heavier may perhaps be found from subsequent developments.

Both Shi'i and Sunni historians—including Ya'qubi, Mas'udi, Mostaufi, and Tabari—agree that the Kufans swore allegiance to Hasan and wanted him to lead their opposition against Syria, as his father had. The Shi'at Ali, with slight adjustments, united the Khawarij of Basra and other companions of Ali around Hasan in order to confront the Banu Umayya in a more powerful alliance than had previously existed. On the other hand, Mu'awiya's denial of the validity of Hasan's designation justified his authority not merely as the leader of the opposition in Syria but also as a power contender and negotiator for the Caliphate. Mu'awiya demonstrated his position by his maneuvering of armed strength, which he, his father Abu Sufiyan, and the rest of the Syrian aristocracy had formed since their accession to power in Syria at the time of Umar. The maneuver of the Syrian might and stability, as well as a *certain mysterious conspiracy* between the agents of Syria and Iraq to debase Hasan's position, convinced Hasan that it would be a mistake to enter at once into a war with the Syrians. The Shi'at Ali was prepared to fight, regardless of the discouragements that had alarmed Hasan, but Hasan refused to trust them.[2] Hasan considered neutrality a more attractive option than accepting terms of war from the Iraqis, whose real motivations he was not sure of. As for his own caliphate, he seemed inclined to give way to Mu'awiya. Upon learning of Hasan's withdrawal from the scene, however, the angry Kufans felt betrayed. Reportedly, some Iraqis even attacked and stabbed Hasan before he left for Medina[3] and some called out to him, "O you humiliator of the Arabs."[4]

Hasan's inclination to negotiate accelerated when he knew he was losing the love of the Iraqis. He began to enumerate various conditions that Mu'awiya must satisfy in order for Hasan to agree to abdicate. This was by no means a peace treaty between the Iraqis (or even the Shi'at Ali on a large scale) and Syria; it was more of a truce between Hasan

---

[2] Mas'udi, II, pp. 1–6; Mostaufi, p. 199.
[3] Ya'qubi, II, p. 142; Mas'udi, II, pp. 4–5; Tabari, VII, p. 2716.
[4] Tabari, VII, p. 2720.

and Mu'awiya. Indeed, between the time of this treaty and the death of Mu'awiya (41/660–60/680), the Kufan Shi'at Ali were led by Hujr b. Adi al-Kindi (51/671), who was eventually arrested and beheaded by the Syrians. The period was also marked by sixteen risings of the Khawarij against the Syrians[5] and by other expressions of opposition on behalf of the dissatisfied Kufans. In fact, upon hearing the decision of Hasan, Hujr was perturbed,[6] though his opposition to Mu'awiya and his governor Ziyad was based more on personal concerns than on sheer loyalty to Ali and his family.[7]

At any rate, Hasan displayed no enthusiasm to defy what subsequent Shi'ites called the tyrannical Umayyads and their false form of Islam. It has been asserted that Hasan was a "peace-loving man of mild temper who hated to see the shedding of Muslim blood."[8] But this characteristic led Hasan to a position contrary to the one Ali adopted in the situation in order to restore Islamic justice and an Islamic way of life. Moreover, it was contrary to the circumstance his brother Husayn in later years experienced that became the source of Shi'i pride in dying for the preservation of the faith. Nevertheless, Hasan made it clear that it was better not to fight. Then he began to set the conditions for abdicating in favor of Mu'awiya. The conditions demanded by Hasan did not favor the Iraqis' opposition, and they also disappointed his father's followers and decreased their respect for him.[9] Nawbakhti and Mostaufi (both of Shi'i origin) indicate that Hasan demanded ready access to the treasury in Iraq, possession of a land in Fars (Persia), and the prohibition of cursing his father, Ali, in his presence.[10]

The concessions are more explicit in the *Kitab al-Akhbar al-Tiwal* of Dinawari (d. 282/895), a contemporary of al-Baladhuri and Ya'qubi. First, Hasan asked for the tribute of Ahwaz (in Persia) as an annual grant (Ya'qubi reports the income of Ahwaz in Mu'awiya's time was forty million dirhams).[11] Second, he demanded an annual grant of one million dirhams for his brother Husayn. Third, he stipulated that Mu'awiya

---

[5] Morony, *Iraq*, p. 487.
[6] Jafri, *op. cit.*, p. 155.
[7] Morony, *Iraq*, p. 487.
[8] Jafri, *op. cit.*, p. 133.
[9] Majlisi, *Jala ul Uyun*, p. 260; Wellhausen, *Religio-Political Factions*, p. 105.
[10] Nawbakhti, p. 61; Mostaufi, p. 199.
[11] Ya'qubi, II, p. 166.

should honor the Banu Hashim with his favors and gifts in the same way that he would honor the Banu Abd al-Shams (Banu Umayya).[12] Reportedly these conditions, with minor adjustments, were accepted by Mu'awiya, who had the leaders of Syria cosign them. Thus the truce was made.[13]

Tabari quotes az-Zuhri as indicating that Hasan had no desire for war. He wanted to make peace, and he expressed this to Mu'awiya by saying "Grant me this [set of conditions] and I shall be totally obedient, provided that you fulfill [those conditions] for me."[14] Mu'awiya had previously sent Hasan a sealed blank scroll on which he might set down any condition he wished; when Hasan received the scroll he doubled his previous conditions.[15] Mu'awiya had kept the letter containing Hasan's original conditions, however, and when they met he refused to grant Hasan the doubled concessions. Mu'awiya said, "I grant you the requests you made originally in your letter to me, for I had done so already when I received your letter." Hasan replied, "[But] I had [additional] conditions when I received your letter, and you agreed to fulfill them.[16] Notwithstanding Hasan's reasoning, Mu'awiya refused to accept the revised terms. One way or another, as Mas'udi indicates, Hasan now had renounced his claim in favor of Mu'awiya and had discouraged the people of Iraq from confronting the Syrian forces militarily.[17]

Thus the Iraqi opposition found itself frustrated when one of its supposedly charismatic pillars fell in passive compromise with Mu'awiya. In this regard, it is interesting to note that none of these concessions Hasan extracted from Mu'awiya is concerned with the Iraqis' status; instead Hasan preferred to establish his influence over financial affairs in Iraq and parts of Persia. Nawbakhti indicates, however, that the people of Basra refused to pay their poll tax (kharaj) to Hasan.[18] One may wonder

---

[12] Abu Hanifa Dinawari, Kitab al-Akhbar al-Tiwal, quoted by Donaldson, Shi'ite Religion, p. 70.
[13] The Shi'a sources agree that upon the acceptance of these conditions the Caliphate was rendered to Mu'awiya.
[14] Tabari, VII, p. 2713 (trans. by Michael Morony, The History of al-Tabari, XVIII, p. 7).
[15] Tabari, VII, pp. 2716–2717.
[16] Tabari, VII, p. 2717 (translated by Michael Morony, op. cit., p. 8).
[17] Mas'udi, II, p. 6.
[18] Nawbakhti, p. 62; see also Tabari, VII, p. 2720.

why Hasan chose to exchange his caliphate and leadership of the Iraqi opposition for substantial financial concessions. He seems to have intended to guarantee prosperity and safety for the Banu Hashim in exchange for their not participating in active politics. According to the Shi'i accounts, both parties agreed that the Caliphate was to be rendered to Hasan after Mu'awiya. Jafri quotes a Shi'i historian named Ibn A'tham al-Kufi (d. 314/926), who states that the restoration of the Caliphate to Hasan after Mu'awiya's death was one of the conditions, but that concerns about Mu'awiya's good faith later arose: "Some time later, the Shi'i, gathering together, showed their disapproval of the fact that Hasan had not asked for sufficient guarantees and had not secured an undertaking in writing from Mu'awiya that the latter would leave him the Caliphate after his death."[19]

It certainly should not be supposed that the Banu Hashim had absolutely abandoned the competition for rulership. Ya'qubi reports that before his death Hasan addressed this message to his sons and his nephews (Husayn's sons): "O my sons and my nephews, you are the children of a clan whose governorship over another clan is upcoming."[20] The rivalry between the Umayya and Hashim clans remained a real (though deferred) issue.

Hasan was wrong if he assumed that power would eventually be transferred to the Banu Hashim or even to the Iraqis. Instead, the Banu Umayya continued ceaselessly to expand their strength throughout the empire for the next ninety years. Furthermore, Hasan's recognition of Mu'awiya as Caliph granted the Umayya a religious legitimacy they had long lacked due to their late conversion to Islam. Hasan thus became known as the matchmaker between the two communities. As the records show, upon receiving the news that Hasan had accepted the truce, Fakhteh, in the court of Mu'awiya, said that this is a reminder of a saying of the prophet who always praised Hasan as the leader of the whole community in paradise, where God, through him, would unite the two groups of the believers (mu'menin) into a pact.[21]

Hasan's compromise has become an issue about which the Shi'ites prefer to remain silent, since he contributed nothing toward preparing

---

[19] Jafri, op. cit., pp. 150–153, quoting Ibn A'tham, Kitab al-Futuh, IV, pp. 158–165.
[20] Ya'qubi, II, p. 157.
[21] Mas'udi, II, p. 4; Jafri, op. cit., p. 156, quoting Bukhari, Tabari, Jahiz, and Amili.

his clan or the Iraqi defense system to confront the Umayya at an appropriate later occasion. He may also be largely responsible for the failure of his brother Husayn, whose charisma—had he had time to gather a forceful camp—might have enabled him to gain prestige and maneuver effectively against the Syrian army. Because Husayn was bound by the terms of his brother's treaty with Mu'awiya, he could do very little to prepare an organized opposition.[22]

As the Shi'i doctrine crystalized over the next century, Hasan came to be considered the second Imam after Ali, but his alleged unlimited knowledge and inheritance of divine virtues in fact failed to assist him and his entourage when it came to dealing with the crisis. Apart from his obscure mission as a leader, his nonpolitical life in Medina (as even some Shi'i sources such as Majlisi concede) was such that even Ali during his lifetime criticized parents who let their daughters marry Hasan, who divorced them constantly. This criticism extended to Hasan himself for his regular practice of divorcing his wives. The same source identifies the total number of Hasan's wives as 250 or 300.[23]

The public and private behavior of Hasan and his retirement in Medina have always remained shadowy, especially once the Karbala tragedy of Husayn gave the Shi'i community the opportunity to focus on retelling the story of Husayn rather than that of Hasan. During the ninth and tenth centuries, many descendants of Hasan led the Zaydi sect. The Sharifs of Mecca were Hasani, and so is the current Imam/King of Morocco, but in a Shi'i community elsewhere—especially in Iran—his descendants (Imamzadeh and Sayyids), when they emigrated there, were considered a less respectable sect.[24]

Shi'ite accounts assert that Mu'awiya conspired to bring about Hasan's death by poisoning him through one of his wives. This may be so, although it has no significance either in a religious sense or in crediting Hasan's standing. Nevertheless Ya'qubi's history indicates that prior to Hasan's death he was seriously ill three times, and the third time convinced him that his death was imminent.[25] There is no indication of his having been poisoned by his wife, however, as the later Shi'i sources

---

[22] Jafri, op. cit., p. 177.
[23] Majlisi, Jala ul Uyun, p. 227; see also Donaldson, op. cit., p. 74.
[24] Aubin, La Perse d'Aujourd'hui, pp. 154–155.
[25] Ya'qubi, II, p. 154.

claim. He died at about the age of forty-five, the exact age varying depending on the source. At least one account states that at forty-five he died of tuberculosis.[26] In any case, Hasan's death (49/669) occurred about nine years after he signed the treaty with Mu'awiya (41/660). Mu'awiya continued his caliphate another eleven years until he died at the age of seventy-seven (60/680).

Husayn

Until the death of Hasan, the split in the Muslim community was political, but with the next series of events—especially those involving Hasan's brother Husayn—new emotional and moral elements began to play a significant role in the subsequent religious orientation of the opposition to the Umayya.

The disorganized opposition remained suppressed under Mu'awiya's austere rule. With Hasan's death, however, the Iraqis once more hoped to find a leader whose bravery and family affiliation would resemble Ali's, who had openly denounced the Umayyad and led battles against them. This early search in Ali's family had no deep religious roots. It had more to do with the Hashimite clan's political ideology, a rivalry with the Banu Umayyads that had its origins in the recent past.

The Iraqis' personal experiences with Ali during his nearly five-year rule in Kufa must be taken into consideration, but the Iraqis had options other than simply choosing from among Ali's descendants. They also followed Hujr b. Adi al-Kindi, who led a revolt against Mu'awiya and his governor of Kufa and Basra, Ziyad b. abu Sufyan (51/671). Later the Kufans also swore allegiance to Mukhtar, then to Ibn az-Zubayr, and so on until the Abbasids came to power in Iraq (132/750).

With Hasan's death, the Kufan turn to Husayn was a spontaneous action based on his being the other son of Ali. But dismay prevailed when Husayn turned down the offer to lead the opposition—at least with respect to the honorable treaty Banu Umayya and Banu Hashim had undertaken. For about eleven years (49/669–60/680), Husayn refused to take part in any opposition. Even when Hujr's expedition failed and

---

[26] *Encyclopedia of Islam*, Lammens, "Hasan," quoted by Donaldson, *op. cit.*, p. 74.

led to his tragic execution, which deeply affected the Kufans, the delegation sent to Husayn returned emptyhanded once again, as Husayn declined to undertake any armed revolt against Mu'awiya.[27]

The atmosphere of suppressed excitement and ambiguity reigned until Mu'awiya decided to obtain allegiance for his son Yazid to guarantee that power was retained within the family. Mu'awiya's persuasiveness in dealing with Ali and Hasan proved him a man of diplomacy and strength, and he was again successful in having his son nominated his successor. According to various versions, Mu'awiya first obtained approval of the multitudes of Medinans for his son's succession. Meanwhile, the four important men of Medina—Abd Allah b. Umar, Abd ar-Rahman b. Abu Bakr, Abd Allah b. az-Zubayr, and Husayn—had fled to Mecca, so Mu'awiya went to Mecca to obtain their consent as well as the Meccans'. Mu'awiya took the four men into a mosque and announced to those who were present, "These four men, without whom no decision concerning the succession can be made, have agreed to Yazid's nomination; so now none of you people should have any difficulty in doing the same." The people then swore allegiance to Yazid, while the four men remained silent, probably out of fear.[28]

When Mu'awiya died in 61/680, the turmoil began with the accession of Yazid to power. The turmoil began partially because a hidden opposition already existed and because of Mu'awiya's reign, which was to be continued through that of his son. Thus the legitimacy of the Caliphate provided both a pretext and a focus for the controversy. The Kufan tribal aristocracy (ashraf) and the other oppositional factions gathered around Sulayman ibn Surad and invited Husayn from Medina to lead these communities and restore the true Muslim sunna. They promised Husayn the allegiance of twelve thousand or eighteen thousand men to follow him.[29] Husayn then wrote back to the Kufans (as well as the Basrans) to confirm that, if they were truthful, he would offer them his guidance. It seems that the political minds of the Kufans underwent a transformation after their unsuccessful military attempt under Hujr. Most notably there appeared a persuasive religious attitude that the opposition against

---

[27] Jafri, op. cit., p. 166.
[28] Ibid., p. 168, quoting Ibn Athir, al Kamil, III, Beirut (965), pp. 508–511; Ibn A'than, IV, pp. 235–249.
[29] Mas'udi, II, p. 58.

The Emergence of Shi'ism

the Umayya must be guided by the theological tenet that they had deviated from the path of the Prophet. Clearly this consciousness could not have had deep roots since it was continuing to grow as the Kufans' failures increased.

Husayn sent a delegation headed by his cousin Muslim ibn Aqil to Kufa to assess the mood and the circumstances there. Muslim ibn Aqil reported to Husayn that the situation appeared favorable. However, Yazid was also informed about this plan. Thereupon he sent Ubaydullah ibn Ziyad to take control of Kufa and to order the Kufan *ashraf* (including those who supported Husayn) to take part in an expedition to Karbala. In Kufa, Muslim ibn Aqil was killed and his body mutilated. Umar ibn Sa'd ibn Abi Waqqas then deployed men to prevent Husayn from entering Kufa.[30]

These developments took place between the time Husayn prepared his party to leave Medina and their arrival at Karbala. Husayn thus knew nothing of the intervening events. Before departing, the Medinans asked Husayn to swear allegiance to Yazid[31] and to ignore the temptation to seek the Caliphate. His family members (Ahl-al-Bayt) began trying to discourage him as well. It appears that they, along with other companions of the Prophet, desired no drastic change in the status quo and felt the cause was not worth dying for. Muhammad ibn al-Hanafiya (whose followers gave rise to the sect of Kaisaniya Ibn Abbas), Ibn Umar, Ibn az-Zubayr (who in the following year began his revolt in Mecca), and others asked Husayn not to proceed.[32] But the communication of the Kufans (Shi'at Ali) had so strongly affected Husayn's psychology and religious contemplation that he now believed going to Kufa would restore the prestige of Ali's Ahl al-Bayt and would probably prevent the Iraqis from charging Ali's family with collaborating with the Umayya in the period after Hasan's treaty. Husayn's decision to go to Kufa might also have been influenced by the thought that, if the Kufans did not receive a favorable response from him this time, they might turn against him and his family forever. Thus the legacy of his father Ali and his Ahl al-Bayt was perhaps at stake.

It is important to note, however, that the stimulus for initial opposition

---

[30] Morony, *Iraq*, pp. 487–488; see also Jafri, *op. cit.*, pp. 180–185.
[31] Mas'udi, II, p. 58; see also Tabari, VII, p. 2916.
[32] Ibn Khaldun, I, p. 430.

against Yazid's government and the Umayya came primarily from Iraq, which compelled Husayn to move on. This process of mobilizing Ali's children—Hasan and Husayn—took nearly two decades after Ali's death to complete. Eventually Husayn was persuaded to proceed to Iraq by the Iraqis' persistence, just as his father had been.

The full religious importance of Husayn's decision to relocate to Iraq cannot readily be analyzed, although the Shi'i point of view emphasizes it, because the Shi'i movement in general was still more a political opposition to the Syrian Umayya rather than a spiritual movement based on a coherent theological framework. In any event, the Shi'i movement (Shi'at Ali) was by nature a heterogeneous political faction defined and understood differently by each group within it.

After his decision to relocate to Iraq, Husayn and some of his family prepared to go first to Mecca, then to Iraq. Prior to his departure, Husayn met with his cousin Ibn Abbas, who offered him reasonable counsel. Mas'udi reports the conversation between Husayn and Ibn Abbas, which may have been constructed after the fact but is still well worth quoting. Ibn Abbas began by saying:

> Cousin, I understand that you are planning to go to Iraq, but let me assure you that the people there are faithless and will not support you in battle. Pray do not act thus hastily; and in case you are determined to fight this tyrant, and if you do not like the idea of remaining in Mecca, then set out for Yemen. There you would be in retirement and there are your brothers and your true helpers. That is a place for you to stay, and from there you could publish your proclamation, and from there also you could write to the people of Kufa and those in sympathy with you in Iraq. They could then dismiss their governor. If they should persevere in this and drive him out from them, there would then be no one to oppose your coming to them. But if they should fail to do this, you could still remain in your place until God would make the way clear. And you would be where there are strongholds and mountain passes.

Husayn replied:

> I recognized the truth and friendliness of your advice, but on the other hand, Muslim Ibn Aqil has written me that the people of the great city had pledged themselves to acknowledge my right and to defend me. I must therefore consent to go among them.

Ibn Abbas interrupted:

But they are a people with whom I have experience. They were companions of your father and of your brother. If you start fighting tomorrow with their governor, as soon as you begin your undertaking, Ibn Ziyad will hear of your expedition and will succeed in frightening them so that they will be afraid to support you. Before God, I bear you witness that the very ones who wrote you are your enemies. At any rate, if you refuse my warning and are determined to go, I pray you not to take the women and the children, for I solemnly declare that I am afraid that you will be killed as Uthman was killed, and his women and children saw it happen.[33]

Husayn left upon receiving the news about the new developments in Kufa; he was already in Iraq. His miscalculated risk reached an early dead end: He was surrounded while encamped to the northwest of Kufa, in Karbala. The grave situation must have demoralized Husayn, for he averred that, if the Syrian forces would just let them go free, he and his party would return to Medina. Tabari indicates that Husayn wanted to return to Medina but that the children of Muslim ibn Aqil were determined to avenge the blood of their father and refused to go back.[34] Notwithstanding variations in certain details among the early sources, they basically agree that Husayn desired no war but insisted upon an honorable return.

Abu Mikhnaf (d. 157/774), a Shi'i Kufan who wrote the first full account of Karbala, reports an account by Sa'id b. Hamdani (who had seen Ibn Sa'd and Husayn together) of Husayn's demands: "Accept one of the three proposals: I would return to where I come from; or I put my hand in the hand of Yazid ibn Mu'awiya, and between us I will tell him my decision (r'ai); or send me by your choice to one of the Muslim lands where I shall bear the same rights and duties as the local residents."[35] This account may be contested by those who have emphasized an uncompromising attitude on the part of Husayn toward Yazid. But the same version is also reported by the Shi'i Nishaburi (d. 508/1125) in his Rawdat al-Wa'izin. He states that Ibn Sa'd and Husayn met for a long period of

---

[33] Mas'udi, II, pp. 58–59. Donaldson translation, op. cit., pp. 80–81.
[34] Tabari, VII, p. 2973. See Nishaburi, Rawdat al-Wa'izin, p. 295.
[35] Tabari, VII, p. 2008, quoting Abu Mikhnaf.

time, after which Ibn Sa'd wrote a letter to Ibn Ziyad, the governor of Kufa. In this letter Ibn Sa'd indicated that Husayn had agreed to return home or to go to another Muslim land, or to meet with Yazid himself to seek a suitable solution.[36] The same source from which later accounts (such as that of Majlisi) were drawn reports: "Husayn with a high-pitched voice said to the messenger of Ibn Sa'd, 'The people of your city (Kufa) have written and invited me here; and now if you wish, I would go back.' "[37]

Husayn's behavior under such difficult circumstances seems to reflect a desire for compromise without guaranteeing any concession to the enemy in its honorable fashion. Many Shi'i accounts (such as those of Ibn Babuya, Sheikh Mufid, and Safar), however, refer to a predestined notion of the fatal developments in Karbala for the grandson of the Prophet and claim that the Ahl al-Bayt had knowledge of this.[38]

The situation existing between Husayn and Ibn Sa'd remained unresolved until the latter received a letter from Ibn Ziyad demanding the unconditional surrender of Husayn's party and their removal to Kufa. Shimr b. Dhil-Jawshan, who delivered the letter from Ibn Ziyad, was instructed to carry out this duty himself, since this was the final decision. It should be noted that there were a number of people in each camp who knew each other from the battle of Siffin between the Banu Umayya and Ali and his followers. Shimr had been injured in the face during the battle of Siffin;[39] now he had Ali's son in his power.

Ibn Ziyad, who had the Kufan *ashraf* and Husayn's supporters brought to the scene to fight Husayn, intended to make this an example of punishment for the subsequent opposition against the Banu Umayya. Mas'udi asserts that "All the troops that took part in the battle that brought about the death of Husayn were from Kufa. There was not a single Syrian among them."[40]

Husayn and his people were warned that they must surrender immediately. Their camps were completely surrounded, and there was no access to water. Their thirst had become unbearable, and the women and

---

[36] Nishaburi, p. 300.
[37] Majlisi, *Jala ul Uyun*, p. 390. See also Nishaburi, p. 229.
[38] See Majlisi, *Jala ul Uyun*, pp. 324–331.
[39] Minqari, *Waq'at Siffin*, p. 365.
[40] Mas'udi, II, p. 65.

children were no longer safe. Yet Husayn and others were fearful of becoming unconditional prisoners of an empire they had aimed to topple. During these crucial moments, Husayn's reluctance to compromise easily (in contrast to his brother Hasan, who quite willingly compromised with Mu'awiya) was most likely a matter of complex human psychology and not necessarily the acting out of a divinely spiritual duty.[41]

In the battle that ensued, Husayn and his companions, including all but a few family members, were slaughtered in a most brutal fashion (61/ 680). Afterward, Husayn was beheaded and Ibn Sa'd ordered his men to trample Husayn's body beneath their horses.[42] This atrocious behavior and wanton bloodshed disturbed even non-Shi'ites.

The martyrdom of Hujr by the Syrians and of Husayn by an army of drafted Iraqis marked the beginning of the injection of many moral, psychological, and emotional issues into the existing political opposition against the Umayya. Such new dimensions also became a fertile ground for moving some groups into a new religious consciousness.

The martyrdom of Husayn meant more to the subsequent Shi'ites than the martyrdom of his father Ali, who was not the son of Fatima, the Prophet's daughter.[43] The Karbala massacre was used in subsequent years by the Iraqi opposition to claim the right of revenge for the blood of Husayn.

As time passed, Husayn's martyrdom was magnified to such an extent that many supernatural anecdotes became attached to it. These supernatural stories connected to the tragedy of Karbala formed part of the system of Arab belief, as well as part of the dogma promulgated by the aggrieved Iraqis known as Penitents (tawwabun).[44] These people began to superhumanize the Iraqi leaders in general, far beyond the pre-Islamic attributes of human excellence asserted by Arabs about their leaders. In this connection, Watt asserts that the attribution of superhuman qualities may rather have come from Persian elements among the Muslims.[45] In any case, Abu Mikhnaf, along with other historians who reported the tragedy of Karbala and Husayn's attitude toward the current political

---

[41] See Ibn Khaldun, I, p. 429.
[42] Mas'udi, II, p. 66.
[43] Wellhausen, *Religio-Political Factions*, p. 116.
[44] Jafri, *op. cit.*, p. 216.
[45] Watt, *Formative Period*, p. 54.

structure, preferred to frame it in a mythological and supernatural for-mat.[46] Jafri interestingly notes that Muhammad b. Ya'qub al-Kulayni (d. 328/939), who compiled the first collection of Shi'i traditions in his book *Usul al-Kafi*, relates many traditions that ascribe supernatural and su-perhuman characteristics to the Imams (Shi'i leaders). Thus Kulayni seems to have based his compilation on transmitted traditions that reached him after having already been elaborated by the exaggerators (*ghulat*) in Iraq (possibly it included Persians, too) before finding their way into the Shi'i literature.[47]

Perhaps it is not so much Husayn's defeat as the way in which he was killed and dishonored that became an agonizing rallying point for the Kufans who had invited him there. This experience not only gave rise to a qualitatively different basis for opposition to the Umayya among the *tawwabun* of Kufa, it also charged the opposition with emotions glorifying Husayn's bravery under difficult political circumstances. Hu-sayn was consequently raised above his predecessors and viewed as de-serving special reverence and respect. This also privileged his descendants to be looked upon as pious men and natural leaders. Further elaborations on Husayn's intentions and actions by the Shi'ites gained precedence for Husayn over the harmonious and cautious tenures of other Shi'i Imams who remained quiet and politically inactive.

Husayn is believed by staunch Shi'ites to have had a complete fore-knowledge of his actions and their outcome. Did he believe he was predestined to die before arriving at Kufa? Did he wish to be martyred for the cause and the persuasion of the Kufans (Shi'at Ali) who deserted him, for Banu Hashim, and for Islam? Did he die because of the stubborn decisions of Ibn Ziyad, Ibn Sa'd, and Shimr as well as his own refusal to surrender, or did divine will decree his martyrdom in order to make the martyrdom a religious virtue? It is difficult to answer these questions without reference to the existing religious dogma and attitude. The as-sessment of historical sources could be put forward: Husayn's stay in Medina for the duration of Mu'awiya's reign, his encouragement and invitation by the Kufans, his dialogues and conditions with the opposing army at Karbala, and other aspects of the record suggest that events were developing extemporaneously as one stage led to the next.

---

[46] Jafri, *op. cit.*, p. 216.
[47] *Ibid.*, p. 303.

But Husayn's interception by the Syro-Iraqi army at Karbala significantly changed the mood and feelings of his father's followers (the Shi'at Ali), causing them to question tremendously the Umayya's morality. Nevertheless, the later religious interpretation of Karbala has argued that Husayn's intentions and actions were foreknown and divinely inspired. A representative religious view of the significance of Karbala runs "A careful study and analysis of the events of Karbala as a whole reveals the fact that from the very beginning Husayn was planning for a complete revolution in the religious consciousness of the Muslims.[48]

While there may be general agreement about Husayn's piety, this element did not touch the Shi'ites the way his murder did. Thus his martyrdom, and not necessarily his religious teaching, became the basis for revering him. Had Hasan chosen to challenge the Umayya in a physical confrontation while he was in Iraq and been named Caliph, his martyrdom would probably have been glorified in the same manner as were his father's and his brother's. Since he did not embrace death, he disappointed many Kufans of his time.

In Shi'i histories the Karbala massacre was analyzed much more thoroughly as a moral, emotional, and religious lesson than with regard to the factors, parties, and interests of the various groups involved. In any event, the post-Husayn era clarifies the position of the Shi'at Ali or the Kufans who turned to Sulayman b. Surad, Mukhtar, and then to Ibn az-Zubayr before turning to Ali's descendants, saying that the latter are to be considered heroes despite the fact that, when they were approached to take active part, they refused. Only later were Ali's descendants given attention, whereas other potential leaders received priority in the days after Husayn's death. "It was only gradually that belief in charismata restricted to the descendants of al-Husayn became predominant."[49] The Kufans' political vision at times varied according to their new religious experiences, which were propagated by the *ghulat*. Turning to each leader, Hashimite or non-Hashimite, alone gave rise to a new sect. But the Kufans as a whole were considered Shi'at Ali, and undoubtedly they were persistently affected by the martyrdom of Husayn because of its bitter political memories more than because of its religious particularities. Wellhausen points out: "There are certain events which exercise amazing

---

[48] *Ibid.*, p. 202.
[49] Watt, *Formative Period*, p. 54.

effect, not because of themselves and their inevitable consequences, but because of their memories in men's hearts."[50]

Was Shahrbanu the Wife of Husayn?

Another established belief in connection with the story of Husayn has to do with his marriage to the daughter of Yazdigird III, the last Sassanid king. The Shi'i tradition attempts to connect Shi'ism with the royal family of Persia and to demonstrate that the nine Imams after Husayn (the third Shi'i Imam) were descendants of the Sassanid princess as well as of the Prophet's grandson. This princess came to be known as Shahr-banu (Bibi Shahrbanu), whose shrine at Ray is still a pilgrimage site for the Shi'ites. (This shrine is not necessarily her tomb, because she is believed still to be alive; as she sought refuge in Persia, a mountain opened before her miraculously and took her inside the rocks.)

A penetrating study on Bibi Shahrbanu has been done by Mary Boyce and a Persian scholar, Sayyid Ja'far Shahidi.[51] Boyce's study demonstrates that the historical accounts prior to the tenth century—specifically, before the time of the Shi'i historian Ya'qubi—do not make explicit references to royal matrimony or even to the name of Shahrbanu (the Lady of the Land).[52] It was Ya'qubi's and the subsequent traditions, despite all of the contradictory versions reporting the story, that fostered the belief that Shahrbanu (other names such as Ghazala and Jehanshah were used by these traditions) was the wife of Husayn and the mother of Zayn al-Abidin. The popular Shi'i version tells that Shahrbanu was captured by the Arabs during the conquest of Persia and brought to Medina, where Husayn took her as his wife and she gave birth to Zayn

---

[50] Wellhausen, Religio-Political Factions, p. 116.

[51] Boyce, "Bibi Shahrbanu and the Lady of Pars," Bulletin of the School of Oriental and African Studies 30 (1967): 30–44. See also Arthur Christensen, l'Iran sur les Sassanides, p. 502.

[52] Petersen, Ali and Mu'awiya in Early Arabic Tradition, p. 117, says "Attempts to parallel the Persians with the Arabs round the Ali figure are not met with until in ad-Dinawari. Correspondingly, al-Ya'qubi tries to establish a family connection between the Prophet family and the Sassanids." This healing reaction may have had to do with previous anti-Persian tendencies among the governing Arabs, especially those who faced revolutionary opposition of Persian origin.

al-Abidin. After Husayn was martyred at Karbala, she is said to have fled to her native Persia with her enemies in hot pursuit. When she approached Ray, "in desperation she tried to call on God; but instead of Yallahu! ('O God!') her weary tongue uttered Ya Kuh! ('O mountain!')" and then the mountain split open to allow her to enter.

This Shi'i version runs counter to two other Shi'i historical references that provide contradictory evidence. One is that the earlier sources such as Ibn Sa'd (d. 844) and Ibn Qutayla (d. 889) record that Zayn al-Abidin's mother was a slave girl (Umm-Walad), who after Husayn's death married Zubaid.[53] Boyce points out that Ibn Babuya (d. 991) tried to reconcile the earlier version with the later one by appealing to the authority of a tradition allegedly transmitted from Reza, the eighth Imam (d. 818), indicating that after the fall of Khurasan the princess of Persia was taken to Uthman (the third Caliph), who gave her to Husayn in marriage. After giving birth to Zayn al-Abidin, Shahrbanu died and the baby was looked after by Umm-Walad. A parallel Shi'i tradition, recorded by Kulayni (d. 940), records that the princess was brought before Umar, not Uthman. Boyce here detects two historical discrepancies: first, with regard to Kulayni's account, that Umar died in 644, whereas Zayn al-Abidin was born in 657; second, with regard to Ibn Babuya's as well as Kulayni's versions, that Khurasan was captured a year after Uthman's death.[54]

The second complicating historical reference can be found in the legend of Shahrbanu in the Zoroastrian tradition. The passage of Shahrbanu from Karbala in Iraq to Ray in Persia after Husayn's death is difficult to establish. In the pre-Islamic period, however, Ray was a Zoroastrian shrine associated with the goddess Ardvisur Anahid.[55] Anahid's cult had gained many followers during the pre-Islamic period. It is believed that Zoroastrians were still living at Ray around the tenth century, and since Shi'ism had gained prominence, the continued worship of Anahid was distasteful to Shi'i believers. The idea of Shahrbanu as a living presence was therefore linked to the Zoroastrian goddess Anahid, and eventually she was claimed as the direct ancestor of nine Shi'i Imams. For the Persians, such a link signified due respect for old patriotism and an

---

[53] Boyce, op. cit., p. 33.
[54] Ibid., pp. 34–35.
[55] Ibid., p. 36.

embracing of the new faith.[56] A similar shrine tied to the story of a Sassanid princess was evolved in the city of Yazd in Iran and was adopted by Shi'i tradition under the name of Banu Pars (Lady of Pars).[57]

The Politics of Opposition After Husayn

Husayn was trapped and killed in Karbala because of the conduct of the Kufans, who apparently were eager to follow a member of Ali's household but retreated from their commitment when new circumstances arose in Kufa. The Kufans began to reorganize themselves partly as a result of having guilty consciences but more importantly as a means of regenerating an effective, ongoing opposition. Members of the Kufan tribal ashraf were equally blamed for shedding the blood of Husayn, and antagonism heightened over their evident collaboration with the Umayya.

Those who pledged to avenge the blood of Husayn called themselves tawwabun (Penitents). They were polarized politically in Kufa and called for support from various other factions. The force of the tawwabun loomed larger when Yazid died (64/683) after about three and a half years of rule and was succeeded by his son Mu'awiya II, who died only six months later. The shift of power in Syria from the Sufyani family to the Marwani family led to loosened control over the province of Iraq. Ibn az-Zubayr, who had already proclaimed himself Caliph in Hijaz, took advantage of the situation by seeking support in Iraq as well. Mukhtar's emergence in Kufa to attract the Kuftan tawwabun gave another dimension to the political consciousness of the opposition to the Umayya. In the politics of the opposition, the ashraf seemed reluctant to let Mukhtar grow in power, perhaps considering him socioeconomically dangerous. They saw Ibn az-Zubayr as a preferable alternative, even though the nature of this attraction toward Ibn az-Zubayr may have been understood as leading to the domination of another Meccan elite party.

The only surviving son of Husayn from Karbala was Ali b. Husayn, known as Zayn al-Abidin.[58] He refused to be identified publicly with any

---

[56] Ibid., p. 38.

[57] See Boyce, "Banu Pars," Encyclopedia Iranica, vol. III, pp. 717–718; see also Boyce, "Bibi Shahrbanu and the Lady of Pars," pp. 38–41.

[58] See Mostaufi, p. 201. (According to this account he was fourteen years old.)

of the opposition factions, including the *tawwabun*.[59] Nawbakhti asserts that, before turning to Muhammad b. al-Hanafiya (Ali's other son), Mukhtar first invited Zayn al-Abidin to support his campaign, but he refused.[60] It appears that Zayn al-Abidin, as well as the Kufans, had not yet clearly defined the guidelines for leadership. Thus the confusion and the power vacuum that existed after Karbala left the opposition (or rather the followers of Ali's Ahl al-Bayt) in conflict over leadership, as they were fragmented into various independent parties.[61]

Why did Zayn al-Abidin refrain from opposing the Umawi government after witnessing the dreadful death of his father, even as others urgently and actively demonstrated their sentiments? One example of such contemporaneous opposition activities involves the *tawwabun* forces led by Sulayman b. Surad (one of Ali's close companions), who clashed with Ibn Ziyad's forces; in this instance, the *tawwabun* were massacred, including Sulayman himself. Zayn al-Abidin's state of mind is difficult to understand in political terms. He may have based his neutrality on the bitter experiences of his grandfather Ali or his uncle Hasan, who diplomatically refused to oppose the government, as well as those of his own father Husayn, whose opposition left the fortunes of the family diminished and badly injured. On the other hand, he also received promises from the government under Yazid—at least after his father's tragedy—of protection for him and his family. Nishaburi reports the contact of Yazid with Zayn al-Abidin after Karbala. Before having Zayn al-Abidin and the rest of his family returned to Medina, Yazid talked to him in private and said:

> May God damn the son of Marjaneh (Ibn Ziyad). I swear if I had known about the affair of your father, whatever he demanded I would have provided him with and would have prevented his death at all costs. But as you see, it was God's will! Write to me from Medina, and inform me of any of your needs.

Then Yazid ordered supplies and clothes for the group's safe journey back to Medina.[62]

---

[59] Jafri, *op. cit.*, p. 229.
[60] Nawbakhti, p. 84.
[61] See Jafri, *op. cit.*, p. 237.
[62] Nishaburi, p. 316; see also Majlisi, *Jala ul Uyun*, p. 450.

From the time of his return to Medina until the overthrow of the Umayyad empire by the Abbasids (61/680 until 132/750), no attempt was made to oppose the ruling system by the descendants of Zayn al-Abidin, who now were considered to have been the Shi'i Imams in the Ithna Ashari (Twelver) line. The same quiescent policy was continued by the Shi'i Imams under the Abbasid empire. In the immediate post-Husayn period, it became evident that Zayn al-Abidin had not attracted followers until the downfall of Mukhtar (d. 68/687).[63] This may be understood better in its practical aspects than in its dogmatic religious ones. Since the majority of the Kufan warriors noted no revolutionary inclination from Zayn al-Abidin, they sought out other leaders to confront the Syrian forces. Zayn al-Abidin's alienation must have sprung from the idea that, as Husayn himself had not fully and formally been sworn to uphold the Caliphate (leadership), he was also not in a position to appoint his son his successor. Jafri comments: "One may doubt the existence of any explicit will of Husayn for the nomination of Zayn al-Abidin as his successor."[64]

The claim of Zayn al-Abidin to the leadership evidently was obscure, but being the only son of Husayn caused him to be invited to assume a leadership role in anti-Umayya activities. Upon his refusal, his uncle Muhammad ibn al-Hanafiya, half-brother of Husayn (his mother was a Hanafite who had been given to Ali as a slave girl by Abu Bakr[65]), was acclaimed the leader of the opposition and was called Mahdi (guided by God) by Mukhtar.[66] Mukhtar at first planned to proclaim himself the leader of the opposition and engineer the freeing of Kufa from Syrian domination, but he was distrusted by the ashraf, and others probably preferred to have another Alid centrally involved. He learned that Ibn al-Hanafiya desired to free Shi'at Ali (the Alids) from their enemies through God's agency.[67] In his campaign, Mukhtar mobilized the mawali (predominantly Persians) in massacring those who were involved in the murder of Husayn, and thus he freed Kufa from the Umayyads.

Members of the opposition organized under the name of Ibn al-

---

[63] Momen, op. cit., p. 64, quoting Kashshi, Al Rijal (Bombay 1317/1879); see also Jafri, op. cit., p. 245.
[64] Jafri, op. cit., p. 246.
[65] Nawbakhti, p. 51.
[66] See Darmesteter, Mahdi, p. 106; see also Wellhausen, Religio-Political Factions, p. 128.
[67] Wellhausen, op. cit., p. 128.

Hanafiya were called *Kaysaniya*, which became a religious sect after the death of Ibn al-Hanafiya. The Kaysaniya believed that Ibn al-Hanafiya had not died, but had gone into concealment (*ghayba*) and would return (*raj'a*). How such a messianic belief emerged among the Kufans will be discussed in detail in the next chapter. Here it suffices that Ibn al-Hanafiya was also looked upon as a son of Ali, and apparently for the Shi'at Ali descent in the male line was what counted. Thus the paternity of Ali received far more consideration than the maternity of Fatima. Because of this belief, all the men in the line of Ali were given precedence, including other descendants of Abu Talib (Ali's father), such as the Abbasids.[68]

With the emergence of the *ghulat* (exaggerators), however, this hereditary tradition took a more religiously fundamentalist direction. Thus, when Ibn al-Hanafiya died his followers were divided into those who believed he was not dead and would return and those who thought he was dead and considered his son, Abu Hashim, his successor as Imam.

After Abu Hashim, according to Shahrastani, the sect broke into five branches.[69] Morony identifies the five subgroups of Kaysaniya in Kufa by naming their leaders: Bayan ibn Sam'an (d. 737); Mughira ibn Sai'd al-Igli (d. 737); Abu Mansur al-Ijli (d. 747); the Janahiyya who followed Abdullah ibn Mu'awiya (d. 747); and the entourage of Abul-Khattab (d. 755).[70] By early in the eighth century, the influence of the *ghulat* on these five groups is quite evident in the sect.

For leadership in opposing the Banu Umayya, Ali's descendants seem to have been selected on the basis of social and tribal traditions favoring hereditary succession, on political grounds, and, with the emergence of the *ghulat*, out of religious preference. But the Kufans looked elsewhere for leadership on some occasions, and in one instance the defeat and death of a non-Alid politicoreligious leader, Mukhtar, by Ibn az-Zubayr, gave rise to a new religious sect—Mukhtariya—which carried a messianic tone.[71] Furthermore, in Hijaz Ibn az-Zubayr's (d. 73/692) claim to the Caliphate, in opposition to the Umayya and to Mukhtar in Iraq, led

---

[68] Hodgson, *How Did the Early Shi'a . . .* , p. 1.
[69] Shahrastani, I, pp. 193–201. See also Ibn Tiqtaqa, p. 191; Petrushevsky, *Islam in Iran*, p. 204; Darmesteter, *op. cit.*, p. 108.
[70] Morony, *Iraq*, p. 498.
[71] See Shahrastani, I, p. 194.

gradually to formation of a religious sect of Zubayrites. Thus it appears that, during the early days of struggle against the Umayya, the Shi'at Ali primarily sought reliable leaders—preferably in Ali's Ahl al-Bayt, but not to the exclusion of all other possible sources of leadership. The willingness of the Kufans to follow non-Alids in certain circumstances is especially significant, considering that post-Ali generations had been continuously developing a distinctive religiopolitical consciousness. The successive emergence of Shi'at Ali, Khawarij, Kaysaniya, Zubayrite, and Hashimite (the other descendants of Ali) was widely appreciated by those who planned to undermine the power base of the Umayyad empire, but the opposition's own dynastic confusion damaged its cohesion.

Zayn al-Abidin, as the only male survivor of the Karbala tragedy, became the guarantor of continuity of Ali's blood through the Husaynid line. Although he did not actively participate in the campaign against the Umayyads, toward the end of Mukhtar's and Ibn az-Zubayr's campaign he gradually gathered a number of people around him.[72] After his death (95/714), his followers rather predictably divided their support between two of Zayn al-Abidin's sons: Zayd b. Ali (the founder of the Zaydi sect) and Muhammad al-Baqir. Apparently the sectarianism due to the lack of any political hegemony in the Islamic community became evident, and diversity in political and religious interests took over in the absence of Muslim unanimity in selecting a leader. It was clear to the followers of each leader that they could not bring about universal recognition for their leader. Thus the followers of each leader decided who should be the successor within their group, until the special designation (nass) of the successor was elaborated by Ja'far al-Sadiq, the son of Muhammad al-Baqir.

Evidence that not all of the followers of the previous leader necessarily turned to his son is scarce, but the diversity in leadership after the death of Ali demonstrates that such things did occur. In the case of Zayd, the son of Zayn al-Abidin, his followers did not even recognize Zayn al-Abidin as Imam or leader;[73] and apart from that the subsequent Zaydi Imams were not Zayd's descendants.[74] Likewise, some people who fol-

---

[72] On the other hand, this did not exclude the non-Alids such as Mukhtar, who was not merely considered a political leader.
[73] Hodgson, op. cit., p. 1, quoting R. Strothmann, Staatsrecht der Zaiditen (Strassburg, 1912).
[74] Ibid.

116

lowed Muhammad al-Baqir then turned to al-Nafs al-Zakiya (a descendant of Hasan), and on these grounds Ja'far al-Sadiq (the son of al-Baqir) rejected them.[75] Thus hereditary succession appears to have been an opposition choice rather than a fixed tradition of appointed Imams promulgated by the sixth Imam. The designation of Muhammad al-Baqir was not a special appointment by his father Zayn al-Abidin but rather a determination reached by judgment and the approval of his followers. The same is true in the case of other Shi'i leaders such as Hasan, Husayn, Ibn al-Hanafiya (and his son Abu Hashim), and Zayn al-Abidin.

The primary goal of the followers in turning to the leaders was at first the political one of deposing the Umayyads. But the life of the opposition could not have been built only on political issues; religious, legal, spiritual, and other matters had to be solved according to the Koran, the *hadiths*, and their interpretation by one leader or another. Though the school of the *mu'tazila* ("withdrawn"; not on either side) did not become an important intellectual trend in theology until about the reign of Harun al-Rashid, the Abbasid Caliph (786–809),[76] the leaders or Imams used their knowledge and authority to resolve disputes and other matters among their followers.

The descendants of Ali, however, had reserved a place of special political prominence in the opposition. Although some of them (notably the Imams of the Ithna Ashari [Twelver] line of Shi'ism) maintained a quiescent policy politically, they nonetheless gained religious prestige because of the special knowledge and virtues attributed to them by the *ghulat* with perhaps the exception of Ja'far al-Sadiq, whose reputation did not rest on virtues attributed to him by the *ghulat* alone. This authorization again did not obscure the position and the role played by certain non-Ithna-Ashari Imams such as Abu Hanifa, Malik, and al-Nafs al-Zakiya (all contemporaries of Ja'far al-Sadiq), who constructed a pious basis for the development of subsequent theology by their followers.

Taking what has just been said into account, the divergence in popular support between the two sons of Zayn al-Abidin may have been based on Zayd's primarily political merits versus Muhammad al-Baqir's primarily religious merits. Although such a generalization may not be completely accurate, the decision to follow Muhammad al-Baqir could not have had a political basis. In contrast, Zayd adopted the policy of his grandfather

---

[75] Lewis, *Origins of Ismailism*, p. 30.
[76] Watt, *Formative Period.*, p. 217.

Husayn to join the Kufans in challenging the Umayya, an adventure in which he perished dramatically (d. 122/740). His son Yahya, who had gone to Khurasan as part of his campaign was killed near the Caspian Sea.[77] There were subsequent differences of opinion about who should be Yahya's successor. Mas'udi quotes Abu Issa Muhammad Harun Waraq as indicating that the Zaydis broke up into eight sects,[78] whereas Shahrastani only reports four.[79] Nishaburi, working on a different scale from a classical Shi'i standpoint, indicates that the movement of Zayd was aimed at ending Shi'i subordination under the Umayya, not necessarily at proclaiming himself an Imam.[80] This view has been equally held about the emergence of various Zaydi sects as representing an unconscious political differentiation. The contradiction becomes apparent when the relationship between Zayd and his brother Muhammad al-Baqir is scrutinized in order to clarify why an earlier Shi'i source such as Nawbakhti *Firaq al-Shi'a* or a Sunni source of Shahrastani *al-Milal wal Nihal* makes reference to the quarrels between the two brothers. It is reported that Zayd asserted that a genuine Imam must revolt and make his appearance public. In response, Muhammad al-Baqir addressed Zayd: "According to your belief (*madhab*), your father was therefore not an Imam, because he never made any open and public struggle (*khuruj*) and did not pursue it."[81]

This disagreement about policy and attitude could by no speculative interpretation be bridged. Zayd was not a quiet tolerator of the conventional existing state of affairs; he was supported by his followers as a revolutionary. At the opposite pole was Muhammad al-Baqir, who throughout his career never attempted any armed struggle. When Ja'far al-Sadiq was informed about his uncle Zayd's activities in Kufa, Ja'far's reply was "Zayd was the best of us and our master."[82]

The designation of Muhammad al-Baqir as Imam by his followers was supported by the criteria of special knowledge [ilm] and hereditary au-

---

[77] Moscati, "Per una Storia dell' Antica Si'a," *Revista degli Studi Orientali* XXX (1955): 261; Shahrastani, I, p. 204.
[78] Mas'udi, II, p. 211.
[79] Shahrastani, I, pp. 205–212.
[80] Nishabrui, p. 439.
[81] Nawbakhti, p. 89; Shahrastani, I, pp. 203–204; Jafri, *op. cit.*, p. 265. For further reading see Abdul Rafi'a Haqiqat, *Jonbesh Zaydiya dar Iran*.
[82] Jafri, *op. cit.*, p. 266, citing Tabari, II, p. 1700.

thority which at this time remained obscure and unconsequential. Evidence of the confusion about the Imamate can be seen when Husayn's followers went over to Muhammad ibn al-Hanafiya and then to his son Abu Hashim.[83] At this stage there was clearly no defined guideline for the succession and the Imamate. At any rate, the information revealed by Nawbakhti about the knowledge of Muhammad al-Baqir is as damaging as his political position among some of his contemporaries:

A group left [the followers of Baqir]. They had listened to one among them called Umar ibn Riyah. This man claimed he had asked Baqir about a certain case and Baqir had given him an answer; then he returned to Baqir after a year and asked him about the same case and received a different answer from the first time. He told Baqir that this was different from the answer he had given him on the point the year before. Baqir said that their [the imams'] answers are sometimes determined by taqiya [dissimulation]. But ibn Riyah was thrown into doubt about Baqir's right, and his imamate; he met one of Baqir's followers called Muhammad ibn Qais and told him [what had happened] and that Baqir had said he did this from taqiya; "but God knows I [ibn Riyah] only asked about it because I am firmly resolved to believe what he decides in cases of conscience for me, accepting it, and acting upon it; there is no reason for his taqiya from me; and that's my situation." Muhammad ibn Qaid said that perhaps there was someone with him who made Baqir need taqiya but Ibn Riyah said, "There was no-one in his room at either of the questions except me. No, his answers are all a matter of luck [tabkhit?], and he doesn't remember what he answered the year before." Ibn Qaid agreed with him and repudiated Baqir's imamate, saying that he is by no means an imam who gives incorrect legal decisions, for any reason and in whatever circumstances. He is no imam who gives other decisions, under taqiya, than what is proper before God; nor who hopes to remain hidden, closing his door; the imam is required to revolt and to command the good and forbid the wrong. For this reason he turned to the position of the Butriya [Zaydis], and several went along with him.[84]

Despite the efforts of the Kufans who had obtained the sympathy of the exaggerating groups (ghulat) for Muhammad al-Baqir, his inactive

---

[83] Ibid., p. 246.
[84] Hodgson, op. cit., p. 12, citing Nawbakhti, pp. 52–53.

role in comparison to Zayd disappointed many of his followers. This is most likely the reason why most of his followers went over to Zayd[85] and after Zayd's death to al-Nafs al-Zakiya. The same group spread the idea after al-Baqir expired (117/735) that al-Baqir was not dead but in concealment and would return. Those who believed in this messianic notion were called Baqiriya.[86]

The revolts of the radical Shi'ites continued in the streets of Kufa, while the direct descendants of Ali through the line of Fatima were busying themselves with the teaching and contemplation of religious matters in Medina. They wished to have nothing to do with the radical Arab and non-Arab enthusiasts and conspirators, and as long as they remained well-behaved they were comforted by the Umayyads and hated by the Zubayrites and their allies.[87] The radical branches of opposition to the Umayya were pursued under the banner of Shi'ism (Shi'at Ali) or under the Khawarij, who continued their fight to undermine the imperial base of the Umayyads. Ultimately the fruits of these unsuccessful revolts were enjoyed by the Abbasids.[88]

After the death of al-Baqir, his son Ja'far al-Sadiq was designated Imam; meanwhile Kufa and other revolutionary centers had absorbed many of the followers of al-Baqir. The Zaydi movement, with its support of a certain mu'tazila; the revolt of one of the descendants of Hasan, Muhammad al Nafs al-Zakiya under the title of Mahdi, whose messianic connotation connected him to other messianic subgroups of the Kaysaniya; and other movements had left Ja'far al-Sadiq with the choice of either following his father's nonrevolutionary policy in Medina or accepting and joining the Iraqis. He chose the former course.

At this time further opposition against the Umayya was developing: that of Abdullah ibn Mu'awiya, who began the Abbasid revolt. Abu Hashim, son of Muhammad ibn al-Hanafiya, was the recognized Imam of one of the subsects of the Kaysaniya but was being held under the control of the Umayya and apparently had no son to succeed him. Ibn Mu'awiya convinced his entourage that the Imamate of Abu Hashim had been transferred to Ibn Mu'awiya's son Muhammad, which eventually

---

[85] Jafri, op. cit., p. 252.
[86] Shahrastani, I, p. 218.
[87] Wellhausen, Religio-Political Factions, p. 161.
[88] Ibid., p. 165.

passed to Abu al-Abbas, who became the first Abbasid Caliph. This gave the Abbasids the necessary legitimacy of a claimed Imamate to enable them to continue their struggle from Khurasan, since Kufa was the center of pro-Alid sympathizers.[89]

Consequently there were two distinct revolutionary movements before and during the time of Ja'far al-Sadiq. First was the Kaysaniya, whose Imam was Muhammad ibn al-Hanafiya; this movement appeared in the struggle of Mukhtar and then in the revolt of Abdullah ibn Mu'awiya, and its followers formed the nucleus of the Abbasid rebellion. Second was the rise of al-Nafs al-Zakiya and the Hasanids, to whom the later Zaydis claimed to be heir.[90] Mas'udi reports that Ja'far al-Sadiq himself (another important descendant of Ali, though a nonrevolutionary one) was invited to accept the allegiance of the people of Khurasan and to join the Abbasids in an alliance to overthrow the Umayyads. Reportedly Ja'far burned the letter and read this poem:

When one lights a fire, are its flames for another? Or does one gather wood in the rope of another?[91]

Nawbakhti also describes Abu Muslim's solicitation of Ja'far al-Sadiq regarding acceptance of the leadership. Ja'far's response to this invitation was "Neither are you one of my people nor has my time come around for such a thing."[92]

Ya'qubi also mentions Ja'far's refusal to undertake the leadership.[93] The Abbasids' political gesture appears to him to have been no more legitimate than the Umayyads', if they succeeded in their enterprise.

The Khurasan and the secret society of Kufa, run by a Persian named Baqir b. Mahan[94] and by Abu Salama (who was eventually assassinated by the Abbasids), paved the way for the revolution to reach its final goals. The complexity of the situation illustrates that the Abbasids' main

---

[89] Jafri, op. cit., p. 272. See also Wellhausen, Religio-Political Factions, p. 153; Nawbakhti, p. 106.
[90] Hodgson, op. cit., p. 9, quoting Strothmann, Staatsrecht, p. 106.
[91] Mas'udi, II, p. 258, Donaldson translation, Shi'ite Religion, p. 130; see also Jafri, op. cit., p. 273.
[92] Nawbakhti, p. 108–110; see also Allamah Tabatabai, op. cit., p. 68.
[93] Ya'qubi, II, p. 329.
[94] Petrushevsky, op. cit., p. 48.

goal of overthrowing the Umayya was identical to that of other groups of Shi'at Ali in Iraq and Medina, but their ambitious strategy and ideology set the Abbasids apart. They asserted that the Caliphate after the prophet belonged to Abbas, Ali's uncle (who was the legitimate inheritor from Muhammad), but that Abu Bakr and Umar had seized power and deprived him of his right. Although they also recognized that the Caliphate of Ali, being from the clan of Banu Hashim, gave them additional grounds for protecting the interests of the Ahl al-Bayt vis-à-vis the Banu Umayya. The strategy of attracting a diverse group of followers for only religious reasons led them to be recognized by the Kaysaniya—especially those from the subgroup of Abu Hashim, which included many religious extremists. The Kaysaniya were primarily a messianic group who asserted the imminent coming of the Mahdi ["guided by God"]. In fact, the first Caliph/Imam of the Abbasids was sworn to the position as the Mahdi who would restore just rule, and he was given the title al-Saffah ("blood shedder," referring to shedding Umayyad blood.)[95]

As an incentive to recruitment to their cause, the Abbasids promised to rule according to the Koran and sunna. They spread the notion of creating an egalitarian social and economic system in which Muslims would not have to pay kharaj (poll tax) and in which non-Muslims' payment of kharaj and jizya (non-Muslim tax) would be reduced drastically. As Petrushevsky put it, these socioeconomic plans had a somewhat Mazdean rhythm toward egalitarianism that attracted many people.[96] The state of affairs under the Umayyads had become so dismal that gradually masses of the deprived and oppressed—the Sunnis, Khawarij, peasants, even Zoroastrians—joined the Abbasid movement in the hope of achieving liberation from the oppressive Umayyads.[97]

Khurasan, as a distant province of the Caliphate, was never under tight control[98] and continued to base its resistance on opposition to Arab hegemony. Even during the Caliphate of Ali, as al-Baladhuri reports, Khurasan's dihgans and dihsalars (those who owned landed estates) refused to pay jizya and constantly rebelled against the Caliphate. This province,

---

[95] Madelung, "Al-Mahdi," p. 1233.
[96] Petrushevsky, op. cit., p. 48.
[97] Ibid., p. 49; see also Nawbakhti, p. 108.
[98] The Persian cultural and political revival indeed began in this province. See Sadiq, The History of Education in Iran, pp. 114–115. See also Frye, The Heritage of Persia.

according to the same source, had remained in a state of chaos until after the death of Ali.[99] By the time of Ziyad in the 660s, twenty-five thousand Kufans were sent to settle in Khurasan as part of the garrison.[100] Around the time the Abbasid revolution was taking place, Shi'ism and the household of Ali received widespread attention. Richard Bulliet states that approximately eight percent of the Persians had converted to Islam at this time;[101] this percentage must have included the pro-Alid (Shi'at Ali) sympathizers as well as nonpartisan Muslims. The pro-Alid movement in Iran at the time of Ja'far al-Sadiq may have functioned only on a religious basis and not necessarily on the basis of political, cultural, and regional resistance to Arab domination. Therefore, apart from the small proportion of converted Persians, there was naturally a diversity of participation in the revolt against the Umayya in hopes of changing the status quo. The efforts of activists in Khurasan to achieve political change attracted them to various religious Shi'i factions in Iraq that were more aggressive and activity-oriented than the Imams and their pacifist branch of Shi'ism in Medina.[102]

The revolution occurred in 132/750. The Umayyad empire was overthrown and virtually all its prominent members were massacred in revenge for various historical wrongs. Abdul Rahman, an Umayyad who survived, left for Spain, where he began a new dynasty of the Umayyads—one that lasted twice as long as the original one in Damascus. At last the Banu Hashim (albeit from a non-Alid line, the Abbasids) prevailed over the Banu Umayya. Nonetheless, according to the early belief of both the Banu Umayya and the Banu Hashim, power was to remain within the Quraysh tribe. This notion had earlier led the Umayya to a position of countering Shi'i beliefs by claiming that the monopoly of the leadership was restricted not to the Banu Hashim clan but the wider clan group of Abd-Manaf.[103] But the charge of the Shi'i (Banu Hashim) against the Umayya was that they had seized the Caliphate by force by ignoring the Hashimites' rights as Qurayshites of the Prophet's clan.[104] Abbasids, as Hashimites on the one hand and as avengers against

---

[99] al-Baladhuri, II, p. 169.
[100] Morony, *Iraq*, pp. 244–245.
[101] Bulliet, *Conversion to Islam in the Middle Ages*, p. 44.
[102] Donaldson, *op. cit.*, p. 121.
[103] Watt, "God's Caliph: Quranic Interpretations and Umayyad Claims," p. 569.
[104] *Ibid.*

the Umayyads on the other, loomed large, but internal conflicts soon diminished their popularity. Certain factions of Shi'at Ali, the Khawarij, the emerging Persian political formation leading to the establishment of the Tahirid (160/776) and Safarid (179/795) dynasties in that land, the establishment of the Fatimids (Isma'ili Shi'a) in North Africa (260/873), and the development of various schools of theology combined to create a more complex set of political preoccupations for the Abbasids than faced their predecessors, the Umayyads.

The early Abbasids invited the Shi'i leaders and the Imams to Iraq to create a religiopolitical coalition and to help identify opposition elements. To this effect, many within the system were identified and either executed or given prison sentences—among them Abu Hanifa, an Imam and the contemporary of Ja'far al-Sadiq. Ja'far Sadiq himself was permitted to remain in Medina, but he, his relatives, and their families were watched although graciously treated.[105]

During the political transition from Umayyad to Abbasid rule, Ja'far attempted to provide a firmer ground for the followers of his sect (while defying the claims to leadership of other sectarian religious groups) by contributing information and methods by which an Imam could be designated. This undertaking was due to Ja'far's observation of the swing of certain groups from one group or Imam to another. Thus Ja'far's codification of the role and qualifications of an Imam had a significant impact in the development of Shi'i jurisprudence and theology.

Ja'far acknowledged that the birth of Shi'ism came at the cost of disunity, but he also recognized that the significant opposition to the Umayyads gave a special character to Shi'ism.[106] He noticed the reality and gravity of the existing Shi'i position of clinging to stagnant ideas in a dynamic world. Although the associated superstitions had been conceived to give the Shi'a the upper hand in religious controversies, they had limited the Shi'ites' vision and their power in the world. Ja'far al-Sadiq, probably the most articulate Shi'i Imam in the Ithna Ashari (Twelver) line, had become acutely aware of the quandary. In response, he tackled two serious problems.

First, he reportedly denounced and boldly rejected the transcendental image of the Imams (referring to the Kaysaniya and their *ghulat* circles)

---

[105] Petrushevsky, *op. cit.*, p. 51.
[106] Mansuri, *Maghz Mutefaker-e-Jahane Shi'a, Ja'far Sadiq*, pp. 95–107.

and the conception of the Prophet as half man and half metaphysical image of divinity. This was notably an implicit rejection of his rivals, who had developed extremist beliefs and messianic notions. To discredit them and to ban the proliferation of extremist assertions among his own followers, Ja'far claimed that all the Imams, including the Prophet himself, were human beings with no supernatural power. Then Ja'far quotes Muhammad, who himself asserted: "I am a human like you." Nonetheless, subsequent Shi'i accounts such as Kulayni's assert that an Imam has the power to perform miracles, is infallible, and uses irrefutable arguments.[107]

The second problem Ja'far singled out for correction was Shi'i isolationism, which closely resembled the custom in the Christian world that monks remained in seclusion within their monasteries and had no outside contacts.[108] Simultaneously, two Imams, Malik and Abu Hanifa, were preoccupied working out cases of religious matters based on the *hadiths* and the *shari'a* (Islamic law), which the Sunni followers looked upon as legal authorities. Working out these legal and religious matters empowered Ja'far al-Sadiq to establish a system that gave him, his predecessors, and his designated descendants a monopoly of legal and religious authority—the system of Imamate or the doctrine of divine right. The Imamate was a justification of the quiescent policies of the household of Ja'far, which had been maintained since the death of Husayn at Karbala. This stipulation enabled an Imam such as Ja'far himself to appoint the next Imam among his qualified children, identifying the one who had the special authoritative knowledge of the religion and (as the Shi'ites put it) the supernatural character. "In this doctrine of the Imamate it was not at all necessary for a divinely appointed Imam to rise in rebellion and try to become a ruler."[109] This system rejected the selection of a leader by a general consensus of the Muslim community (*ijma*) and instead prescribed a special designation (*nass*) by the household of the Prophet (Ahl-al-Bayt). Therefore the hereditary authority and guidance must likewise remain with his family. This connotated a denial of the legitimacy of the descendants of other Imams such as Ibn al-Hanafiya, Hasan (notably al-Nafs al-Zakiya), and Zayd. Henry Corbin, a French

---

[107] Jafri, *op. cit.*, p. 294, quoting Kulayni, *al-Kafi*, I, pp. 205, 207, 304.
[108] Mansuri, *op. cit.*, pp. 95–103.
[109] Jafri, *op. cit.*, p. 293.

Islamicist, explains that the followers of the house of Ja'far al-Sadiq chose the idea of the hereditary Imamate to give certain continuity to the legacy of the prophecy in its spiritual sense and to justify considering an Imam the inheritor (wasi and warith) of the Prophet.[110]

Thus the abandoning of violent rebellion and the establishment of an esoteric belief system led the followers of Ja'far to accept the notions of nass (designation) and ilm (knowledge). Reportedly, Ja'far designated one of his sons, Isma'il, to the position of Imamate, but Isma'il died (d. 143/760) before Ja'far did. Some Shi'i accounts assert that the Imamate of Isma'il was in fact annulled by Ja'far as a result of Isma'il's reckless wine-drinking and misbehavior.[111] In turn, fundamental questions were raised about Ja'far's own special knowledge by his naming as his successor a man who died before him.[112] The opinion that Isma'il was nonetheless a legitimate Imam caused followers to leave Ja'far, eventually resulting in a schism within the sect. Certain believers in the Imamate of Isma'il argued that Isma'il was not dead but had gone into concealment and would return when the world came to an end.[113] Others believed that the Imamate of Isma'il had passed to his son, Muhammad; proponents of this view were called Mubarakiya.[114]

Ja'far's position was substantially weakened when many of his followers left him on the grounds that Isma'il's Imamate was valid; in subsequent stages this notion gave rise to a very important sect in Shi'i history, the Isma'iliya, which still exists today. Another factor that led to criticism in certain Shi'i circles was Ja'far's refusal to denounce the first two Caliphs, Abu Bakr and Umar (considered by some to have seized power by force and afterward to have failed to comply fully with the tradition of the Prophet). In part Ja'far's reluctance stemmed from the fact that his mother was the daughter of Abu Bakr's grandson, Qasim.[115] Moreover, Ja'far's father al-Baqir and his grandfather Zayn al-Abidin not only did not denounce the two Caliphs but indeed confirmed that they were

---

[110] Corbin, En Islam Iranien, I, p. 221.
[111] Mostaufi, p. 203.
[112] Hodgson, op. cit., p. 12.
[113] Shahrastani, I, p. 222; see also Chapter 5 of this book.
[114] Shahrastani, I, p. 222; see also Nizam al-Mulk, Siyasat Nama, p. 208.
[115] Mas'udi, I, p. 657; see also Shahrastani, I, p. 219.

Caliphs.[116] Ja'far equally appreciated the merits of the first two Caliphs.[117]

Ja'far al-Sadiq's Imamate ended in 148/765, some fifteen years after the establishment of the Abbasid dynasty. His death at the age of sixty-five was denied by some of his messianic followers (called Nawusiya).[118] But in the aftermath of his death, another dispute over leadership broke out, this time in Ja'far's own household.

Reports of the number of Ja'far's children vary. However, each of his sons apparently gained followers and emerged as the head of a rival sect. Ibn Tiqtaqa and Mas'udi indicate that one of Ja'far's sons, Muhammad, proclaimed his authority in Mecca and gained Meccan consensus in his favor against the Abbasids. During the Caliphate of al-Ma'mun the seventh Caliph (813–833) Mecca was regained, but Muhammad was pardoned by the Caliph.[119]

While Musa al-Kazim, another son of Ja'far, undertook the Imamate in Medina, Musa's older brother Abdullah asserted that the Imamate belonged to him.[120] Meanwhile, the contingent who believed in the Imamate of Isma'il bitterly left the rest of Ja'far's family altogether; they proved themselves able in developing a distinct theology and in pursuing their political aspirations to the extent of damaging the Caliphate on the one hand and giving rise to powerful dynasties in Egypt, Bahrain, Persia (Alamout Ismaili-Hasan Sabbah), and other regions of Central Asia on the other. The dispersing members of the Ahl-al-Bayt and their developing animosity toward one another (for example, Isma'ili versus Ithna Ashari Shi'i), could raise questions about the later Shi'i assertion of the descendants of the Prophet, Fatima and Ali and all their offspring, as a special human order gifted with divine knowledge. The broken strategy of the Ahl-al-Bayt definitely created one of the most multi-branched sects in history and left Shi'ism vulnerable to a variety of religious and historical criticisms.

In the line of the Ithna Ashari (Twelvers) Imamate, the Imamate of

[116] Jafri, op. cit., p. 252, quoting Ibn Kathir, Bidaya, IX, p. 311; Dhahabi, Tarikh, iv, p. 300; Ibn al-Jawzi, Sifat as-Safwa, II, p. 61; Abu Nu'aym, Hilya, II, p. 185.
[117] Donaldson, op. cit., p. 130, quoting as-Suyuti, History of the Caliphs (trans. Jarrett, Calcutta, 1881), p. 125.
[118] See Shahrastani, I, p. 218; Majlisi, Bihar al-Anwar, XIII, p. 423.
[119] Ibn Tiqtaqa, pp. 304–305; Mas'udi, II, p. 440.
[120] Sayyid Muhammad Mahdi, Khulasatu'l Akhbar (Karbala 1879, Ch. xxxv), quoted by Donaldson, op. cit., p. 154.

Musa al-Kazim was recognized following that of Ja'far, after a great lapse of time during which followers diverged into various sects. Significantly, the death of Musa al-Kazim in 185/799 was itself not free of extremist accusations and resulting divisions. Those who hesitated to believe he had died were called *Mamtoriya*. Those who believed he was dead but was the last Imam were known as *Qat'iya*. Those who believed he was the hidden Imam and would return were known as *Waqifiya*.[121] Another group, however, recognized the Imamate as having passed to Reza (born 148/765), one of Musa's sons.[122] Reza's mother was a slave girl named Marisa, one of the many concubines of Musa al-Kazim.[123]

Some four decades after the birth of Reza, the household received the news that the Abbasid Caliph, al-Ma'mun, had invited Reza to accept the right of succession to his throne (202/817). Al-Ma'mun, half Persian himself and a follower of the school of the *mu'tazila*, may have felt a sincere admiration for the household of Ali; but in diplomatic terms, as some Shi'i sources indicate, he may have hoped to reduce Shi'i opposition throughout the empire by appointing Reza his heir.[124] In any case, al-Ma'mun gave his daughter in marriage to Reza. Some Shi'i sources report that, when al-Ma'mun invited Reza to accept this arrangement, Reza at first refused but later gave his consent.[125] It is interesting to note how the esoteric practice of the religious Imamate was to be transferred into the broader context of the political Caliphate. This collaboration requires political, social, and religious explanations (including consideration of Reza's own reasoning) in a comprehensive study to corroborate the Shi'i versions, which have always tried to stress the uncompromising attitude of their Imams.

Reza and his entourage did not constitute a significant threat to al-Ma'mun or the Abbasids, but al-Ma'mun's uneasiness stemmed from other Alid revolts—especially that of Muhammad, the son of Ja'far al-Sadiq and the uncle of Reza.[126] By designating Reza Al-Ma'mun expected to gain the sympathy and support of those who wished to have a leader

---

[121] All instances from Shahrastani, I, p. 224.
[122] Musa al-Kazim had eighteen sons and nineteen daughters.
[123] Nishaburi, p. 386.
[124] See Majlisi, *Jala ul Uyun*, p. 546.
[125] Ibn Tiqtaqa, pp. 300–301; Mas'dui, II, p. 441.
[126] Housain, *Occultation of the Twelfth Imam*, pp. 74–75.

from the house of Ali.[127] In fact, al-Ma'mun's appointment of Reza as his successor (engineered by his Persian vizier Fazl b. Sahl) served a multitude of Abbasid goals. Perhaps foremost among these was to absorb the pro-Alids, if it proved impossible to divide them by the tactical moves without confronting them militarily. In prayers, al-Ma'mun's name and the names of those in the household of Ali were to be mentioned. Furthermore, at least two brothers of Reza advanced their fortunes by favoring al-Ma'mun's Caliphate. Abbas b. Musa al-Kazim took over the governorship of Kufa, while Ibrahim b. Musa al-Kazim assumed the governorship first of Mecca and then of Yemen under al-Ma'mun.[128]

Despite the intelligence of this policy, al-Ma'mun faced fierce opposition to it in his own court at Baghdad where his uncle Ibrahim proclaimed himself Caliph—probably in part as a reaction to al-Ma'mun's own tendencies (it has been asserted that al-Ma'mun's ideas were close to those of the Zaydis[129]) and in part to prevent the announced succession (which may have called for the Caliphate, after Reza, to pass to his descendants).

After Reza and al-Ma'mun spent time together in Khurasan, al-Ma'mun headed toward Baghdad and Reza died shortly afterward (203/818). Shi'ites have claimed al-Ma'mun conspired in Reza's death. Ya'qubi reports that when Reza reached Nughan (later called Mashad), he became fatally ill and died after three days. The author goes on to assert that Ali b. Hisham offered a poisoned pomegranate to Reza.[130] However, Tabari reports no such story of death by poison.[131] Ibn Babuya quotes Khadim asserting that Reza had become ill before arriving in Tus (near Mashad), and that his condition became critical there.[132] Ya'qubi's report at the same time indicates that al-Ma'mun became despondent upon learning of Reza's death. He prayed, cried, and said at the grave of Reza:

---

[127] Watt, *Formative Period*, p. 176.
[128] Housain, *op. cit.*, p. 76. It is said that al-Ma'mun ordered the adoption of green outfits to replace the Abbasids' black ones in order to satisfy the pro-Alids. The pro-Alids usually wore white, but green was the symbol of the Sassanid Persians, which may again point to the suggestion of al-Ma'mun's vizier Sahl as a policy to gain support of the Persians. *Ibid.*, pp. 75–76.
[129] Watt, *Formative Period*, p. 176.
[130] Ya'qubi, II, p. 471.
[131] Tabari, XIII, p. 5675.
[132] Majlisi, *Jala ul Uyun*, p. 554.

"O Abul Hasan [Reza] after you who will there be for me to depend on?"[133]

The rumor of Reza's death being caused by poison must be assessed in light of the belief that, according to Shi'i assertions, all the Imams except Ali and Husayn (who were killed) and the twelfth Imam (who is believed to have gone into occultation) were victims of death by poisoning: "Imams are said to have been put to death by poison, which is consistent, not with any law of probability, but with the accepted traditions that none of the Imams should die a natural death."[134]

Their martyrdom is believed to be a manifestation of their excellence and so represents a divine virtue for the cause of the Shi'ites. Given the early ghulats' preaching about the superhuman power of the Imams and their messianic missions, it may well be that the ghulats are also responsible for the notion of the Imams' martyrdom by poison. (If they had superhuman power, how could they be poisoned?)

After Reza's death, his nine-year-old son Muhammad al-Taqi (d. 220/835), known as Jawad the generous, then the latter's son Ali al-Naqi (d. 254/868), and then his son Hasan al-Askari (d. 260/873), were recognized in the tradition of the Ithna Ashari Shi'a as the ninth, tenth, and eleventh Imams, respectively. Shi'i traditions categorize them as infallible Imams of the same divine order as other Imams, but at least in Iranian Shi'i society, these three have not been endowed with mythological characteristics to the extent of other Imams, nor did any major divisions occur within the sect during their imamates.

In the time of Hasan al-Askari, the eleventh Shi'i Imam, a drastic change took place. A sudden interruption occurred in the Imamate when Hasan al-Askari left no successor, and this produced widespread acceptance among staunch Shi'i believers (apparently influenced by the ghulat) that the twelfth Imam (the alleged son of Hasan al-Askari) had gone into occultation; meanwhile skeptical Shi'ites refused to believe that any such child was ever born. Nevertheless, the messianic belief that for a long time had been adopted by subsects of the early Shi'i (notably within the Ithna Ashari line) now conclusively became part of the religion. This principle subsequently made possible a new development in theory expounding the messianic notion in Shi'ism; its special character led to

---

[133] Ya'qubi, II, p. 471.
[134] Donaldson, op. cit., p. 141.

a new and speculative theology that is the subject of the next chapter of this book.

This Shi'i sect became known as Ithna Ashari Shi'i (Twelver), distinctly recognizing Ali as the first Imam and tracing his descendants through his wife Fatima, the daughter of the Prophet, down to the last or twelfth Imam, who was believed to have gone into occultation but who would return before the Day of Judgment. In light of what has been just said about this tradition, we now must draw some conclusions about how the early political opposition of the Iraqis, Banu Hashim, the dissatisfied, and various anti-Umayya parties evolved into sectarian religious beliefs, especially that of the Ithna Ashariya.

A Final Comment

No single firm judgment is possible in assessing the emergence of Shi'ism out of its complex social, political, religious, tribal, and moral background. Nevertheless, these factors must be considered instead of evaluating the sect by preconceptions (as the Shi'ites prefer to do) or in terms of linear progression. Succession to the Prophet played a pivotal role in the formation both of authority (the Caliphate) and of its opposition (united under the banner of Shi'ism). The program of *Shi'ites* of whoever defied the existing system was dictated by the interests of the tribe, region, family, and religious faction involved. Historically, it is important to distinguish the nature of the Shi'i opposition in its own times from the way it came to be viewed later, influenced by subsequent developments. Even the early sources provide only a sketch of events up to their own time, indicating that the issues, events, number of sects, and number of Imams had not yet been settled.

For example, the title of the Ithna Ashari (Twelvers) sect was decided only by later tradition—not before or even immediately after the death of Hasan al-Askari, the eleventh Imam, when the belief grew that the twelfth Imam had gone into occultation. Earlier than this, no Shi'i sources indicate either the number of Imams or the occultation of the last (twelfth) Imam.[135] Nawbakhti's *Kitab Firaq al-Shi'i* and al'Qummi's

---

[135] Kohlberg, "From Imamiyya to Ithna-Ashariyya," *Bulletin of the School of Oriental and African Studies* 39 (1976): 522.

Kitab al-Maqalat wa'l Firaq, the two earliest sources that mention a belief in twelve Imams, were both completed around the year 900 (about twenty-five years after the alleged disappearance of the twelfth Imam), yet neither makes any explicit reference to the length of his occultation, to the two phases of occultation (minor and major [see the next chapter]), or even to the claim that the number of the Imams was to be final at twelve.[136] It was only the later traditions of Kulayni (d. 329/940), Ibn Babuya (d. 381/991), Sheikh Mufid (d. 413/1022), and so on that supplied the details of the Ithna Ashari sect that were to serve as the basis of its future theology.

When the Shi'i motif began has been disputed by scholars. Some (including the Shi'i scholars) believe that the Shi'i existed around Ali following his exclusion from the initial reconciliation when Abu Bakr was designated Caliph after the Prophet died. Others believe that the Shi'i sentiment emerged identifiably after the death of Uthman, when Shi'at Ali confronted Shi'at Uthman. Still others regard the unresolved settlement between the Banu Umayya and the opposition as the beginning—especially after the death of Husayn. Ali and the Banu Hashim indeed had associates and partisans in Medina and Mecca. But if this is sufficient to constitute a movement, then each tribe and each companion of the Prophet—including Abu Bakr, certain *ansars*, and Uthman—had his own Shi'a. Moreover, when the issue was brought up, each potential candidate or tribe pressed for succession. Thus the aspirations and loyalty of Ali's close associates and his party, seen as part of the natural fabric of rivalry and conflict among other companions of the Prophet, gained significance only because of subsequent developments in Iraq against the Umayya in Syria.

Another point to be considered is that the Shi'at Ali had no widespread popularity in the Arabian Peninsula (among the Hijazis), and for this reason Iraq welcomed and honored Ali and his associates as natural allies complementing each other's opposition to various elements from the Hijaz (battle of Jamal) and the Umayya (battle of Siffin). Even in the time of Ali's children Hasan and Husayn (and his son Zayn al-Abidin), the Hijazi still preferred the son of Zubayr (Ibn az-Zubayr) to any son of Ali (until the time of Zayd [123/740]).[137] The failure of the Iraqis vis-

---

[136] *Ibid.*, pp. 521–522.
[137] Hodgson, *op. cit.*, p. 3.

à-vis the Umayya and the maintenance of the idea of the Ahl-al-Bayt (notably with respect to the house of Banu Hashim, from which the Prophet came) fostered a political climate more receptive than elsewhere to extremist religious ideas in the Iraqis' vicinity, where the *ghulat* emerged. By attributing divine characteristics to various leaders from Ali's family or even to others, the *ghulat* satisfied their religiospiritual tendencies and also laid the groundwork for a legitimate argument. In its early stages, the Shi'i community within a large so-called Sunni empire conceived of its existence as a bona fide divine recognition of its proper place in Islamic society. Meanwhile, its political purpose was to challenge the legitimacy of both the Banu Umayya and even the successors to Muhammad (notably Abu Bakr and Umar). The antagonistic slanders, the cursing of the Banu Umayya and of Uthman by the Shi'a, and the cursing of Ali and his party by the Umayya may describe only the initial animosity that led ultimately to the formation and interpretation of Islamic doctrine with each side holding its own disparate, conflicting beliefs (excluding that of the neutralist *mu'tazila*). Iraq itself, as a result of its diverse historical background of ethnic groups, religious minorities, races, and languages, provided some of the conditions for cultural creativity.[138]

Sociologically and anthropologically speaking, the Iraqis of the post-Islamic era retained a complex combination of pre-Islamic characteristics, carried and practiced in a conditioned Islamic context.[139] Such cultural behavior and the simultaneous opposition to the existing ruling bodies (from Uthman to the Umayya era) significantly and spontaneously determined the course of events in which the Shi'at Ali was gradually transformed from a political opposition into a religion defiant (Shi'ism) of the Umayya. The old Meccan aristocracy—notably the Umayya headed by Mu'awiya—attained the Caliphate, which automatically put them into conflict with their tribal counterpart, the Banu Hashim headed by Ali, as well as with the diverse Iraqi interest groups.

The descendants of Ali may have symbolized one thing to their contemporaries and another to posterity as a result of developments in the religiopolitical domain. The swing of the followers from one descendant of Ali to another was a means for them to reach precision in their religious

---

138 Morony, *Iraq*, p. 19.
139 *Ibid.*, pp. 6–19; see also Moscati, *op. cit.*, p. 265.

leanings without falling back from their political ideals. Those who had followed Mukhtar under the banner of Muhammad ibn al-Hanafiya (the Kaysaniya) turned to Zayn al-Abidin before turning to Abu Hashim, Ibn al-Hanifiya's son.[140] Some of those who had followed Muhammad al-Baqir left after his death to join the movement of al-Nafs al-Zakiya, one of the descendants of Hasan. Indeed, this was one of the fluctuations in popular support against which Ja'far al-Sadiq reacted.[141] But even so, the most consequential split in Shi'i history occurred after Ja'far's death: that of the Isma'ili, who seceded from the mainstream of the Shi'a following the disputes over the legitimacy of various descendants of Ja'far al-Sadiq. The divisions and relocations of the Shi'i groups support the idea that there were various ways to match religiopolitical aspirations to a movement.

Nonetheless, these excessive numbers of divisions gave importance to a *hadith* attributed to Muhammad. Shahrastani reports that, according to the Shi'ites, Muhammad had predicted that the Islamic community would be divided into seventy-three factions, of which only one would be legitimate.[142] However, according to Lammens, who quotes Maqrizi (d. 1442), the number of Shi'i sects eventually reached three hundred.[143] The religious justification, despite supporting *hadiths*, cannot bypass the fact of spontaneous division, which can only be explained socio-historically.

The Shi'i Imams in the line of the Twelvers withdrew from active politics after the death of Husayn, despite constantly being importuned by the radicals to take up arms. The Abbasid revolution, which rose as a huge wave of opposition to the Banu Umayya, significantly absorbed or crushed many of the existing Shi'i sects within itself after overthrowing the Umayyads. At this time, the moderate Shi'i community in the line of Twelvers was under suspicion but deemed relatively harmless. Its preference for esoteric religious leadership was left under surveillance but at peace, whereas the Isma'ili and Zaydi movements distinctly took measures to promote their own theology and dynasties throughout the Muslim empire.

---

[140] Moscati, *op. cit.*, p. 258, quoting Ash'ari, *Kitab Maqalat al-Islamiyyin*, I, p. 23.
[141] Lewis, *Origins*, p. 30, quoting Nawbakhti.
[142] Shahrastani, I, p. 7.
[143] Lammens, *op. cit.*, p. 187.

During the Abbasid Caliphate, there remained some *ghulat* Shi'a who attributed various supernatural characteristics to the Abbasid Caliphs. Rawandi Shi'ites, for example, believed that God was in human form and asserted that God and the Caliph were one entity. Mansur, the Abbasid Caliph, upon being questioned about this notion, rejected it, whereupon the Rawandites attacked him in his palace.[144] Other *ghulat* gathered around the Imams (descendants of Ali), to whom they attributed superhuman qualities and, after their deaths, messianic possibilities.

The later followers of the Shi'i Imams gradually incorporated these superhuman attributes into their descriptions of the Imams and developed a very important thesis that the right of succession belonged to Ali and his descendants. It is said that Abdullah ibn Saba', a companion of Ali and an extremist, propagated the notion that Ali was not dead and regarded him as a messianic figure. Shahrastani mentions that Ali was also considered to be God. These beliefs emerged as a sect known as Saba'iya.[145] In later stages the Saba'iya put forward the assertion that Ali was the rightful claimant to the Caliphate after the death of Muhammad, although Watt notes that there is no reference to Ali making such a claim himself in any of the early historical sources.[146] Many other leaders—whether from the house of Ali or not—were approached by the *ghulat* and thereafter attributed many supernatural virtues. This included the Shi'i Imams (Twelvers), whose legitimacy as rulers was supported by the claim of Ali to the Caliphate. Because of either their failure or their disinterest, the Shi'i Imams were considered by the zealots to be infallible, divine, and from another human order.[147]

In their own times, the Shi'i Imams attracted fewer people because of their inactive political careers. But, interestingly, they gained more attention in subsequent stages, even though other branches of Ali's descendants had more significant records in fighting the Caliphs of both the Umayyad and Abbasid empires. An important historical reason may be that, since the Shi'i Imams rejected the notion of armed struggle after the death of Husayn, their spiritual leadership, although meager, re-

---

[144] See *Iranshahr*, I, p. 337.
[145] Watt, *Formative Period.*, pp. 59–60; see Shahrastani, I, pp. 232–233. See also Chapter 3.
[146] *Ibid.*, p. 61.
[147] Corbin, *op. cit.*, I, p. 59.

mained consistent and continuous in contrast to those adventurous radicals who sporadically appeared in the arena to revolt and met defeat.
Their own notion of Ahl-al-Bayt, based on being the descendants of Ali
and the Prophet through Fatima, was complemented by the propagation
of *ghulat* extremist ideas that distinguished them from others. Arab attention traditionally was directed toward the male line of descendants,
but the introduction of Fatima was a way to legitimize the connection
with the Prophet as well, even though some of the mothers of the Imams
were of obscure background. For example, the mother of the twelfth
Imam, the Imam allegedly hidden and returning as savior, was a Christian
woman of Roman background called Narjis.

To the staunch Shi'i community, after the Ithna Ashari form of the
Imamate was established (and even to present-day Shi'i believers), the
mothers of the Imams never played a significant role in the religious
orientation of the sect. What really counted (as Nawbakhti indicates)
was that an Imam must be recognized in accordance with three essential
criteria: (1) being a member of the Banu Hashim clan, (2) being an
Arabic-speaker, and (3) being a direct descendant of Ali and Fatima.[148]
These criteria not only negated the importance of genealogy on the
mother's side (except that of Fatima, who symbolically linked them with
the transcendental image of Muhammad) but also excluded all other
relatives—even other branches of Ali's descendants (including Hasan's)
from a legitimate claim to the Imamate throughout the three centuries
of struggle after Muhammad.

The twelve Imams were singled out by their subsequent followers and
were revered as the progeny of the prophets: Adam, Noah, Abraham,
Ismael, and Muhammad.[149] After the occultation of the twelfth Imam
Shi'i scholars expounded on the sinlessness and perfect knowledge of the
Imams, their miracles, and their superhuman powers—naturally under
the influences of *ghulat* propaganda—although Nawbakhti, an early Shi'i
author asserts that claims about the Imam's performing miracles were
far-fetched.[150] The link of the Shi'i sect to other biblical religions was
another attempt to establish external legitimacy. Nishaburi, in authen-
ticating the role of Ali and his two sons with regard to the succession

---

[148] Nawbakhti, *op. cit.*, p. 77; see also Aubin, *op. cit.*, p. 153.
[149] Moosa, *The Extremist Shiites*, p. 99, quoting Kulayni.
[150] Momen, *op. cit.*, p. 80, quoting Nawbakhti.

to Muhammad, draws a parallel vindication with the family of Moses. He points out that Ali's and Harun's similar positions as successors on the one hand, and Hasan's and Husayn's names as Arabic translations of the Hebrew names of Moses' grandchildren (by God's choice) on the other[151] indicate that the whole structure of the Shi'i sect was divinely preconceived and selected to echo the earlier legitimacy of another biblical religion.

The monopolization of knowledge by the Imams, their infallibility, and their other divine attributes raise the question of whether these Imams acted and reacted extemporaneously to the circumstances inflicted upon them and their followers or whether everything took place inevitably within an abstract divine plan. For example, it is asserted that Husayn (as well as the Prophet and Ali) had prior knowledge of Husayn's death at Karbala. It thus appears that God willed and predestined Husayn to die tragically at this time and place, and that He informed His Prophet and Ali's family about it. Even Hasan's truce with Mu'awiya was conditioned by a reading of the circumstances that reflected Hasan's unlimited divine knowledge and his recognition that such a treaty would ultimately serve the divine cause. But for centuries these and other beliefs have forced people to choose between an understanding of the past based on divine intervention or predestination (in which the whole course of events is determined by God Himself in an otherwise unintelligible way) and one reflecting an uncertain world that depends on the laws of cause and effect or of probability. When Husayn was slain, was the whole historical scene a divine setup for the grandson of the Prophet to be killed? Did Hasan enter into his truce with Mu'awiya to promote a special virtue?

Answering such questions requires a metaphysical and philosophical vision, but this should not obscure the need for objectivity in seeking concrete answers. Ibn Sina (Avicenna), the great Persian physician and philosopher of the tenth century, introduced a logical outlook concerning metaphysics and believed that an active intellect could understand and overcome the passivity of the soul and its weakness.[152] In other words, applying one's own sense of judgment and reasoning—even to the con-

---

[151] Nishaburi, pp. 256–257.
[152] Ibn Sina (Avicenna), *Livre des Directives et Remarques* (Kitab al-Isarat wal'Tanbihat), Paris, 1951; see also *La Metaphysique du Shifa*, books 1–5, Paris, 1978.

duct of the Imams—may produce fewer clear-cut conclusions than are obtained by accepting the allegedly divine ideas, but it significantly provides a choice for people living in the dynamic world. Nonetheless, the issue of free will and reasoning is part of Shi'i theology, even though this Koranic verse implies that people do not make distinct decisions without the will of God:

> And whosoever it is Allah's will to guide, He expandeth his bosom unto the surrender, and whomsoever it is His will to send astray, He maketh his bosom close and narrow as if he were engaged in sheer ascent. Thus Allah layeth ignominy upon those who believe not. [6:126]

This invites the feeling that human beings live in a world of illusion whose process is futile and where they make no decision that is truly their own. Detailed discussion of this issue would, however, exceed our focus on the role and the emergence of the Imams. But an important question similarly needs clarification by the theologians, whose presumptions about and understandings of Shi'i religion arise from information derived from books and contemplation, not necessarily as a result of any divine enlightenment. If one bases an argument on careful scrutiny of historical events reflected in the works of early historians, one may venture to ask why Muhammad succeeded in delivering his message without having his mission aborted. And if we accept the argument that the twelve Imams were also the appointees of God after Muhammad, then the objective of such appointment—to govern Muslim people—not only did not receive a widespread recognition but also resulted in the Imams' being forced into isolation by the repressive competition of their rivals. Did God will this, or did it just happen that way?

Objectivity of argument in light of reported historical circumstances and sober reason should prevail over speculation in trying to answer these questions. The lack of any universal declaration of such an Imamate in the Koran necessarily gave importance to the collection of *hadiths* about the Imams and their private mission. Nonetheless, the Shi'i argument indicated in Chapter 3 states that proper resolution of the issue of the succession to the Prophet depends on *hadiths* and anecdotes reported by earlier Shi'ites. Furthermore, on the matter of the occultation of the twelfth Imam, it is asserted that the Prophet and Ali both knew about this but kept it a secret tradition passed down to the succeeding Imams.[153]

In our discussion of the Imams and the emergence of Shi'ism we have sought to understand the modality by which the Shi'at Ali as a political force underwent a transformation, in the presence of existing religious and moral forces, into a diverse religious sect. As the leadership of the Iraqi opposition was gradually being molded around the descendants of Ali, the movement gave rise to various subsects and provided the grounds for an esoteric leadership, the Imamate. For each sect or subsect, the number of the Imams corresponded to their situation, vision, interest, and interpretation of a recognized religious truth. The Ithna Ashari Shi'i Imams in their own times were each identified and recognized as Imams to one group as opposed to another; their number and the nature of their succession were determined only by the later Shi'ites, who believed that Hasan al-Askari (the eleventh Imam) had left behind a son who could not be seen in public because he was in *ghayba* (concealment)—an idea first formulated by the *ghulat*—and who thus stood as the twelfth and last Imam.

Further, in the absence of the Prophet and any new revelation, these Imams undertook the responsibility of maintaining the prophetic laws as well as interpreting the revelation in its spiritual profundity.[154] However, this approach gradually crystallized the doctrine of the Imamate into a theological form, and the Imams were attributed a superhuman character replete with supernatural qualities.[155] The Shi'ites understandably prefer to think of the development of Shi'ism as being wholly predestined, with very little or no mark of external influences. From a more practical viewpoint, it has been difficult if not impossible to determine to what degree the various internal and external forces, Arab and non-Arab elements, and Islamic and non-Islamic beliefs contributed to the final form of Shi'i religious belief.[156] Nevertheless, it would be incorrect to assume that external non-Arab and non-Islamic elements, other cultural borrowings, and further elaboration contributed to expediting Shi'ism as an opposition to the existing forces at different intervals in its history. All of this has been the product of Muslim people, not of Islam itself.

---

[153] Goldziher, *Le Dogme*, p. 179.
[154] Corbin, *op. cit.*, I., p. 54.
[155] Gibb, *Mohammedanism*, p. 123.
[156] Moscati, *op. cit.*, p. 265.

As Michael Morony eloquently states: "It is more productive to think in terms of what Muslims did than in terms of what Islam did."[157]

Finally, it is to be hoped that further research will be undertaken by the Shi'ites to rationalize and criticize those who gave hyperbolic images to their Imams—if only as a way to make Shi'ism reasonably understandable to a broader audience.

---

[157] Morony, *Iraq*, p. 6.

CHAPTER 5
Mahdi: Shi'i Messianism or Ghayba

In order to understand the sociopolitical development of the Shi'i doctrine, three men—Muhammad, Ali, and Husayn—must be seen in perspective. But to understand the doctrine's dogmatic aspect, the notion of Mahdi and its relationship to the hidden Imam must be understood. The notion of Mahdi or the returning savior formed a vision to which many Shi'ites (and to a certain extent, Sunnis) demonstrated a strong psychological attraction and established a theological framework for future religious scholars. This dual focus came to occupy almost the whole of Shi'i socioreligious life.

The theory of the disappearance of the Mahdi and his return to this world before the Day of Judgment plays the central role in the development of Imami Shi'i thought. Given the failure of the Imams to bring about an ideal government on the part of the rulers of the time (the Abbasid Caliphs), the Shi'ites, defeated and deserted, believed that divine intervention must occur to reverse their unhappy condition. Even though many divine attributes were ascribed to the Imam himself, Shi'i followers still believed that divine intervention, amid mysterious circumstances, would be the cure for Shi'i sufferings. The twelfth Imam had gone into hiding, but upon his return he would launch a bloody campaign against the enemies of the Shi'ites and against the nonbelievers. He would also restore the right of the Imams and the work of the Prophet.

Any attempt to trace the belief in the Mahdi or the returning savior, who stands as the predicted redeemer of the Imami Shi'ites, breaks down into two important areas. The first is the origin of the doctrine of a redeemer, which can be traced through Zoroastrian, Judeo-Christian, Buddhist, and other regional religious roots, finally to emerge among the early Shi'i sects. The second is the final formulation of the doctrine in Ithna Ashari (Twelver) Shi'ism and its specific causes.

The doctrine of the returning savior (Mahdi) was a prominent feature of many important world religious philosophies as well as many ancient mythologies. The incorporation and development of such a notion in Shi'ism could be attributed to the physical circumstances in which the Shi'ites found themselves.

With these two aspects in mind, we must follow the idea of the Mahdi from its first use in early Shi'ism to its final formulation, and then we must investigate the confusing circumstances following the death of the eleventh Imam, Hasan al-Askari (d. 260/873), the father of the alleged twelfth Imam, whose birth was doubted by some and strongly espoused by others.

Doctrine

It is useful to distinguish various world religions' concepts of an impending savior who is expected to come as a final deliverer from various historical figures who have already claimed to be the savior. The roots of both may be found in the same line of thought: that man has always sought a powerful ally in his life who could save his physical existence in this world and his soul in the other world. The idea of a savior can be traced in many cultures and mythologies. Often the Persian and Selucid kings gave themselves the title *Soter* (Savior), which represented a living liberator. On the other hand, the notion of a savior in its eschatological form was used by Judaism, Christianity, Zoroastrianism, and Buddhism.[1] In each of these religions a savior is divinely designated to come in due time to end the sufferings of believers and to establish the "divine rule." Each of these religions has developed a series of messianic doctrines that should be understood in an undivided context. James Darmesteter, the nineteenth-century French orientalist, although controversial, indicates that the return of the dead hero was an enriching Aryan myth and a favorite of Iranians in particular.[2] If this is true, then such a notion must have had a strong religious connotation, and its link as a prerequisite to the regional religions must be sought. It is also interesting to note that

---

[1] See Nawbakhti, p. 154; see also von Grunebaum, *op. cit.*, p. 193.
[2] Darmesteter, *op. cit.*, pp. 22–25.

the Persian king Cyrus has been mentioned in the Hebrew Scripture as Messiah (Isaiah 45:1).

The notion of a final savior in Islam is thus not completely abstract. It shares its roots with the heritage of other major religions. Monotheism, a doctrine Muhammad preached throughout his prophetic career, was also a belief that several world religions already preached and shared, although each gave the notion a different coloring depending on historical conditions, cultural restrictions, and the social transitions to which they were subject. The idea of a savior in Islam definitely gained a different coloration as a series of events evolved that determined the final elaboration on the concept: the twelfth Imam of the Shi'ites.

In this discussion, Mahdi will be used instead of "the returning savior," while acknowledging and considering that various messianic ideas are applied to the notion of Mahdi in Shi'i Islam. The word Mahdi, which means "guided by God," at first was used merely in its political and religious senses with respect to the early Imams—Ali, Hasan, and Husayn.[3] Many scholars assert that the first use of Mahdi in its Shi'i eschatological sense was in 66/685 by Mukhtar, an Iraqi revolutionary who attributed the title of Mahdi to Muhammad b. al-Hanafiya, the son of Ali (of a non-Fatimid line).[4] However, Tabari asserts that the first use of Mahdi was by Sulayman b. Surad, who referred to Husayn as the Mahdi after his death.[5] The Encyclopedia of Islam asserts that after the Mu'awiya's death, the term Mahdi came to be used for an expected ruler who would restore Islam to its perfection. According to the Kufans, the Mahdi would be from the Alids, and it was reported in Medina that, if there was any Mahdi, he would be from the Abd as-Shams (Umayya) family.[6] Regardless of this controversy over primacy, such usage of the notion of the Mahdi in Shi'ism was not the first and significantly not the last to maintain a dependence on a superhuman person through religious belief and practice. Many religious sects and political formations in various lands (for instance, Egypt, Sudan, and Iran) have embraced the concept of the Mahdi through the centuries. As recently as the

---

[3] Lewis, Origins of Ismailism, p. 25; A. Sachedina, Islami Messianism, p. 9, both authors quoting Snouck Hurgronge, Der Mahdi: Verspreide Geschriften (Bonn, 1923).
[4] Darmesteter, op. cit., p. 20; Petrushevsky, op. cit., p. 22; Allamah Tabataba, op. cit., p. 75; Lewis, op. cit., p. 25; Sachedina, op. cit., p. 9.
[5] Tabari, V, p. 589; cited in Sachedina's note, p. 204.
[6] W. Madelung, "al-Mahdi," Encyclopedia of Islam, p. 1231.

1930s, a black man from Detroit by the name of Wallace D. Fard—who denounced whites as "blue-eyed devils," "cavemen," and "Satan"—was believed by some to be the Mahdi.[7]

From the time of Mukhtar, the ill-defined notion of the Mahdi was used, elaborated, and ascribed in a messianic context for the next two hundred years of Shi'i development, until the time the alleged son of the eleventh Shi'i Imam, Hasan al-Askari, who was expected to be the Mahdi, was believed to have gone into concealment. Since he never revealed himself, the messianic notion of return was ascribed to him. Historians point out that the idea of the Mahdi marks the beginning of a whole new stratum of eschatological thinking in Islam, especially in Shi'ism. This notion owes its advancement to the difficult conditions of life for which man seeks superhuman remedies. The introduction of the idea of Mahdi into Shi'ism came during such a difficult period, and the belief offered itself as an alternative to the oppression of the Umayyad and then the Abbasid Caliphates.

When the idea of Mahdi was used by Mukhtar for the benefit of Muhammad b. al-Hanafiya, it seems not only to have garnered the religious legitimacy necessary for his political campaign against the Umayyads but also to have introduced a new religiopolitical element into Shi'ism, which was at that time primarily a political party. Mawali (non-Arab subjects) are believed to have played an important role in Mukhtar's campaign for justice and equality, which marked the breach with the Kufan tribal aristocracy (ashraf).[8] Sabatino Moscati asserts, however, that the notion of the Mahdi used by Mukhtar may have derived its influence from the non-Arab population.[9]

Darmesteter[10] asserts that the presence in Iraq of mawali, predominantly Zoroastrian Persians, contributed to the political as well as to the religiophilosophical development of the region. By participating in various political campaigns during the Arab domination, the Persians became involved with a group of radical Iraqis who called themselves the Shi'ites of Ali (Shi'at Ali). This group's appeal to the Persians lay in their fierce opposition to the Syrian Umayyads. These Iraqis seemed to

---

[7] Zafar Ishaq Ansari, "Aspects of Black Muslim Theology," Studia Islamica 53 (1981): 137–176.

[8] Hodgson, op. cit., p. 3. See also J. Wellhausen, Religio-Political Factions, pp. 128–131.

[9] Moscati, op. cit., p. 257.

[10] Darmesteter, op. cit., p. 18.

be looking for a hero to defeat their ancient rival and their present Syrian patrons. For the Persians, this became a favorable ground for saving both themselves and their religious and cultural beliefs in the face of the Arab Muslim threat.

Persians and Christian groups were characteristically the dominant minorities in certain tribes of Kufa—especially the tribe of Banu Ijl, with which in later years Abu Muslim had contact.[11] This Persian domination, together with the existence of other religious minorities in Kufa, intensified the Shi'i opposition in the former city. In Kufa, Mukhtar was believed to be a bright and ambitious man, and his knowledge of many philosophies and close collaboration with the mawali gave him the essentials of an informed leader and enabled him to exploit this cultural situation.[12] It is interesting that, when Mukhtar was defeated by the Zubayrites and killed in battle, his followers, called Mukhtariya, asserted that he would come back to save them.[13]

It is now appropriate to discuss how the notion of Mahdi might have been conceived in Iraq. Iraq as a cosmopolitan region provided a breeding ground in which a number of religiopolitical sects emerged. Prior to the Arab conquest, this region was the home of Christians (Monophysites and Nestorians), Jews, and Magians, along with Hellenistic antecedents that had preserved some roots there.[14] Furthermore, the Zoroastrians and Manichaeans were considered important religious communities whose influence (quite apart from having a political basis in the emergence of non-Muslim mawali as oppositional forces) remained to be exerted in the area of religious dogma. Thus Iraq was a center of world religions and cultural dialogue at the end of the Arab Conquest. "In Iraq the ancient Babylonian religious systems, Zoroastrianism, Mazdakism, Manichaeism, Judaism and various forms of Christianity all contributed to a kaleidoscope of religious debate and religious speculation probably unequalled in the ancient world."[15]

In those early stages, when Shi'ism was still essentially a political

---

[11] Moscati, op. cit., p. 267. See also Watt, The Formative Period, p. 46, quoting Goldziher.
[12] Browne, A Literary History of Persia, I, p. 347; Darmesteter, op. cit., pp. 20, 25. See also Wellhausen, Religio-Political Factions, pp. 131, 149.
[13] Shahrastani, I, p. 194.
[14] Morony, "Religious Communities in late Sasanian and Early Muslim Iraq," Journal of the Economic and Social History of the Orient, XVII, Part II (1974), pp. 113–135. See also Morony, Iraq After the Muslim Conquest.
[15] Momen, op. cit., p. 65.

opposition, Iraq with its huge population of non-Arabs witnessed the dreadful defeat of Ali, Hasan, and Husayn at the hands of the ruling Syrians. This left the Iraqis doubtful of ever achieving victory in their battle against their enemy. The Persians came to share this belief—like the Zoroastrians, who believed that Soashyant, the expected savior from the family of the prophet Zoroaster, would upon his coming bring justice. Darmesteter asserts that, while certain names were changed, the main idea of the Mahdi was translated into the early Shi'i doctrine by the Persians.[16] This viewpoint, of course, was a product of premature nineteenth-century scholarship; today, it is recognized that the roots are more complex. Goldziher adds little more to this understanding when, in addition to Zoroastrianism, he considers the influence of Judeo-Christianity on the origin of the notion of Mahdi fundamentals.[17]

Moscati concurs that there are foreign—Judeo-Christian and Persian—as well as domestic elements in the formation of the notions of Mahdi, ghayba (occultation), and raj'a (return),[18] but he does not point out these elements in their specific format, nor can he tell us what proportion of these elements was of Arab origin and what proportion non-Arab.[19] Marshal Hodgson at least recognizes one Arabian idea that was upheld by the Arabs of jahiliya: the notion of raj'a, the messianic idea of Mahdi's return. But the depth and recognition of this idea among the pre-Islamic Arabs, as in other major regional religions, cannot be measured. Hodgson says:

> There was the notion of raj'a—that a hero might return to this life from the dead; as in the jahiliya, this was not necessarily restricted to one messianic figure, though it was readily adapted to the whole messianic idea.[20]

In his study of the return of the hero in pre-Islamic Arabia, M. M. Bravmann argues that it is certain that the Shi'i doctrine of the "hidden Imams" and the idea of "the return" are Islamic versions of a genuinely

---

[16] Darmesteter, op. cit., p. 18.
[17] Goldziher, op. cit., pp. 184–185.
[18] Moscati, op. cit., p. 266.
[19] Ibid.
[20] Hodgson, op. cit., p. 6.

Arab pre-Islamic idea.[21] This tradition raises questions as to why the Prophet as an "Arabian hero" was never attached to this doctrine.

Having noted the vague definition of savior in the Hijazi–Iraqi region, we must now consider the political upheaval that existed as the Kufan movement against the Umayyads of Syria failed and the followers of Ali (Shi'a) desperately sought charismatic leadership. Among these followers, the emergence of an important religious group or series of groups, the *ghulat* (exaggerators), must be recognized. *Ghuluww* (exaggeration) or *ghulat* was the term that the later Twelver Shi'ites used for these people in contrast to themselves and their supposedly more moderate ideas.[22]

In any event, the opposition against the Umayyads took shape in various religiopolitical channels. The *ghulat* placed their belief in the continuation of divine leadership after Muhammad and in the eschatological expectation of the return of a hero.[23] (Both of these ideas were carried into Twelver Shi'ism.) These religious aspirations of the *ghulat* gradually found roots in the new socioreligious understanding of the Iraqi–Hijazi area. Messianic figures were sought by the *ghulat* elsewhere than among Muhammad's descendants.[24] The introduction of the title *Mahdi* for Ibn al-Hanafiya was even more wildly exaggerated by some *ghulat* members such as al-Barbari, who calls Ibn al-Hanafiya the god for whom he is the prophet. (He also believed in *raj'a*, the return.)[25] William Tucker indicates that, following the revolt of Mukhtar in Kufa, the messianic aspect of Mahdi—the return—had become an integral part of Shi'ism. Thus, Abu Hashim, the son of Ibn al-Hanafiya, was also believed to be the returning Mahdi.[26]

How such eschatological ideas developed among the early Shi'ites,

---

[21] Bravmann, *The Spiritual Background of Early Islam*, p. 287. (Cf. the assessment by Morony [*Iraq*, p. 497] of Bravmann's argument in *Spiritual Background*, p. 265, that "the belief by some of the followers of Muhammad b. al-Hanafiya that he would return was based most directly on the Pre-Islamic Arab concept of the Arthurian return [*raj'a*] of the hero.")

[22] Hodgson, *op. cit.*, p. 4.

[23] *Ibid.*, p. 8.

[24] *Ibid.*, p. 5.

[25] Ibid. See Watt, *Formative Period*, pp. 48–49. Watt mentions Hamza b. Umara (of whom Bayan was a follower) as having held such view of Ibn al-Hanafiya.

[26] Tucker, "Bayan b. Sam'an and the Bayaniyya," *The Muslim World* LXV, 4 (1975): 244–245.

who were making new divisions based on their situation on the one hand and were receiving new ideas from sources outside Shi'ism on the other, ultimately becomes an essential question to answer if we are to understand the entirety of messianic belief in Islam. There is no agreement about the extent to which these eschatological ideas should be ascribed to sources outside the Islamic sphere. Yet the notion of a final savior—whether a promised one or one who has already lived in this world and is now expected to come back—has been found in other major world religions. The invention and the growth of the idea of the Mahdi in the fifth and sixth decades after the death of Muhammad, while civil war raged among Muslims, would sound far-fetched in abstract terms if influence from non-Islamic elements were denied.

Massignon considers the messianic development of the Mahdi to have grown out of the Koran, the Muslim tradition, and Arab folklore under the stimulus of social conditions.[27] This idea might have been regarded as legitimate had subsequent information corroborated it. But the information provided by more modern scholarship reinforces the theory that many ideas shaping the doctrine and purpose of Shi'ism were contributed by the superficially Islamicized *mawali*.[28] Of course, this still suffers from the general lack of evidence. Mahdism in its messianic context may have been a combination of early metaphysical Islamic visions with strong non-Islamic elements. The early *ghulat*, who seemed to be an eager instrument for spreading the eschatological idea of *raj'a*, return, extracted their streams of thought from outside Islam. Moscati treats the phenomenon of *ghuluww* as one of the many crises of Islamic religious thought that finds its roots outside Islam.[29] On the other hand, Tucker mentions that the Bayaniyya sect, which believed Abu Hashim to be the returning Mahdi, also believed in Bayan's claims to prophecy and in the continuation of prophecy—themes seemingly connected with the parallel idea of prophetic succession held by the Manichaeans, who are known to have been present in Iraq during this period.[30] Sachedina, a Shi'i scholar, describes the extreme fluidity of Islamic society during and after the time of Mukhtar, when the organizers of religiopolitical parties introduced

---

[27] Massignon, Lectures at College de France, cited by Lewis, *Origins of Ismailism*, p. 25.
[28] *Ibid.*, p. 24.
[29] Moscati, *op. cit.*, pp. 254–255.
[30] Tucker, *op. cit.*, p. 245.

non-Islamic elements in attributing to leaders semidivine virtues and a messianic mission.[31]

Thus Iraq, as the cosmopolitan center for religious minorities, was a fertile ground for the development and elaboration of eschatological notions. Since the development of such eschatological notions coincided with a political struggle against the oppressive domination of the Umayyads, the Shi'at Ali observed and responded favorably to such notions, as it suited their political cause. Once it became clear that the Umayyads showed no sympathy for and did not wish to compromise with the minority subjects, Arab or non-Arab, Shi'ism as a form of political opposition underwent its fundamental change. Shi'ism went from a minor party founded on an Arab dispute over the succession of Ali to the Caliphate to a major opposition bloc of subjects belonging to a lower economic stratum. In this new role, Shi'ism also represented the aspirations of unprivileged non-Arabs and religious minorities whose faith and culture were at stake under the powerful Muslim Arab rule. Furthermore, the opposition became reoriented from a political to a religious realm as the early political and military campaigns failed. The adoption of the idea of Mahdi (in its military sense) under these circumstances became almost inevitable. After several military attempts against the Umayyads led to severe defeats, the Shi'at Ali gradually incorporated the idea of the return of those martyred Imams while looking to the future for a promised Mahdi. This vision maintained the political spirit of the Shi'ites while a religiophilosophical change was occurring at the outset of their struggle.

During the formative period, many religiopolitical and purely religious sects emerged whose leaders were given the title of Mahdi one way or another. Shahrastani provides an account of these sects in his book, *Al-Milal wal Nihal*.[32] Among others, Zayd, the son of Zayn al-Abidin, the fourth Imam from the Ithna Ashari line, was considered a Mahdi. However, other sects that had shown zeal toward *ghulat* messianic ideas subsequently adopted the notion of the return of their Imams after death or never acknowledged that their Imam was dead. In short, they had consolidated the doctrine of occultation (*ghayba*) with that of return

---

[31] Sachedina, *op. cit.*, p. 10.
[32] Shahrastani, I, pp. 191–224.

(raj'a). These sects are too numerous to be listed exhaustively, but a few along the line of the Imami Shi'ites are worth mentioning.

Of the nonrevolutionary Imams (in the Twelver line), each of the three Imams after Zayn al-Abidin, the fourth Imam—Muhammad al-Baqir, Ja'far al-Sadiq, and Musa al-Kazim—were expected by certain followers to return after ghayba. The three sects were called, respectively, Baqiriya, Nawusiya, and Waqifiya or Musawiya.[33] The distinctions in definition of the return in these three sects are vaguely stated; nonetheless, these sects were extinct shortly after their emergence.

Now Shi'ism was established as something of a religious sect growing alongside the huge Muslim empire of the Umayyads. The Shi'ites at this stage, from two standpoints, could be divided into two categories: the Fatimiya, who followed Imams who were direct descendants of Fatima and Ali; and the Hanafiya, the followers of Muhammad b. al-Hanafiya's descendants. (The emergence of other lines of Shi'ites, such as the Talibites—followers of direct descendants of Abu Talib—are not included.) Another division that could be made would recognize on the one hand those subsects that adopted a messianic belief in the return of their Imams and on the other hand those that simply did not.

Probably one of the major factors that hindered the Iraqi opposition to the Syrians was the religious and political confusion that disintegrated the main oppositional force into various smaller sects. Among the sects, the Imami Shi'ites of the Twelver line had neither adopted nor rejected any exaggerating messianic attributes with respect to the Imams. However, only a century later the same Twelver Shi'ites adopted and developed the notion of the returning Mahdi, providing a firmer theological basis for it.

Before continuing our discussion about the Twelver Shi'ites, it would be valuable to examine briefly the emergence of two sects in whose development non-Islamic influences are evident and strong: the Isma'iliya and the Muslimiya.

Among the most important sects of this period was the Isma'iliya, which emerged near the end of the Abbasid revolution (132/750) against the Umayyads—a revolution in which the Persians and the Iraqis played major roles. Isma'il, the son of Ja'far al-Sadiq, the sixth Imam of the

---

[33] Shahrastani, I, pp. 218–223; Majlisi, Bihar al Anwar, XIII, p. 423, provides further details concerning the Nawusiya. See also Momen, op. cit., pp. 47–60.

Twelver line of Shi'i Imams, died before the death of his father. Twelver Shi'i sources cite al-Sadiq's decision to disinherit Isma'il from the Imamate because of his reckless drinking and other behavior.[34] Ja'far al-Sadiq appointed another son, Musa al-Kazim, as his successor. (Other sons of Ja'far al-Sadiq were later recognized as Imams by some.) However, Isma'il's death—even when evidenced by the exposure of his dead body in public—did not convince the loyalists and by no means annuled his Imamate. But others believed that Isma'il had died in Ja'far's lifetime, that he had gone into concealment, and that he would return.[35] This group called itself pure Isma'iliya (al-Isma'iliya al-Khalisa). Majlisi indeed reports that, among the supporters of the Isma'ili's Imamate, one group believed that Isma'il's death was a ruse and that he was al-Qaim, al-Muntazar (the hidden, the expected).[36] Another group believed that the Imamate was transferred to Isma'il's son Muhammad. This group considered Muhammad the last Imam and the returning Mahdi; members were called Mubarakiya.[37] Nonetheless, the main Isma'ili sect that survived has continued under the leadership of living Imams to the present day.

Many historians trace the roots and tendencies of the Isma'ili sect to non-Islamic or even non-Arab origins. One scholar cautiously asserts that the Isma'ilis were initially an Arab group that had assimilated elements from the Kaysaniya, Mukhtariya, Zaydiya, and (in later years) Muslimiya sects, which had exerted their influence widely outside Islam.[38]

As a revolutionary Shi'i sect within the Abbasid empire, the Isma'ili sect attracted many Persians, Berbers, and Arabs. This eventually divided the Isma'ilis into two groups: those in Egypt, who gave rise to the Fatimid empire (260/873), and those in southern Persia and eastern Arabia, who did not recognize the Fatimids as their Imams.

Apart from upholding the messianic notion of Mahdi that the early Isma'ilis adopted through roots traced to pre-Islamic times, they were

---

[34] See Chapter 4.
[35] Lewis, *Origins of Ismailism*, p. 40, quoting Nawbakhti.
[36] Majlisi, *Bihar al Anwar*, IX, p. 175, quoted by B. Lewis, *Origins*, p. 41; *al-Qa'im* in Aramaic Samaritan text and gnostic usage means "the living one," see Madelung, "Al-Mahdi," p. 1235.
[37] Shahrastani, I, p. 222; see also Lewis, *Origins*, p. 41.
[38] Lewis, *op. cit.*, pp. 27, 24.

also, in the latter part of their development (particularly in Persia), heavily influenced by various Persian doctrines. The fragments of historical evidence in, for example, Nizam al-Mulk's *Siyasat Nama*, in Biruni's *Athar al-Baqiya*, in Shahrastani's *al-Milal wal Nihal*, in Rashid al-Din Fazlollah's *Jama' al-Tawarikh*, and others support the view that the Isma'ilis in the Persian Gulf area were influenced by Persian Mazdaki, Manichaean,[39] and Arab *mu'tazilite* doctrines.[40] Rashid al-Din Fazlollah (d. 718/1318) gives another account (which may not be free of bias), concluding that there was a Persian face behind the mask of Isma'ili faith. Although the assertion is controversial, he describes how many Persians of Manichaean and Mazdaki faith disguised their beliefs upon joining the followers of Ali (various Shi'i sects), who were leading the revolt against the legitimacy of the Caliphate.

Persians resisting the Arab Islamization tried to maintain their cultural identity. For this reason, according to Fazlollah, they seized the opportunity to join the Shi'ites of Hasan, Husayn, Muhammad b. al-Hanafiya (sons of Ali), Abu Muslim, and finally the Isma'iliya, who had separated from other Shi'i sects.[41] In later centuries, the Persian Isma'ilis became an important rival of other Shi'i factions, notably the Ithna Ashari. The Isma'ilis remained a strong political force in Persia until the Qajar period, when they made their last attempt to seize power in the nineteenth century and their movement was finally crushed. Eventually, the remaining Isma'ilis emigrated to India.[42]

Another element that seems to have influenced the Isma'ilis of the Persian Gulf and Iraq—even though it sounds Muslim—was the teaching of an unknown man from Khuzistan. This unknown teacher fasted during the day and worshiped at night, working hard to gain a living. Eventually he gathered around him a great number of people whom he inspired to join the Isma'ili cause. Ahmad Qarmat succeeded this unknown man and propagated Isma'ili teaching in Iraq.[43]

While Persian influences were strong in the Isma'ili movement, such influences in the movement were not restricted to Persia and the Persians.

---

[39] Biruni, *op. cit.*, p. 312.
[40] Browne, *op. cit.*, I, p. 574.
[41] Fazlollah, *Jama' al-Tawarikh*, pp. 72–74.
[42] See Hamid Algar, "The Revolt of Agha Khan Mahallati and the Transference of the Ismaili Imamate to India." *Studia Islamica* 29 (1969); 55–81
[43] Tabatabai, *op. cit.*, pp. 79–80. See also Shahrastani, I, p. 261.

The Isma'ilis benefited from and appealed to a multiplicity of races and religions.[44] However, the practice of communism and other elements of the Mazdaki program might have been preached and prescribed in certain areas under Isma'ilis, particularly in Bahrain (around fifth/eleventh century).[45]

The Muslimiya sect's non-Islamic character was largely Persian. When Abu Muslim, a Khurasani war hero in the revolt against the Umayyad empire, was assassinated by order of the Caliph al-Mansur of the succeeding Muslim Abbasid empire, sympathizers in later years (137–160/ 755–778), including al-Muqanna, Sanbad, and Ishiq Turk, all attributed to Abu Muslim the title of returning Mahdi.[46] This became the nucleus of the Muslimiya movement.

As the modern British orientalist Edward G. Browne explains, the title *Mahdi* was given to Abu Muslim more in its Zoroastrian than its Shi'i sense; his followers believed him to be from the household of Zoroaster. It has been suggested that the followers of this sect were also called the Khurramdin and shared the Mazdaki doctrine.[47] Nawbakhti points out that most of Abu Muslim's army during his uprising against the Umayyads consisted of Zoroastrians, Khurramdins, Kaysaniya, and Sistani Khawarij.[48] This could explain how the Muslimiya sect, with its messianic overtones, drew influence from non-Arab religious and cultural philosophies and other regional elements.

On this ground, it may be asserted that, the more non-Arabs became involved in the Islamic political scene, the more they exerted their cultural influence on Arab religious and political consciousness. On the other hand, doctrines from various lands and societies were similarly incorporated into the Islamic body as a whole. But it is possible that Shi'ism, because of its oppositional nature and emphasis on immediate political and religious solutions, itself began to embrace the doctrine of Mahdi that may have been a non-Islamic product.

As part of their religious scheme, the Shi'ites, a minority within the empire, were constantly seeking a pious hero to lead them to victory

---

[44] Lewis, *Origins of Ismailism*, p. 93.
[45] *Ibid.*, pp. 96–98.
[46] Browne, *op. cit.*, I, p. 465.
[47] *Ibid.*, pp. 359, 368. See also Nizam al Mulk, *Siyasat Nama*, p. 238; Shahrastani, I, pp. 200–202.
[48] Nawbakhti, p. 109.

THE EMERGENCE OF ISLAM

over what they considered an illegitimate Caliphate. On the other hand, the Imams, after Husayn's dreadful defeat, isolated themselves from active political and military activities. The Shi'ites faced a dilemma: accept the Caliphate, which now for religious reasons they would not willingly do, or stage a rebellion without the charismatic appeal of the Imams—a rebellion they could not win.

Nevertheless, the Shi'i opposition managed to produce results upon which subsequent generations could build. There can be little doubt that, when these Shi'i rebels witnessed the death of their leaders (whether the Imams themselves or the Imams' relatives), their incomplete victory left them frustrated but with the eschatological hope that a hero never dies and must come back to achieve complete victory. The Shi'ites' heros were of the household of the Prophet from the clan of Banu Hashim, whose piety and sinlessness was (and still is) attested by God. Some children of Zayn al-Abidin, of Muhammad al-Baqir, and of Ja'far al-Sadiq performed heroic acts, leading armies against the Caliphate, but they all fell short of their goal. Nevertheless, these revolutionary leaders were looked upon by their zealous followers as both the descendants of God's messenger and war heroes, and so they could not die.

On the conservative side of the Imamate (Ithna Ashari), pacifism was the standard. The basis of their doctrine was to learn the true path of living that Muhammad had preached. While military action was also part of Muhammad's teaching, the hopelessness of the Imams' situation left them with no realistic alternative to pacifism—although these Shi'ites still appeared to hope that their Imam would one day defeat their oppressors, although this never happened. The death of their Imams without a defeat of the ruling system was inconceivable while the Caliphate continued to exist (which it did until Mongolian forces defeated the Abbasid empire in 1258). Inevitably the followers of certain passive Imams who were not warriors, such as the Baqiriya or Nawusiya, adapted the widely held messianic belief in the Mahdi to match the notion that their Imams were immortal and would return.[49]

Meanwhile, the Isma'ilis, who had denied the appointment of Musa al-Kazim (the younger son of Ja'far) as the new Imam, had also become critical of the Imams and their quietist attitude of dissimulation (taqiya).

---

[49] See Lewis, *Origins of Ismailism*, p. 30. (Nawusiya believed in the immortality of Ja'far, who was a returning Mahdi.)

154

Often the local movements against the empire never developed into broad-based Shi'i revolt, and the Imams, as charismatic leaders, were blamed for their lack of audacity in the face of the usurpers. These Imams never openly declared war against the empire. The political temerity of these conservative Shi'ites caused a rift between the Isma'ilis and the other Shi'i sects.

Eventually, the Isma'ilis felt justified in separating from the main sect. Among other things, they had learned, according to Kulayni, that Ja'far al-Sadiq had been exacting a religious tax (*khums*) in secret from his followers[50] while making no attempt to organize a revolutionary force to topple the unjust government under which they were living. Even worse, Ja'far al-Sadiq's son Musa al-Kazim had sworn to the Caliph that, in exchange for a promise of safety, he would never initiate any armed struggle against the Caliphate.[51] In fact, the Ithna Ashari Shi'ites suggest that Musa al-Kazim's later arrest was engineered by the Isma'ilis.[52]

It is extremely significant that the Ithna Ashari Shi'i traditions assert that the promise of the Mahdi was already established in the time of the Prophet and the early Imams. Secret *hadiths* reported this. Kulayni (d. 329/940), a Shi'i traditionist (or collector of *hadiths*), quotes Ja'far al-Sadiq as having expressed the idea of an expected Mahdi who will return (the historic role attributed to the twelfth Imam). This was a secret matter until the Kaysaniya became aware of it and propagated it.[53] Such a belief implies that a divine connection had been made between the misery and stagnation of the Shi'ites under the Umayyads and Abbasids on the one hand and the need during the period of both empires for a strong Shi'i leader and final deliverer on the other.

Another important disagreement caused confusion among the Shi'ites: They did not know whether the savior would actually appear during the tyranny of the Caliphs or would simply give signals during this period and make his final appearance sometime in the future. This ambiguity

---

[50] Kulayni, *al-Kafi*, vol. I (Tehran, 1381/1961), pp. 203–204, 545–556, quoted by Jasim Housain, *op. cit.*, p. 64.
[51] Khatib Baghdadi, *Tarikh Baghdad* (Bayreut, 1931), vol. 13, p. 31; Tabari III, p. 533; Ibn Tulun, *al-Shadharat al Dhahabia* (Bayreut, 1958), p. 96, quoted by J. Housain, *op. cit.*, p. 66.
[52] Housain, *op. cit.*, p. 69.
[53] Kulayni, *al-Kafi*, vol. II, p. 223, quoted by J. Housain, *op. cit.*, p. 47.

could not have been resolved by any of the Shi'i sects who had adopted the messianic belief in Mahdi, but there was a strong hope that the Imam would return to overthrow the tyrannical Caliphate that was still in power and establish justice.[54]

The Ithna Ashari line of Shi'ites continued to believe in the leadership of the living Imams in the hope that these leaders would change their situation in the present world. As time went on, however, the remaining Imams—Musa al-Kazim, Reza, Naqi, Taqi, and Hasan al-Askari—did not attempt to overthrow the power of the Caliphate. Reza, the eighth Imam, did manage to penetrate into the Caliphate circle under the Caliph al-Ma'mun, but he did not live long enough to inherit power. When the eleventh Imam (Hasan al-Askari) died, the situation became critical. From this time on, Hasan al-Askari's Shi'ites were deprived of a tangible Imam, and the notion of the Mahdi was adopted to further the goals of the sect.

Causes

Having examined the evolution of the doctrine of Mahdi, we now need to consider the circumstances that led the moderate Shi'ites to adopt a notion they had previously rejected. The Imami Shi'ites in the Ithna Ashari line witnessed an increasing number of small groups breaking away for various reasons while adopting the dogma of the savior who would return to bring justice to the world. This situation was unsettling enough, but the lack of a fixed guideline for the succession of the Imamate created even more confusion. In 260/873, the last visible Imam, Hasan al-Askari, died without having appointed a successor. As we have seen, it had been the tradition that the father would appoint his son as the succeeding Imam, but there was no apparent son. Before long the subsequent confusion divided the sect. Shahrastani indicates that, after the death of Hasan al-Askari, his Shi'ites were divided into eleven subsects. Each of these subsects either adopted some form of messianic belief or considered Hasan's brother Ja'far and his descendants the rightful suc-

---

[54] Jafar B. Mohammad b. Sharih Hazrami, *Kitab Jafar b. Sharih* (Tehran Univ. Library, no. 262/1262, p. 239), quoted by Housain, *op. cit.*, p. 51.

cessors.[55] Nawbakhti gives an account of fourteen subsects;[56] Mas'udi even reports the number to have reached twenty.[57]

The main reason such confusion prevailed within this last Shi'i group was that staunch believers could not accept that Hasan al-Askari had left no son. Sachedina's assessment:

> Hasan al-Askari died in 260/873–74 in Samarra, apparently having left no son whom people had seen to take his place. Consequently, the most immediate and sensitive problem facing the Shi'ites at this time was to determine the successor of al-Askari.[58]

Shahrastani also says that Hasan al-Askari left behind no son when he died,[59] but rumors to the contrary abounded. When Hasan al-Askari died, the Caliph Mu'tamid ordered that his house be sealed and searched. He checked to see whether the female servants of Hasan al-Askari were pregnant, and if they were, he placed them under surveillance.[60] When it became clear that there was no physical evidence of a son the Shi'ites despaired, while the Caliphate breathed a sigh of relief. Despite the assertions by some that this alleged son had been born, the general consensus among the Shi'ites, even the companions of Hasan al-Askari, was that no son had been left behind to succeed him.[61]

Nevertheless, a small number of zealous Shi'ites maintained that this son had been born but could not be seen in public, though still no proof was presented. A number of undecided Shi'ites, joined to one subsect or another, waited patiently to see whether this mysterious son would appear before making up their minds.

The ambiguous nature of the birth is underscored by the discrepancy in historians' reports of the exact date of the event. Saduq (Ibn Babuya) gives the eighth of Shaban 256 A.H. as the date of birth; Ibn Khallikan gives the fifteenth of Shaban, 255 A.H.; Nawbakhti gives the month of Ramadan, 254 A.H.; and Kamal al-Din in his Kashf al-Ghuma reports

---

[55] Shahrastani, I, pp. 227–229.
[56] Nawbakhti, p. 160.
[57] Mas'udi, II, p. 599.
[58] Sachedina, op. cit., p. 39.
[59] Shahrastani, I, p. 226.
[60] Nawbakhti, p. 160.
[61] Housain, op. cit., p. 116, quoting Nawbakhti.

the twenty-third of Ramadan, 258 A.H.[62] The discrepancy in determining the exact date or even the place of birth of the son was inevitable because of the lack of concrete information, direct contact with the family of the baby, or any eyewitnesses.

The adoption of the notion of *ghayba* (concealment or occultation) avoided the dispersal of the Shi'ites' small community and thus, in the end, saved the doctrine of the Imamate, even though any uncautious assertion about *ghayba* or the concealment of the alleged son could have jeopardized the future of the community and faith altogether. But the works of the intelligent men of the post-*ghayba* period guaranteed the success of the doctrine.

At any rate, the reports of post-*ghayba* Shi'i scholars, based on scattered anecdotes, indicate that the child went into concealment at an age variously reported to be four, five, or eleven years, depending on the source.[63] Henry Corbin reports a tradition that, when the child was descending a ladder of several steps toward the basement of his father's residence, he suddenly disappeared although there was no explanation of how and why such a thing happened.[64] It could not, of course, have been explained in purely human terms; rather, it was ascribed to divine will. The staunch Shi'ites meanwhile asserted that this young boy, the concealed Imam, was alive but lived in concealment. However, his absence from public view would not deprive his followers from his benediction and guidance. He still, through his representatives (*wukala*, *sufara*) would carry out his duty. For the Shi'ites, it seems that having faith in such an unusual divine concept was more spiritually satisfying than receiving detailed and logical explanations.

It is not clear exactly when during this confusing period the idea of Mahdi was tied to the concept of *ghayba*, a synthesis that held out the hope that the concealed child could be the promised Mahdi for whom all the sects had been so anxiously waiting. At some point this connection was made, however, and this son (whose name was not clearly given but was revealed as Muhammad)[65] was asserted to be the promised Mahdi. Although no man had ever laid eyes on him in public, the belief was becoming stronger that, if he was the Mahdi, the Shi'ites would soon

---

[62] All instances are quoted from Majlisi, *Bihar*, XIII, pp. 207–221.
[63] *Ibid.*, pp. 207–227.
[64] Corbin, *op. cit.*, IV, p. 322–323.
[65] Kohlberg, *From Imamiyya . . .*, p. 522.

demolish the Abbasid usurpers. With this concept the Shi'ites tried to disarm the Abbasids psychologically, asserting that the Mahdi would guarantee a quick Shi'i victory. It is interesting that this happened at about the same time an Isma'ili Imam emerged in public. It also must be noted that the first Isma'ili Caliph was called al-Mahdi and the second al-Qa'im.[66]

It is reasonable to assume that, since the twelfth Imam never appeared in public and left no descendant behind, the notion of *ghayba* was probably formed in the two or three decades following his reported disappearance. The Shi'ites were becoming convinced that there would probably be no other visible Imam after the twelfth, since there was no marriage and no son. To this effect, Henri Lammens, in his dry and shrewd way, indicates that the notion of *ghayba* grew out of the Shi'ites having been deprived of a visible leader.[67]

Six or seven decades after the young Mahdi allegedly disappeared, a Shi'i traditionist, Kulayni, completed a work based on the theory of *ghayba* and utilizing the *hadiths* that provided support for the theory. In other words, Kulayni completed his *Usul al-Kafi* and reports on *ghayba* when Mahdi was still thought to be in "minor occultation" (260/873–329/940), before he went into the so-called major occultation (329/940–??). This indicates that there was an understanding during these six or seven decades that Imam Mahdi had not explicitly declared his political intentions and had not named a successor. It was not completely clear that there would be no more Imams after him. The time of his reappearance was also vague. Therefore, the work of Kulayni and the Shi'i scholars immediately after him concentrated on establishing that the concealed Imam was indeed the promised Mahdi rather than on the details of his reappearance and his political intentions. Such details were significantly elaborated by scholars of a much later period. The authoritative work of Kulayni thus established *ghayba* as a divine and preconceived concept within Shi'i doctrine and provided a doctrinal basis for the subsequent Shi'i scholars to develop the *ghayba* doctrine: "The crystallization of the doctrine of *ghayba* (occultation) occurred in about 300/912. Prior to that date Shi'i books make no reference to this doctrine."[68]

When Momen indicates that, prior to about 300/912, no reference

[66] Lewis, *Origins of Ismailism*, p. 52.
[67] Lammens, *op. cit.*, p. 192.
[68] Momen, *op. cit.*, p. 75.

had been made to the notion of *ghayba*, he means the *ghayba* of the twelfth Imam specifically—not the concept of occultation of the Imams in general, as developed in other sects. The concept of Mahdi had been promulgated by other Shi'i sects prior to the occultation of the twelfth Imam. It should also be noted that the early Shi'i works around this date make no assertions that the total number of Imams was twelve (or any other number) or even any references to the idea of occultation.[69] It is clear that the beginnings of these doctrines, both as to the total number of Imams and as to the occultation of the twelfth Imam, were so shrouded in ambiguity that no one can be thought to have known the true nature of the doctrines at their source. It was only in later stages that the number twelve was appropriately connected to ideas asserted to be from a divine source, such as the twelve months of the year in the Koran (9:36), or even that Isma'il, the Hebrew prophet, was parallel to Muhammad, the Prophet of Islam, and that his twelve sons prefigured the twelve Imams, descendants of Muhammad.[70] Nevertheless, Corbin suggests that we should not require this kind of precision from the Shi'i books on this point.[71]

The ground on which the notion of *ghayba* grew, apart from the lack of the Imam's physical presence, was the assertion by Shi'i scholars that, because of the Abbasid's continued pressure on the household of the Prophet, God deemed it necessary for the Imam to live in concealment. In many Shi'i traditions it is suggested that Hasan al-Askari did not report the birth or succession of his son because of the Abbasid intrusion and the consequent violence against the Imams. Thus Hasan al-Askari's concealment of his son was a means to protect his heir and successor, about whom many eschatological theories eventually developed. The idea of the concealment was perfectly logical, given the tumultuous circumstances under which the Shi'ites had to survive. Most of the movements of the Shi'ites had been crushed throughout the empire, and the Imams were believed to be under surveillance by the Abbasid Caliphs. And as time went by, the eschatological fervor of the Shi'ites only intensified.

Another plausible explanation for the idea of concealment of the Imam

---

[69] Kohlberg, *op. cit.*, p. 522.
[70] *Ibid.*, p. 527.
[71] Corbin, *op. cit.*, IV, p. 322.

concerns Ja'far, the brother of Hasan al-Askari, who had been proclaimed the new Imam when Hasan al-Askari was thought to have left no son to succeed him.[72] Ja'far's Imamate was denied by certain Shi'ites, who eventually adopted the notion of *ghayba*. But still, without clear evidence of a son, Ja'far was the closest kin who could succeed to the position of the Imamate. After all, turning to the brother as successor to the Imam, while by no means common, did have precedent: Hasan and Husayn, the sons of Ali, had been recognized as the second and third Imams. Furthermore, Ja'far was also thought to carry the "holy" blood of the Banu Hashim clan in his veins; he was the son of the tenth Imam, al-Naqi; and he was the descendant of Fatima, the daughter of the Prophet. Theoretically, then, it was natural to turn to Ja'far. But the Shi'i theologian Majlisi (d. 1111/1699) slanders Ja'far, calling him a gambler, a drinker, and an evildoer.[73] Such anger on behalf of the Shi'i scholars who developed and believed in *ghayba* is understandable, for once the theory of *ghayba* was completely developed, no other claim to the Imamate could be accepted.

Nawbakhti indicates that Ja'far and his mother stepped forward to take charge of his brother's belongings before the Caliph could get control of them.[74] The staunch Shi'ites disapproved of this move because it implied that Ja'far was also convinced that Hasan al-Askari had no other inheritor—that is, no son. The Shi'ites rejected Ja'far's Imamate and condemned his indifference toward the *ghayba* of his nephew. But the many people desperately searching for an Imam during this confusing time never accused Ja'far of being indifferent.

In later accounts of the early Shi'ites, it is asserted that the *ghayba* of the twelfth Imam was divinely conceived and known through *hadiths* passed down from one Imam to the next. It remains a puzzle how these *hadiths* became known to future Shi'i scholars and not to Ja'far, the concealed Imam's own uncle. The traditions indicate that the concealed Imam was seen by and remained in touch with certain individuals called *wukala* (representatives) during the next seven decades after his alleged disappearance. According to the traditions, no *wakil* (singular of *wukala*)

---

[72] Majlisi, *Bihar*, XIII, p. 394; Shahrastani, I, pp. 226–227; Allamah Tabatabai, *op. cit.*, p. 76.

[73] Majlisi, *Jala ul Uyun*, p. 578.

[74] Nawbakhti, p. 160.

could claim a genealogy that reached back to the Banu Hashim clan, the family of the Imam; whereas Ja'far, a highly regarded man of the prophet's own household, never saw his nephew or reported any *hadiths* of any kind concerning him or his concealment. Moreover, those Shi'ites who believed in the Imamate of Ja'far are testimony to a moment in history when no other tangible claim to the Imamate was being made. It certainly seems unfair that the supporters of the *ghayba* doctrine, who never saw any physical evidence to prove the existence of the concealed Imam, became so ardently critical of their fellow Shi'ites who supported Ja'far—a man whose Imamate was real, who actually lived, and who stood in the face of the Abbasids' oppression.

The Hadiths

It is difficult to judge the validity of the *hadiths* concerning the concealed Imam and their relevance to history. It is explained in certain traditions that the Imams came under such tremendous pressure from the Caliphate that a policy of *taqiya* (dissimulation) was generally adopted. One of the explanations that helped develop the notion of *ghayba* was that Hasan al-Askari wanted to protect his son from the plot and conspiracy of the Caliphs. This decision led to the development of the messianic notion that the alleged son was the promised Mahdi and the savior of the Shi'i community. Regardless of whether this son existed, the motive of preserving his safety caused a certain obscurity about the reported *hadiths* with regard to the preconceived notion of the *ghayba* in contrast to the actual historical circumstances (that is to say, the Abbasid pressure inflicted upon the Imams as a whole and the eleventh Imam in particular). In other words, if the idea of *ghayba* was preconceived by God, as the Prophet and the Imams were informed through the *hadiths*, it leads us to believe in an abstract vision of the world as a place that moves in a linear progression not based on cause and effect. Furthermore, it is an indication of the role of prediction in the formative period of Shi'ism as a distinct and divinely privileged sect, as well as an indication of the developing conception of the predestined fate of the Shi'ites in the face of the atrocious Caliphate, which caused the concealment of the twelfth Imam and eventually necessitated a Mahdi to save the sect.

The *hadiths* on *ghayba* and Mahdi were promulgated after the twelfth

Imam was supposed to have gone into occultation. There had been, however, certain reports on the notion of Mahdi by earlier traditionists of other messianic Shi'i sects. The eminent traditionists or *muhaddithun* of the Ithna Ashari Shi'i sect were Kulayni (d. 329/940), Ibn Babuya (d. 381/991), Sheikh Mufid (d. 413/1022), and Sheikh Tusi (d. 460/ 1067). These transmitters of the *hadiths* based their works on oral reports of certain notable people in the holy circle as well as on written works of earlier traditionists in other sects.[75] Kulayni's *Usul al-Kafi* was predominantly based on oral reports gathered while traveling in various regions of the Islamic world. However, sometimes the reports from other sects written prior to the concealment of the twelfth Imam were used, with the explanation that their true Mahdi was the twelfth Imam and not the Mahdi they had hastily designated. An example of such an argument occurs when Kulayni takes issue with Hasan b. Muhammad b. Sama' Taii Tatari, who asserted that the Mahdi was the seventh Imam, Musa al-Kazim.

The tradition of Sama' had already developed the notion of the Mahdi to some extent prior to the doctrine of the concealment. This was used by Kulayni to support his argument, by arguing that Sama' had mistakenly declared that the promised Mahdi was the seventh Imam, whereas the true Mahdi was the twelfth Imam instead.[76] In other words, the theory of the Mahdi finally adopted by the Ithna Ashari traditionists was based in part on previous traditions that they adapted to their own cause by changing the name of the expected Mahdi.

As the written works of the Shi'i traditionists increased, the Sunni scholars, in their attempts to clarify the point of view of the Ithna Ashari Shi'ites, began to use compiled works. Works such as Baghdadi's *al-Farq Bayn al-Firaq*, Ibn Hazam's *al-Fasl fi Milal wal-Hawa al-Nihal*, and Shahrastani's *al-Milal wal-Nihal* are Sunni attempts to portray the Shi'ites' doctrine. Subsequent Shi'i accounts of *ghayba* are sometimes based on these Sunni works, extracting only those parts favorable to the Shi'i cause.[77]

The study of the reported *hadiths* on the Mahdi by Ibn Khaldun ad-

---

[75] Obviously, late Shi'i sources, such as Majlisi's *Bihar al-Anwar* of the seventeenth century, are for the most part based on written traditions of early Shi'i works.
[76] Housain, *op. cit.*, p. 22.
[77] For partial explanation, see *ibid.*, p. 28.

dresses two other serious problems. First, he asserts that the chain of transmission of these *hadiths* is controversial.[78] Second, he indicates that *hadiths* concerning the Mahdi do not conform with the works of *Sahih* by al-Bukhari and al-Muslim, which have been widely accepted as authentic and authoritative by the Muslim community.[79]

Later in this chapter we will examine the implications of some of the *hadiths* concerning the place of residence and the intentions of the Mahdi upon his return. However, the following *hadith* provides an example of the vagueness of some of the sources. According to Tusi, Imam Ja'far al-Sadiq had asserted:

> I [Ja'far al-Sadiq] was assigned to carry out this duty [*ghayba*], but God decided to postpone this matter and to leave it to my descendants.[80]

Here Tusi ascribes to God what may well have been Ja'far al-Sadiq's own indecisiveness.

In light of all of this, it is possible that many of these *hadiths* were constructed in the post-*ghayba* period. The Umayyads, after all, had fabricated *hadiths* after the death of the Prophet, and this had become a pattern during subsequent controversies. The Shi'ites were not far behind in spreading their own versions of *hadiths*, which ultimately led to contradictory and sometimes unimaginable versions of the truth, each evidently serving only the interest of the party supplying it. With regard to the subject of the Mahdi—his birth, concealment, Imamate, and return—there was no trace of tangible evidence to rely upon. Future Shi'ites trying to assess the situation had to depend on those versions transmitted by the *muhaddithun*, and they were often contradictory. In this regard, Moojan Momen says: "Even for the committed believer, it is difficult to decide which of the many and often contradictory versions presented in the traditions to follow."[81]

---

[78] Ibn Khaldun, II, p. 633.
[79] *Ibid.*, p. 634.
[80] Housain, *op. cit.*, p. 48, quoting Tusi, *Ghayba*.
[81] Momen, *op. cit.*, p. 161.

The Two Phases of *Ghayba*

The important early Shi'i sects that adopted the notion of the Mahdi only theorized about the occultation and return of their Imams. But the Ithna Ashari Shi'ites, due to their special circumstances, approached the notion of *ghayba* somewhat differently than their predecessors. When the alleged son, the twelfth Imam, was reported to have been born, no one had seen him. In order to prevent any doubts in later years, it was reported that the young Imam had gone into concealment to protect his life. In later years other divine aspects were connected with his concealment. However, the word *death* was never used in connection with the twelfth Imam in an effort to keep the Shi'ites together and to maintain the impression of having a single Imam at all times. Nawbakhti, in fact, believed that the twelfth Imam died in concealment while his children uninterruptedly continued to lead the community of believers until God should direct the reappearance of the Mahdi.[82] Of course, this never became the common belief among the more zealous Shi'ites.

As the doctrine of *ghayba* was introduced, new circumstances evolved around it. Now the Imam was reported to be living and transmitting his messages to the Shi'ites through his representatives (*wukala*). In popular versions, it is reported that the concealed Imam, from the time of his alleged disappearance (260/873), selected one or another person as a *wakil* (representative, mediator) to the Shi'i community. The many reports show that, during the period of sixty-nine lunar years known as the "minor occultation," the Imam selected only four representatives to give instructions and to answer questions. After this period, the Imam was apparently silent, and it was reported that he had entered into a second phase of *ghayba*, which in a much later period was known as the "major occultation." The four representatives of the minor occultation were introduced only by later Shi'i accounts, notably Uthman b. Said Amari (d. 260/874), Muhammad b. Uthman Amari (d. 304/916), Husayn b. Ruh al-Nawbakhti (d. 326/937), and Ali b. Muhammad al-Samarri (d. 329/940).

In the early Shi'i traditions there is no specific mention of the exact

---

[82] Nawbakhti, p. 161.

number of representatives. Rather, the works of Kulayni, Ibn Babuya, Tusi, and Numani refer to an active network of representatives throughout the land.[83] It seems, then, that it was later Shi'i scholars who determined the number of representatives and gave the doctrine and the period of the minor occultation a more definite form. By this means, the theories about the deputyship of the Imam were placed in a more practical framework:

From the several reports in these early sources two points become evident: First, the deputyship of the Imam was not confined to the Four Agents in this period. The stress laid on the four seems to be because of the influence they exerted on the Imamate of this period. Second, in all probability, the institution of the deputyship (niyaba) was a later explanation to solve the meaning of al-ghaybat al-qasira, as interpreted by al-Nu'mani.[84]

It appears that, during the sixty-nine years of the minor occultation, these four representatives were the main khums collectors of the Imam. Nevertheless, after the death of al-Samarri no eminent personage was able to take over this position,[85] and this temporarily put an end to the issue of deputyship. Still, many others later asserted that they were in contact with the Imam during his occultation—among them, as Majlisi reports, Abu Muhammad Hasan Sharii, Ahmad b. Hilal Karkhi, Muhammad b. Ali b. Bilal, Husayn b. Mansur Hallaj, Muhammad b. Ali Shalmaghani, and Abu Bakr Baghdadi.[86]

Mas'udi's report, after the death of Hasan al-Askari, that the number of subsects had reached twenty reflected the early confusion among the Shi'ites. Without a clear leader, many pretenders proclaimed themselves either the Imam himself or his deputy, resulting in a situation that temporarily led the Shi'i sect astray. Before the concept of ghayba was cemented into a theological framework, the astonished Shi'ites may well have thought of the ghayba of the twelfth Imam as merely another ruse, like many of the other messianic claims.

At any rate, once the Shi'ites established the concept of concealment

---

[83] Sachedina, op. cit., p. 86.
[84] Ibid., p. 87.
[85] Ibid., p. 99.
[86] Majlisi, Bihar, XIII, pp. 697–718.

of the Imam while at the same time asserting that he was in contact with his representatives, they still needed to convince the community. Thus we come to the second phase of *ghayba*, the major occultation. It was asserted that the Imam was not dead but had decided to remain in concealment until God ordered him to reveal himself and bring justice to the world. According to this notion, the Imam Mahdi would live until the last episode of human history.

But there was one serious disagreement concerning the second phase of *ghayba*: how long it should last. The early Shi'ites believed that the Mahdi would reappear in the near future in order to crush the whole Abbasid state. (How the reappearance of the Mahdi was going to effect revenge upon the already faded Umayyads of Damascus was another question.) Some thought the second phase might even be shorter than the first. Some remained undecided. About thirteen years after the end of the first phase of occultation (342/953), Nu'mani was undecided about which of the two phases would be longer. He in fact quoted Ja'far al-Sadiq that the first phase of occultation would be longer than the second.[87]

The available *hadiths* did little to help the early Shi'ites elucidate the sequence and the precise periods of the two phases of *ghayba*. But the doctrine of *ghayba* in its two parts was by now established. As time went by, the Shi'ites became more and more curious about the notion of the reappearance, or the end of the second phase.

Because of the uncertainty, it was suggested by the early Shi'i scholars that the *khums* that belonged to Imam Mahdi be kept aside until his return, which they considered imminent. Some Shi'i theologians remarked that the *khums* were secretly given away by the believers at their death. Sheikh Mufid suggested that part of the *khums* might be used as a donation to the poor and the rest could be burned at the time of death or kept in a safe place, or even deposited with some third person, so that when the Imam should make his appearance, one might submit to him the accumulated *khums*. This practice was popular among the theologians until about the thirteenth century A.D., when Muhaqiq Hilli solved the problem (since the period of *ghayba* was becoming lengthy and the sums accumulated unwieldy) by volunteering to receive the *khums* himself in order to spend it in the conduct of religious affairs.[88]

---

[87] Kohlberg, *op. cit.*, p. 528.
[88] Housain, *op. cit.*, p. 228.

During the early crucial days of the second phase of occultation, many followers noted that sixty-nine years, the period of the minor occultation, seemed to be the average life of a man, even an Imam, who might have died, and so the *ghayba* was conceived.[89] This belief could have jeopardized the credibility of the Imamate in the future. On the other hand, the conservative position of those Imams who had practiced dissimulation (*taqiya*) in the face of the Caliphate had already disappointed more revolutionary Shi'ites. Furthermore, the defeat of Ali and Husayn, the *taqiya* of the remaining Imams, and the concealment of the last Imam altogether created a political malaise and had deadened the people's enthusiasm to fight for a just society. The dismay at no longer having an Imam had an enormous impact both on the minds of the Shi'ites and on the development of their theology. To overcome the notion of the death of the Imam on the one hand and to reduce the pressure of the Abbasids on the other, introduction of the second occultation, which carried many messianic overtones, was indispensable. It may even be relevant that shortly afterward the Buyids came to power in Persia and patronized Shi'ism. In any case, the Shi'ites were not to be deprived of an Imam and the just society that only he could achieve. Sachedina notes: "The growth of such a hope among the group which had been wronged and oppressed was the inevitable outcome of the consistent stress in Islam on the realization of the just society under the guidance of divine revelation."[90]

Therefore, the doctrine of occultation in two phases was introduced and inevitably the doctrine of return accompanied it.

Return and the Ideal Rule

The messianic doctrine of *ghayba* came to include a belief in the physical absence of the Imam from this world and his return to establish an ideal rule (which the Shi'ites had never experienced under the visible Imams). The exasperation of the Shi'ites in their fight against the Abbasids, as well as bitter memories of the Umayyads, paved the way for the devel-

---

[89] *Ibid.*, p. 221.
[90] Sachedina, *op. cit.*, p. 3.

opment of such a messianic belief. During his minor occultation not only did the Mahdi not carry out a military expedition, he also left his Shi'ites to their own devices in their worldly challenge until such time as he and God should deem it necessary to end worldly affairs. Then he would return, on God's order, to retaliate against the enemies of the Shi'ites and thus bring the world to an end.

The concept of a final return in other religions—even in Sunni Islam—generally employs a subtler way of treating the enemies of righteousness. In Imami Shi'ism, the return of the Mahdi signifies only vengeance and bloodshed against the enemies of the Shi'ites as well as against nonbelievers. Physical force is apparently the only instrument of justice that could satisfy the Shi'ites—precisely because it is so very worldly. The Mahdi's transcendental dimension is limited to enabling him to achieve military victory. Thus it is essentially through military might that an ideal rule could be established at the end of the world.

This hope developed because no significant military victory was ever achieved by the Shi'i Imams in the Ithna Ashari line as the Isma'ilis established their Caliphate in Egypt. Ali, Husayn, and other Alids were plagued by failures and eventually massacred by the ruling Caliphs (except for the Isma'ilis and Zaydis). The last Imam became the last hope to carry out what other Imams could not accomplish. However, during his minor occultation, while the Imam was said to be intervening in worldly affairs through his representatives, no military instructions were given. Furthermore, his alleged divine attributes never managed to further the cause of the Imami Shi'ites. In fact, the Imam himself was reported to have gone into concealment out of fear of the Abbasid conspirators. According to one tradition, the Imam was constantly changing location in order to avoid harassment. At one point, the Caliph's soldiers forcibly entered the Imam's reported residence in Samarra, but the Imam managed to escape to the capital (Baghdad).[91] He apparently was in no position to help his people militarily.

While the Shi'ites saw a need to maintain a belief in the return of the Mahdi, their political situation actually improved after his disappearance, and a certain cohesion emerged within their community. However, this new messianism changed the Shi'i consciousness, which now

---

[91] Housain, *op. cit.*, p. 180, citing Rawandi, *al Kahraij wal-Jaraih* (Bombay, 1301), p. 67.

embodied an element of hope and a dream that the conservative method of *taqiya* practiced by the Imams never had, even though the concept and the process of *ghayba* paralleled that of *taqiya* in its passivity and sense of stagnation. But while there may have been little hope in *taqiya*, *ghayba* held out a potent promise. Certain Shi'i traditions indicate that the reason the Imams practiced *taqiya* was that they had advance knowledge of a coming Mahdi and therefore chose to delay the final revolution until his coming.[92] The question that remained was when this revolution would take place. To this question there was no answer. For the present, the promise of a revolution was vain, for the Shi'ites still lived under the Abbasids. (Although, indeed, the Abbasids under the Buyid dynasty of Persia were just as powerless.)

Still, the Shi'i theology was taking shape and preparing the grounds for the time of revolution. Certainly, since the beginning of the major occultation (329/940), the Mahdi had not shown any sign of reappearing and had made no specific assertion as to when he would return. This wide gap in time [from 329/940–??] left the field open for the development of a sophisticated theology with the appropriate ritualistic and legal trappings. In light of this development, the role of *faqih* (legal scholar) was expanded to include prescribing the essentials of faith and law until the return of the Mahdi.

In terms of spiritual and psychological development, it was during this chronological gap that there appeared in the Shi'i literature the eschatological anecdotes that attempted to bolster the argument for the return of the Mahdi and to reduce the amount of skepticism. This eschatological literature made important contributions to maintaining religious unity among the Ithna Ashari Shi'ites and reinforced the role of the *faqih* as the sole representative of the Imam in this world (*naib al-Imam*). Thus was accomplished a successful and impressive transition from the institutional Imamate to an indefinite and tumultuous period with no visible Imam. But the lack of a visible Imam did not alter the Shi'ites' view about the Imamate. Indeed, the absence of the twelfth Imam had not kept the Shi'ites from having any Imam at all: the Imamate was maintained through the *faqih*.[93]

---

[92] Housain, *op. cit.*, p. 182.
[93] As the theology developed in later stages, the role of *faqih* became more explicit in taking responsibilities in interpreting the Koranic laws and in acting as the esoteric leaders of the Shi'i community.

This continuity in the Imamate beyond the death of the last visible Imam also contributed to the belief that God had not deserted His creation. According to Corbin, this belief has been described as one in which the earth can never be deprived of an Imam, because humanity itself would cease to exist and would lose contact with Heaven.[94]

During the major occultation, the Imam is believed to live on and watch over his community until he receives orders from the Deity to make his glorious reappearance. Majlisi, in Volume XIII of his *Bihar al-Anwar*, has tried to fit as many traditions as possible into his apocalyptic chapter on the sequence of the Mahdi's return. The events following the reappearance of the Mahdi may sound hyperbolic, but its propagation in the Shi'i literature as well as through oral folk culture has had an immeasurable impact on the psychoreligious belief of the Shi'ites.

Majlisi: The Return[95]

Muhammad Majlisi's account of the return of the Imam Mahdi consists of several traditions that contain discrepancies in reporting the names, places, and circumstances of the Imam's reappearance. In Majlisi's compilation, the return begins in this way:

> [This event] will take place at sunrise, when the sun comes out. An announcer from the corner of the sun would speak with eloquent Arabic which all the heavens and earth would hear. Then he would say: "O people of the world [*alam*]! This is Mahdi, of the household of Muhammad." Then Mahdi would be called upon by the names of his forefathers from the prophet to Husayn to his own father [Hasan al-Askari].[96]

The Mahdi will arise from Mecca. He will be accompanied by 313 men, the number of men who participated in the battle of Badr with the Prophet. The Mahdi will also have the angels Gabriel and Michael on either side. He will carry the old flag, armor, and sword of the Prophet (*zulfiqar*) while leading men to the battlefield. His intentions will be to create a government in which all other religions fade away, their disciples

---

[94] Corbin, *op. cit.*, I, p. 59.
[95] Majlisi, *Bihar*, XIII, pp. 1066–1239.
[96] *Ibid.*, p. 1154.

convert to Islam, and nonbelievers become believers. The people of the East and the West will obey him, and a great number of the dead who had been nonbelievers and oppressors will return to life in order for the believers to avenge themselves upon them. Finally, in his government, the Mahdi will carry out the unfinished work of Ali, Husayn, and other Imams. Mufadhal's tradition indicates that the Mahdi will choose Kufa as his capital (probably because Ali also chose Kufa as his capital). Other cities in the area are to come under his jurisdiction, and the people of those cities will give him their oath of allegiance—all except the people of Basra (probably because they gave rise to Kharijism as they turned their backs on the descendants of Ali).

According to Ayyashi, who quotes Imam Muhammad al-Baqir, after having established his ideal rule the Mahdi will live ninety years. After his death, chaos will reign for fifty years. Sheikh Mufid, in his *Irshad*, asserts that the Mahdi will die forty days prior to the Day of Judgment, and during this forty-day period the dead will be rendered up to justice. However, both Ibn Babuya in his *Kamal al-Din* and Tusi in his book of *Ghayba* quote Ja'far al-Sadiq asserting that, after the Mahdi (the twelfth Imam), there will be eleven or twelve more hidden Imams or Mahdis.[97]

A Critique of Return

Based on various and sometimes conflicting traditions, several observations can be made here. First, it seems that the return of the Mahdi would be a reincarnation of Arab rule by the Quraysh tribe, particularly the clan of Banu Hashim, since this was the privileged clan from which the Shi'ites believed the Prophet and his successors were chosen by God. But the Prophet's successors, the twelve Imams, failed to carry out their divine mission. Consequently the Mahdi, the last supposed Imam who was the direct descendant of Muhammad's daughter Fatima, was to undertake this duty. Upon his return he would restore the tarnished prestige of the Quraysh and the Banu Hashim family. This idea certainly fueled hopes of a final restoration of Islamic rule in the hands of the Banu Hashim. It also helped justify the delay in the return of the Mahdi and his fulfillment of a final triumph.[98]

---

[97] All instances are quoted in Majlisi, *Bihar*, XIII, pp. 1066–1239.
[98] Sachedina, *op. cit.*, pp. 151–152.

The unsuccessful efforts of the Imams to achieve a final victory or to establish the ideal rule led many of the traditional accounts to suggest that it would be a superhuman Mahdi who would save the Shi'i community. These accounts also report that the Shi'ites believed that the Imams could predict both events in the near future and the details of the Mahdi's victory at the end of the world.

Some of the traditions report that the reappearance of the Mahdi will be a prelude to resurrection rather than the resurrection itself. The question then remains: How will the dead of Badr, twelve thousand of Ali's Shi'ites,[99] and many others, be brought to life? Of course, in later periods, the return of the Mahdi was divided into two consecutive sequences: *zuhur*, the appearance; and *raj'a*, the return and the establishment of the ideal rule by means of a mass resurrection aimed at settling old scores. This concept enabled believers who were unable to confront nonbelievers in this world to look forward to exacting vengeance at the return of the Mahdi. In this regard, the *mu'tazilites* criticized the Shi'ites and sought a clearer explanation for this view of the Mahdi. According to Sachedina, the *mu'tazilites* asked how the Shi'ites could be sure that, when the Mahdi returned, people such as Yazid or Ibn Muljam (who had killed Ali, the first Imam) and Shimr (who had killed Husayn, the third Imam), would not repent of their sins and agree to obey the Imam Mahdi.

Despite many attempts to answer this question, only Sheikh Mufid managed to provide an answer that could begin to satisfy the *mu'tazilites*.[100] He offered a twofold answer. First, when God returns the nonbelievers to life in order to allow the believers to avenge themselves, He will not reconsider their guilt or acknowledge their repentance. Second—as revealed by certain Koranic verses (29:39, 38:78, 38:85)—the fate of people like Yazid and Ibn Muljam has been determined: They will burn in the fires of hell.[101]

In this context, the philosophical discourse on the issue of predestination and free will could continue and yet no concrete explanation could be provided upon which the Shi'i vindications could be based. Later theological work elaborated on the doctrine of free will without compromising the power of God to determine man's final destination. But

99 According to Mufadhal, cited in Majlisi, *Bihar*, XIII, p. 1153.
100 See Madelung, "Imamism and Mu'tazilite Theology," p. 23.
101 Sachedina, *op. cit.*, pp. 170–171.

Shi'i theological thought still has not clarified the many ambiguous notions about God's guidance of man and man's freedom to go astray.

Another uncertainty about the rule of the Mahdi relates to the specific names of the cities to be involved in the final events as reported in the *hadiths*. The cities of Baghdad, the capital of the Abbasids, and Samarra, the reputed birthplace of the Mahdi, were built *after* the Abbasids established themselves in Iraq in 132/750.[102] Therefore, reports concerning these cities quoted from the Imams prior to Ja'far al-Sadiq (whose life coincided with the establishment of Abbasid rule) cannot be accepted, since these cities did not yet exist. In addition, cities such as Mecca, Medina, and Kufa, regardless of their Islamic importance, may not survive the centuries to come should the Mahdi delay his return. Further, the discovery of the Americas, the emergence of Africa, and the further development of Europe and Asia have all rendered the geographic and political importance of ancient Rome, Persia, and the Islamic empires significantly more remote. The modern world extends itself around the globe. Many Islamic cities that were extremely important at the height of Islamic rule, while maintaining their symbolic importance in Islamic religious thought, now play a much less significant role in global political affairs.

And of course, from a technological standpoint, one can no longer conceive of the Mahdi leading an army in the classic Islamic fashion, with such accoutrements of war as dagger, sword, and horse. Still, the religious can argue that faith in the unknowable and unimaginable power of God will make anything possible. But this subjective argument should not undermine the workings of *aql*, the intellect, which by its very nature reflects and searches for a convincing explanation.

Other historical discrepancies raise similar questions. For example, certain reported traditions indicate that the hidden Imam was seen by

---

[102] See Majlisi, *Bihar*, XIII, Ch. 33. Majlisi detects Mufadhal's discrepancy with regard to the city of Samarra. The origin of the site and the name of Baghdad are not fairly clear (it is asserted that the name is of Persian origin). Nevertheless, Baghdad was built for military, economic, and climatic reasons under the Abbasids. Furthermore, Baghdad was given prominence by the Abbasid Caliphs over the turbulent pro-Alid Kufa. See Dori, "Baghdad," *Encyclopedia of Islam*, 1960, pp. 894–908. However, Mostaufi in his *Nodhat al-Quloub*, pp. 34 and 44, indicates that the site of both cities of Baghdad and Samarra were found under Sassani though under different names. They were destroyed during the Abbasid period and they were built again under their current names.

certain individuals in various countries. According to Tusi, one of the *wukala* reported that in order to see the Imam he had to go west. Another reported that the Imam was last seen in Syria; a third person even mentioned Egypt.[103] Majlisi presents various traditions that the Mahdi, during the minor occultation, was seen by dozens of people in Mecca, Medina, Egypt, and Iraq.[104] Sheikh Montakhib al-Din's *Kitab Fihrist* (twelfth century A.D.) reports that Mehdi b. Thar Billah Husayni Jili, the leader of the Zaydiya movement in the province of Gilan (Persia), who had been converted to Ithna Ashari Shi'ism, also saw the hidden Imam.[105]

It seems that the Imam Mahdi changed location from one country to another—presumably because of his fear of the Abbasids. But, strangely enough, he was recognized and identified in different countries by unknown people who could never have seen the Imam before, while his hometown Shi'ites never knew who he was and could never themselves be certain about his existence.

Moreover, it is reported that the Imam, during his major occultation, would nevertheless be present during the *hajj* ceremony every year. Ibn Babuya, who based this tradition on the *hadith* of Ja'far al-Sadiq, indicates that the Mahdi is among the people on the pilgrimage every year; but while he sees others, he remains invisible himself. Nu'mani and Tusi both confirm this version in their book on the *ghayba*.[106] However, Mutawakkil's *Kitab Kamal al-Din* reports that the Imam appears in every pilgrimage and that, while he is seen among people, he cannot himself be recognized.[107]

These assertions, which have mostly remained unscrutinized, had tremendous influence on the masses, helping to resolve their doubts. The roots of their faith may be found in the historical psychology of the Shi'ites. The doctrines try to affirm that the Imam lives, that he is everywhere, that he can make himself known to whom he wishes, and (most important) that he will return for the final victory over the oppressors.

---

[103] Cited in Housain, *op. cit.*, p. 181.
[104] Majlisi, *Bihar*, XIII, pp. 719–825.
[105] *Ibid.*, p. 825.
[106] *Ibid.*, p. 929.
[107] *Ibid.*, pp. 929–930.

It was on this faith in God and the supernatural power of the Mahdi that the people depended for many centuries, and it has had an enormous effect on the people. There are reports that, in the thirteenth and four-teenth centuries A.D. the people of Kashan and Sabzavar in Persia put a saddle on a white horse just outside the gates of the city every day at sunrise, in case the Mahdi should appear.[108] A similar ritual used to take place at al-Hilla in Iraq in the thirteenth century.[109] In the sixteenth century, after the eschatology of the return of Jesus had been merged with the idea of the return of the Mahdi, the Safavid dynasty of Persia, whose members considered themselves the representatives of the Mahdi on earth, always had two horses prepared, one foi the Mahdi and the other for Jesus as his vice-regent.[110]

For those who believed that the return of the Mahdi and the estab-lishment of his ideal rule were inevitable, no hard evidence or intellectual explanations were required. It was purely the flame of faith and a complex psychological need that had convinced them. Nevertheless, examples both in history and in contemporary society make it clear that the Mahdi has been thought to be the savior of last resort when times are hard, and his reappearance may be expected whenever people need most to believe in him. But the eschatological nature of the beliefs about the Mahdi (both the return itself and the restoration of an ideal rule) holds out a promise only to be fulfilled at the end of the world, and this without tangible benefit in the contemporary lives of those who are suffering. Though the argument dates back to an earlier time, eighteenth century theologians in Iran hoped to clarify this paradox; however, the conclu-sions of their debates remain obscure to this day.

Since the length of the major occultation could not be determined, the conflict between the believers and the skeptics increased. The the-ologians' political role, after the fall of the Safavids, came into conflict with a desire for change, giving rise to the two schools of thought among the theologians of eighteenth-century Iran: the Usuli and the Akhbari.[111] For the Usulis, social protest and participation in the sociopolitical pro-

---

[108] Petrushevsky, op. cit., p. 226, quoting Yaqut, Mu'jam al-Buldan, IV, p. 15.
[109] Mostaufi, Nodhat ul-Quloub, p. 42.
[110] Darmesteter, op. cit., p. 39.
[111] See Scarcia, "Intorno alle controversie tra Akhbari e Usuli presso gli Imamiti di Persia," Rivista degli Studi Orientali, XXXIII (1956): 211–250.

cess became a religious mandate. The Akhbaris prescribed a quietist policy and advocated bearing hardship peaceably until the return of the Mahdi. When the Usulis emerged victorious, the *mujtahid* (a designated theologian) began to gain power, and his intervention in social and political matters was legitimized.

Perhaps it was the central orthodoxy of the theologians, together with their unaccountable interpretations in countless books, that gave the notion of return a peculiar mythological aspect. In any case, the philosophy of the return and the teaching of Shi'i doctrine have not sufficiently answered certain questions. Why was the twelfth Imam even born? Why was he concealed for sixty-nine years? And why was it the will of God that he go into major occultation? Can there ever be a just and ideal rule by well-intentioned human beings in this world? Or can this only be achieved by the Mahdi upon his return?

To these questions and many others, only a speculative method of theology known as *kalam* (rhetorical speech formulation) can provide subjective answers. This method was used by theologians to reach speculative philosophical or theological conclusions in order to respond to questions on controversial dogmatic problems. The words of the theologians substituted for concrete documentation in the attempt to solve the dilemma of the Mahdi and his return.

After *Ghayba*

For the Imami Shi'ites, the popular belief in the occultation of the twelfth Imam has not required sophisticated dialectical explanations concerning its origins in Shi'i history. It is, in fact, remarkable that the primitive Arab tribal culture lent itself to this kind of apocalyptic vision—a kind of vision undeveloped in the Arab past. Although zealous Shi'ites profess that the Prophet and God refer implicitly in the verses of the Koran to a savior and Mahdi, this assertion was only put forward after the twelfth Imam went into major occultation.

The concept of occultation, however, never achieved a widespread general consensus among the Muslim community. Ibn Khaldun, a Sunni scholar, did not hesitate to criticize the Shi'i exaggerations—unlike Sunnis such as al-Ghazali (d. 505/1111), who for political reasons never touched the subject of Mahdi.[112] After all, nearly every Shi'i sect had adopted the same kind of messianic belief about their own Imams. In the Sufi circle, Ibn al-Arabi (d. 638/1240), in his *Futuhat al-Makkiya*, asserts that the expected Mahdi would be a descendant of al-Hasan as the seal of saints (Khatam al-awsiya).[113] From Ibn Khaldun's writings it is understood that the Sunnis, apparently parallel with Shi'i doctrine, vaguely expressed a hope that some member of the family of the Prophet would rise up and return again.[114]

To counteract the disagreements over the idea of the true Mahdi (particularly since this had become the main concern of the Ithna Ashari Shi'ites) new *hadiths* and new interpretations of them were constantly released until the Shi'i writers succeeded in establishing the Mahdi theology, though on rather shaky and speculative grounds. Only after the death of Hasan al-Askari, the eleventh Imam, and the realization that there was no longer a physical, living Imam was the messianic doctrine incorporated into the body of Islamic theology, essentially to prevent the threatened dissolution of the Shi'i sect.

The need to elaborate on the idea of *ghayba* and to develop a theology distinct from other branches of Islam led to a speculative theological construction known as *kalam*. It evolved because there was no more legislative prophecy, no new revelation to serve as law.[115] Consequently, first the Imams and then the theologians established themselves as the protectors and interpreters of the law. To ease their task, the theologians ultimately sought a speculative theological method that could adapt the existing laws to current needs while providing updated philosophical and religious explanations concerning the faith. This was the art of *kalam*, which was borrowed from the *mu'tazilites*; and those who practiced it were called *mutakallimun*. This theological transition following the advent of the major *ghayba* was divided into two periods. The first consisted of reporting the *hadiths* and the traditions by the early scholars, called *muhaddithun*. The second period was that of the theologians, in which they developed a speculative interpretive method, or *kalam*, to apply to both the *hadiths* and the Koran itself. These were the *mutakalimun*.[116]

---

[112] Madelung, "Al-Mahdi," *Encyclopedia of Islam*, p. 1235.
[113] *Ibid.*
[114] Ibn Khaldun, II, p. 632.
[115] Corbin, *op. cit.*, I, p. 249.
[116] For the roots of the technique of *kalam*, see Watt, *Formative Period*, pp. 182–186; for *mu'tazilites*, see *ibid.*, pp. 209–250.

Before the Shi'i theologians arrived at a definitive theology, earlier Shi'ites had prevaricated under the influence of two important groups: the *ghulat* and the *mu'tazilites*. The *ghulat* (exaggerators), whose many ideas were rejected at first by the Shi'ites, developed the doctrines of *tanasukh* (the transmigration of souls), *ghayba* (concealment), *raj'a* (return), *hulul* (the descent of the spirit of God into man), and *imamate* (the Imamate of divinely inspired leadership and guidance). The *mu'tazilites*, on the other hand, had a firmer belief in free will and human reason, and maintained that speech (*kalam*) can determine a person's decisions without the power of God being undermined. Both groups played an important role in the formation of Shi'i theology.[117] The post-*ghayba* period clearly opened the way for both groups to maneuver in an attempt to influence the views of their Shi'i contemporaries.

In much of Shi'i doctrine, contradictory *ghulat* and *mu'tazilite* influence can be detected. For example, the Imams were seen to be divinely inspired and to possess supernatural power, as *ghulat* thinkers conceived them, yet the *mu'tazilite* concepts of free will and human reason were taken as the basis of human decisions. The final solution was to except the Imams as being from the ordinary human realm. In practice, the *mu'tazilite* school of thought ultimately exerted more influence in the formation of Shi'i theology than did the *ghulat*, but *ghulat* influence can very clearly be seen in the formation of Shi'i eschatological thought.

A clash became inevitable between the traditionists, who rejected the speculative theology of the *mu'tazilites*, and the early theologians, who ultimately introduced the *mu'tazilite's* concept of *kalam*. Ibn Babuya, an early traditionist, was antagonistic to the *mu'tazilite's kalam* and to speculative theology in general.[118] He opposed those supporters of the *mu'tazilites* who tried to reconcile reason with revelation, most notably Sheikh Mufid (d. 413/1022), Sheikh al Murtada (436/1044), and Sheikh al-Taifa (460/1067).[119] The broad argument was over the conflict between God's predetermination of man's fate and the doctrine of free will. The *mu'tazilites* came to believe that "God changes His mind over certain matters that He had decreed" (the classic case being that of Isma'il, who was first designated al-Sadiq's successor, only later to be replaced by Musa

---

[117] Momen, *op. cit.*, pp. 78, 66. See also Madelung, *Imamism*, pp. 13–29, Wellhausen, *Religio-Political Factions*, p. 154.
[118] *Ibid.*, p. 78.
[119] Madelung, "Authority in Twelver Shiism in the Absence of the Imam," p. 167.

al-Kazim).[120] This idea, according to the traditionists, appeared to con-
tradict certain Koranic verses: "It is not for any soul to believe save by
the permission of Allah. He had set uncleanness upon those who have
no sense" (10:101).

There are many other verses in the Koran that testify to the immu-
tability of the will of Allah, yet man has continued to try to find a way
to assume control over his own life. To this day, the puzzle of free will
and predestination remains unsolved. The contemporary Shi'i scholar
Allamah Tabatabai has tried to take a middle road by quoting the sixth
Imam, Ja'far al-Sadiq: "It is neither determination nor free will but
something between the two."[121] Tabatabai goes on to quote the fifth and
sixth Imams again: "God loves his Creation so much that He will not
force it to commit sin and then punish it."[122]

The battle over these unresolved philosophical issues became part of
a theology conceived on speculation. The theologians used the *hadith*
and the Koran, together with the process of *ta'wil* (spiritual interpretation) and *tafsir* (technical interpretation) to systematize a theological
structure that would be convincing and at the same time legitimize their
own historical position in the world of Islam. The Koran and the *hadith*,
however, did not always provide answers to the technical social, philosophical, or political questions that presented themselves to each successive generation. Thus the theologians of one generation left enough
room for future theologians to use their own judgment in confronting
contemporary problems. This amorphous role of interpretation and leadership, although confusing at times, gave a special authority to an individual *faqih* (learned theologian), lifting him up above a different *faqih*
in another time or in another place. It must also be noted that the
increase in the authority of the theologians coincided with the ever-
increasing duration of the major occultation. Eventually an important
waiver was obtained: no longer did the leading theologians have to be
from the Banu Hashim family; they only need to acquire the knowledge
of *fiqh* (theology) and be just.[123] The theologians came to represent the
physical reality of Ali as well as the spiritual reality of the twelfth Imam.[124]

---

[120] Momen, *op. cit.*, p. 77; see also Hodgson, *op. cit.*, p. 12.
[121] Tabatabai, *op. cit.*, p. 135.
[122] *Ibid.*
[123] Housain, *op. cit.*, pp. 66, 78.
[124] Corbin, *op. cit.*, IV, p. 325.

The *velayat*, the designated leadership, had passed from the Prophet to the Imams, and finally, in the later days of the major occultation, to the learned theologians.

A Final Comment

Despite the Shi'i claims that the doctrine of *ghayba* had a divine source, it must be admitted that Arab, non-Arab, and Iraqi religious and philosophical ideas tremendously influenced the development of the messianic aspects of Shi'ism. The Iraqis' and the Persians' early involvement in the struggle against the Umayyads contributed many religious, philosophical, and dogmatic concepts to the group later known as Shi'ites.

Aside from being a battleground for the fight against the Syrians, Iraq was an ancient center for philosophical debate. Many sects adopted messianism in one form or another as a political and spiritual defense against the rule of the Umayyads and the Abbasids. In the early days, several people introduced the notion of the Mahdi; among these, Mukhtar's assertion and use of the Mahdi on behalf of Muhammad b. al-Hanafiya were especially significant. If we assume that the messianic approach to the concept of the Mahdi, as Massignon describes, was through the internal spiritual development of Muslims and through Koranic interpretation, then Mukhtar (acting more as a political than as a religious leader) must have reached that understanding in its spiritual sense and seen the time as being appropriate to regard Ibn al-Hanafiya as the Mahdi or the messiah. Thus the assertion that the notion was divinely conceived is contradicted. Some historians observe that this event could have been influenced by non-Islamic messianic ideas that were introduced by *mawali*, while others prefer to say it was an extension of the Saoshyant of Zoroastrianism. Yet others consider that the influence of Judeo-Christian messianic notions was important in the development of Mahdism as well, particularly the Christian doctrine of the second advent of Christ. So it may be said that the notion emerged spontaneously,[125] but it would be wrong for these influences on Islamic thought to be ignored.

---

[125] Fazlur Rahman, *Islam*, p. 133; see also Lewis, *op. cit.*, p. 24, quoting Hurgronge, *Der Mahdi Verspreide Geschriften* (Bonn 1923) I, p. 152.

On the other hand, Islam as a political religion provided the ground for many religious notions to be developed for political purposes. Mukhtar, because of his position, depended on the *mawali* forces, who affected and readjusted his political goals with derivatives of their ancestral beliefs, religious and political. Thus Mukhtar became a Kharajite, a Zubayrite, and then a Shi'a, yet emerged as though he were a prophet.[126] It cannot be said that he had been anything other than Muslim (although he was called a Jew by one of his enemies),[127] but for his political purposes he did not hesitate to use the notion of Mahdi (even though its source might have been non-Islamic) on behalf of Ibn al-Hanafiya, whose vice-regent he considered himself to be.

The Persians who had brought Zoroastrian, Manichaean, and Mazdaki religious beliefs; the Iraqis who upheld religious beliefs in Judaism and Christianity; the Gnostics who believed that adherence to spiritual doctrines would save men from rule by material forces; and finally the belief in the return of the dead hero in the pre-Islamic *jahiliya* all supplied ideas for the intelligent men of religion and politics in Iraq to assess before deciding which elements to adopt and which to reject. The messianic notion of a Mahdi was adopted by the Muslims and disguised Muslims, e.g., the Muslimiya, and played a crucial role in Islamic development for about two hundred years while their hereditary leadership, the Imamate, was interrupted, until the emergence of the last main Shi'i sect —the Ithna Ashari, with its elaboration of this messianic concept.

According to the Ithna Ashari Shi'ites, God made them the messianic promise of a Mahdi through His prophet and the Imams. Why, then, did it never overcome the confusion experienced by many followers of various sects who never understood where this notion came from and its practical purpose or why God Himself could not settle the affairs of the end of the world instead of relying on an unseen Mahdi? The Koran and the *hadith* were used to support one argument against another, yet at the same time they contradicted each other. Von Grunebaum states that Muslims found themselves in utter confusion with the verses of the Koran and suggests that, had Muhammad anticipated such a difficulty in the future, he might have revised his statements and made them less vul-

---

[126] Wellhausen, *Religio-Political Factions*, p. 147.
[127] *Ibid.*, p. 157, notes.

nerable to misuse and speculation.[128] It seems that the notion of the Mahdi was used in the face of failure against the enemy, as the Shi'ites were struck by political failures within a powerful empire that they thought belonged to them rather than in the context of spiritual and religious salvation.

The Ithna Ashari Shi'ites in subsequent stages developed a particular doctrine of the Mahdi that not only made powerful worldly governments (Umayyad, Abbasid, and other non-Shi'i systems) look unjust and wrong but also denied and attacked the rightfulness of any Mahdi and savior whom other Shi'i sects awaited. Indeed, generally speaking, their denial extended itself to savior figures in other religions, since the Mahdi or the Shi'i hidden twelfth Imam had been pronounced the sole savior of the world. In justifying this belief, the Shi'ites assert that the true source of this idea was the clan of Banu Hashim of the Quraysh tribe in Mecca.

Even though many savants throughout Islamic history have tried to create bridges between philosophy and theology and between literature and metaphysics in order to intellectualize and work out a persistent dogma in the Islamic world, we must conclude—with great respect for those brilliant thinkers—that the intellect is still being awaited to un-dogmatize itself in religious science. The concept of the Mahdi, complete with its eternal overtones, is one of the most serious religiopsychological issues that Shi'ites have to come to terms with for themselves, in our time and in the future.

---

[128] Von Grunebaum, op. cit., p. 85. Some verses of the Koran have a clear meaning that is accepted by all Muslims. They are called Ayat al-Muhkamat, as opposed to those unclear verses that require interpretation, called Ayat al-Mutashabihat. See Jafri, op. cit., p. 295.

CHAPTER 6
Conclusion

To understand the set of beliefs that constitute Islam, one must consider factors broader than religious doctrine. Such factors include the historical, cultural, anthropological, political, economic, and psychological that must be taken into account in order to understand their influence on a particular event in a particular time. Reexamining religious history using the new methods of research established by social scientists can provide numerous insights.

The interplay of historical circumstances and religious inspiration that influenced the Muslims (Shi'ites in particular) and shaped their religious beliefs needs to be summarized here. The institution of Islam, as conceived by Muhammad, could not have evolved as it did were it not for various historical events that occurred during the time in which he lived. Similarly, without Muhammad's own religious inspiration, the outcome of the conflict between Muhammad and the Meccans would certainly have been different. The success of his stance against Meccan polytheism owes a great deal to the subsequent developments in Medina, without which Muhammad's attempt to organize an army to confront the Meccans would have been impossible and his voice would have been suppressed as it had been in his Meccan years. His ideas became more explicit after he sought refuge in Medina, and certainly those ideas determined the sociopolitical direction of affairs. Nonetheless, Muhammad did not have a wide range of choices; his own ideas were constrained by the reality of Arabian life. In addressing the question of what role divine assistance played in these events, one is still far from an answer—particularly when faith and feelings are the sole proof offered to back up various pious assertions.

The same assessment applies to the development of Shi'ism. The turn of events in Iraq—the assassination of Uthman, the great ambition of the Umayyad family headed by Mu'awiya—and an interconnected series of other events dictated the policies whose by-product was the emergence of Shi'at Ali as an early political opposition. After Ali's assassination, the appeals of a significant group of Iraqis to the descendants of Ali for leadership—from the line of Fatima, the daughter of the Prophet (from both Hassanid and Husaynid lines) and from descendants other than Fatima (such as Ibn al-Hanafiya)—became a pattern that not only muddled the opposition's direction because of their internal rivalry in combating the Banu Umayya but also gradually gave rise to a new religiomoral consciousness after Husayn's death.

The argument about whether Shi'at Ali initially aimed to create a religious sect or simply to legitimize its political opposition by backing the household of Ali (a brave fighter from the Quraysh tribe, a cousin of the Prophet, an early convert, the husband of Mohammad's daughter Fatima, and a pious and righteous Muslim) can perhaps be resolved on the basis of the historical record. The course of events demonstrates that the Iraqis (not necessarily Hijazis), in response to changes in their stage-to-stage situation, eventually generated a latter-day religious belief that accommodated their political opposition. Ali's descendants, especially in the Ithna Ashari line, detached themselves from involvement in the political realm after Husayn's death and chose instead to maintain an esoteric religious life to an extent that matched and fed the religious (if not the political) desires of the Iraqis. Shi'ism thus became a stream of religious opposition to the Umayyads—one that systematically attracted the political dissidents of the day. Shi'ism only received widespread attention when the Abbasids came to power 132/750, although the already-formed religiopolitical debates continued during the reign of the Abbasids.

The development of messianism in Shi'ism was the product of a gradual synthesis of various Islamic and non-Islamic local and external elements that over time enlisted first the notion of *ghayba* (concealment) and then the idea of *raj'a* (the return). The first recorded uses of the notion of Mahdi in its eschatological sense were by Mukhtar and subsequently among the Kaysaniya sect, whose penetration by the *ghulat* (exaggerators) was obvious. Sporadic messianic assertions of the *ghulat* continued to appear in other sects as well—even in the proto-Ithna Ashari line of Shi'ism, which gave rise to short-lived subsects such as the Baqiriya, the Nawusiya, and the Waqifiya. Only when Hasan al-Askari, the eleventh

185

Imam, left no son behind were the *ghulat's* old elaborations of the idea of *ghayba* propagated to explain that a son had in fact been born but for the time being would remain in concealment. As decades passed, it became clear that the concealed twelfth Imam had no intention of appearing in public, and even the series of representatives (*wukala*) who claimed to have been in contact with the Imam was discontinued. Consequently, the notion of the return and (understandably, under the prevailing conditions of repression) the desire for just rule were incorporated into Shi'i eschatological belief, particularly in Ithna Ashari Shi'ism.[1]

This book has discussed the historical context in which Islam and Shi'ism as a sect emerged, borrowing cultural antecedents from various host lands as they evolved; it has also noted the occurrences in history that led events from one stage to the next. But it is necessary to continue the search to illustrate the historical conditions more clearly and more completely, in order to better understand the formation of the religious doctrine. This book, then, is an attempt to identify certain relevant threads in the historical and sociopolitical fabric of Islam and to examine them in connection with popular belief and the assertions of religious leaders.

---

[1] For historiographical analysis see Mostafa Vaziri, "Dogma Islamico e Problemi di Storiografia," *SYNESIS VII* (1990/2) pp. 29–33.

Personal Remarks

Here I would like to describe an evolution in my own perception and evaluation of religious chronicles. In the course of writing this book, this adjustment occurred gradually as I began to feel doubtful about how one could logically dissect and scrutinize certain religious beliefs that serve as significant psychological instruments within which believers find spiritual, mental, and moral security.

On the other hand, reexamination of Islamic history from a more objective standpoint is useful in understanding the birth and overall evolution of Islam instead of depending on anecdotes that sometimes take on epic proportions.

True, the ideas herein may receive mixed reactions from people whose religious doctrine has been scrutinized; various communities and individuals have developed a unique behavioral and intellectual reactive mechanism. Therefore, the hope that all Muslim people may respond in unity to and cope with the arguments in this book is unrealistic. Nonetheless, it is my sincere wish that this study serve the purpose of furthering our collective understanding of Islam. This work may also be viewed as a test of the degree of tolerance for religious discourse within Islam.

GLOSSARY

adalah   integrity

Ahl-al-Bayt   tribe members, here referred to prophet's household

Ajam   non-Arab

akhbar   transmission of traditions

ansar(s)   helper(s)

aql   intellect

ashraf   tribal aristocracy

Ayat al-Muhkamat   verses of the Koran that have concrete meaning

Ayat al-Mutashabihat   verses of the Koran that have speculative meanings

azwaj   temporary marriage

Caliph   successor and representative of the Prophet

Caliphate   institution and government of Caliphs

dihgan   feudal landlord

dihsalar   feudal landlord

faqih   theologian

fiqh   theology

ghayba   occultation, concealment

ghulat   exaggerators

ghuluww   exaggeration

ghusl   washing the cadaver before burial

Glossary

hadith sayings and deeds of the Prophet and Imams

hajj pilgrimage

hanifs pre-Islamic monotheists

higra migration of the Prophet from Mecca to Medina

hulul the descent of the spirit of God into man

ijma concensus

'illah defect

ilm knowledge

Imam leader

Imamate esoteric Shi'i leadership

Imamzadeh son or descendant of an Imam

Islam submission

isnad documents

Ithna Ashari Twelver Shi'ism

ittisal asanad chain of transmitters

jahannam inferno

Jahiliya pre-Islamic period of Arabia—Age of Ignorance

jizya non-Muslim tax

kahin religious functionary of Pagan Shrine

kalam speech, rhetorical formulation

kharaj poll tax

khums a fifth of earnings, religious tax

khuruj reappearance, coming out

kitab book, the holy Scripture

madhab belief, religious, school of thought

Mahdi guided by God: refers to the returning savior

mawali non-Arab subjects under Islamic government

mawla master, friend

Medinat al-nabi city of the Prophet—in short, city of Medina

muhaddithun transmitters of *hadith*; traditionists

muhajirun Meccan emigrants to Medina

mujtahid a clergy who has learned jurisprudence and exercises interpretic judgment, designated theologian

mu'menin believers

mutakalimun clerics who practiced speculative theology using the method of kalam

mu'tazilite - mu'tazila "withdrawn" the school which applied the speculative reasoning for the interpretation of Koranic doctrine

nabi informer, Prophet

nafaqah alimony

naib al-Imam representative of the Imam

nasab nobility of descent

nass designation

niyaba deputyship

qibla the direction of Ka'ba, which the Muslims face to perform prayers

r'ai decision

raj'a return of the Imam

rasul messenger

rawda preachment

sabiqa early conversion, past profile

sadaqa donations for the poor, charity

Sahih book of Bukhari, means the correct ones

saj rhyme

sayyid descendant of the Prophet

sha'ir poet

Glossary

shari'a   Islamic law

shura   council

sufara   representatives of the twelfth Imam

sunna   practices of the Prophet

sura   a chapter of the Koran

tafsir   technical interpretation of the Koran

taqiya   dissimulation

tanasukh   transmigration of souls

ta'wil   spiritual interpretation of the Koran

tawwabun   penitents

ulama   religious leaders

umma   Islamic community

velayat   designation of leadership

wakil   representative, mediator

warith   inheritor

wasi   guardian

wukala   (plural for wakil) representatives of the twelfth Imam

zakat   alms

zuhur   appearance of the Mahdi

zulfigar   Ali's sword (given by Muhammad to Ali)

Chronology of Early Islamic (Shi'i) History

A. H. (after Higra)

570 A.D.
Muhammad born

610
Declaration of Muhammad's prophecy

622
Migration from Mecca to Medina

2/624
Battle of Badr

3/625
Battle of Uhud

8/630
Fall of Mecca

11/632
Muhammad dies in Medina

11/632–40/661
Reign of four Caliphs: Abu Bakr, Umar, Uthman, Ali

11/632–13/634
Caliphate of Abu Bakr

13/634–23/644
Caliphate of Umar

23/644–35/656
Caliphate of Uthman

35/656–40/661
Caliphate of Ali

Chronology of Early Islamic (Shi'i) History

35/656
Battle of Jamal (first civil war)

37/657
Battle of Siffin (second civil war)

38/658
Battle of Nahrawan

40/661
Ali assassinated by a member of Khawarij

40/661–132/750
Reign of the Umayyad Caliphs

132/750–656/1258
Reign of the Abbasid Caliphs

11/632–260/873
The Imamate of the twelve Shi'i Imams*

49/669
Hasan (second Shi'i Imam) dies

61/680
Husayn martyred at Karbala

260/873
Alleged birth of the twelfth Imam (Mahdi)

260/873–329/940
Minor occultation

329/940–?/?
Major occultation

---

* Considering Ali as the first Imam after Muhammad's death through his descendants to the disappearance of the twelfth Imam

QURAYSH TRIBE (HASHEMITE AND UMAYYAD)
(12 SHI'I IMAMS)

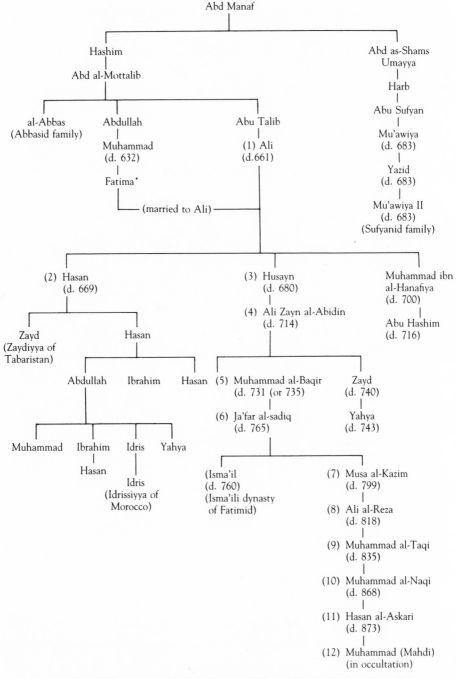

* Fatima (Ali's first wife) gave birth to Hasan and Husayn. Muhammad ibn al-Hanafiya, the other son of Ali, came from another wife.

BIBLIOGRAPHY

al-Baladhuri, Ahmad b. Jaber. *The Origins of Islamic State* (Futuh ul-Buldan). Vol. I, New York: AMS Press, 1968–69. Vol. II, New York, 1916–24.

————. *Futuh ul-Buldan* (section on Iran). Tehran: Soroush, 1364/1985.

Algar, Hamid. "The Revolt of Agha Khan Mahalati and the Transference of the Ismaili Imamate to India," *Studia Islamica* 29 (1969); 55–81.

Ali, ibn Abu Talib (compiled by Sayyid Razi). *Nahj ul-Balagha*. Isfahan: Entesharat Mas'al, 1360/1981.

Amini, Sheikh Abd al-Husayn b. Ahmad. *Al-Ghadir*. Vols. I–XXII, Tehran (1340/1961–1365/1986).

Andrae, Tor. *Mohammed: The Man and his Faith*. New York: Harper, 1960.

Ansari, Zafar Ishaq. "Aspects of Black Muslim Theology," *Studia Islamica* 53 (1981): 137–176.

Arberry, A. J. "Teachers of Al-Bukhari," *Islamic Quarterly*, II (1967): 34–39.

Armavi (Mohades), Mir Jalaledin Husayn. *Ta'liqat Naqz*, vols. I, II, Tehran: Zar Publishers, 1979.

Arnold, T. W., *Preaching of Islam*, 2nd ed., London: Constable, 1913.

Aubin, Eugène. *La Perse d'Aujourd'hui*. Paris: Libraire Armand Colin, 1908.

Avicenna (Ibn Sina) Husayn b. Abdullah. *Livre des Directives et Remarques* (Kitab al-Isarat Wal Tanbihat). Paris, 1951.

————. *La Metaphysique du Shifa*. Vols. I–V, Paris, 1978.

Azami, Mustafa. "Hadith: Rules for Acceptance and Transmission," *The Place of Hadith in Islam*. International Graphics Printing Service, 1977.

Bibliography

Benda, Julian. "The Betrayal of Intellectuals," *History of Western Civilization*, a handbook by William H. McNeille. Chicago: University of Chicago Press, 1986.

Biruni, Abu Rayhan. *Athar al-Baqiya*. Tehran: Amir Kabir Publishers, 1363/ 1984.

Boyce, Mary. "Bibi Shahrbanu and the Lady of Pars," *Bulletin of the School of Oriental and African Studies* 30 (1967): 30–44.

———. "Banu Pars." *Encyclopedia Iranica*, Vol. III. London and New York: Routledge & Keagan Paul, 1989, pp. 717–718.

Bravmann, M. M., *The Spiritual Background of Early Islam*. Leiden: E. J. Brill, 1972.

Brockelmann, Carl. *The History of Islamic Peoples*. New York: Capricorn Books, 1960.

Browne, E. G. *A Literary History of Persia*, Vols. I–III (translated by Ali Pasha Saleh and Ali Asghar Hekmat). Tehran: Amir Kabir, 1354–5/1975–6.

Bulliet, Richard. *Conversion to Islam in Middle Ages*. Cambridge, Mass.: Harvard University Press, 1979.

Caetani, Leone. *Annali dell'Islam*. Vols. I, II. Milan, 1905–1907.

Christensen, Arthur. *l'Iran sur les Sassanides*. Copenhagen: Levin & Munksgaard, 1936.

Cook, Michael. *Muhammad*. Oxford: Oxford University Press, 1986.

Corbin, Henry. *En Islam Iranien: Aspects Spirituels et Philosophiques*. Vols. I–IV, Paris: Gallimard, 1971–72.

Crone, Patricia. *Roman, Provincial, and Islamic Law*. Cambridge: Cambridge University Press, 1987.

Crone, Patricia, and Michael Cook. *Hagarism: The Making of the Islamic World*. Cambridge: Cambridge University Press, 1977.

Crone, Patricia and Martin Hinds. *God's Caliph*. Cambridge: Cambridge University Press, 1986.

Darmesteter, James. *Mahdi*. Tehran: Adab Ketab Co., 1938.

Donaldson, Dwight M. *The Shi'ite Religion*. London: Luzac & Co., 1933.

Bibliography

Donner, Fred. *The Early Islamic Conquests.* Princeton, N.J.: Princeton University Press, 1981.

Dori, A. A. "Baghdad," *Encyclopedia of Islam.* Leiden, 1960, pp. 894–908.

Ejtehadi, Abolghasem. *Vaze Mali va Malieh Muslemin.* Tehran: Soroush Publishers, 1363/1984.

Emadzadeh, H. *Chehardah Ma'sum,* 5th ed., Vol. I. Tehran, 1339/1960.

Fazlollah, Rashid al-din. *Jama'al-Tawarikh.* (section on Hasan Sabbath va Janeshinan uo). Nashre Alborz, 1366/1987.

Fischler, Kurt. *A'isha After the Prophet.* Tehran: Amir Kabir, 1360/1981.

Frye, Richard. *The Heritage of Persia.* Cleveland: World, 1963.

Gibb, H. A. R. *Muhammadenism.* London: Oxford University Press, 1949–1950.

Goldziher, Ignaz. *Le Dogma et la loi de l'Islam.* Paris: Librairie Paul Geuthner, 1920.

Haqiqat, Abdul Rafi'a. *Jonbesh Zaydiya dar Iran.* Tehran: Entesharat Falsafa, 1363/1984.

Hasegawa, Ichiro. "Catalogue of Ancient and Naked-eye Comets." *Vista in Astronomy,* 1980, pp. 59–71.

Hodgson, Marshal. "How Did the Early Shi'a Become Sectarian?" *Journal of American Oriental Society* 75 (1955): 1–13.

Housain, Jasim. *The Occultation of the Twelfth Imam* (Tarikh Siayasi Ghayabat Imam Davazdahom). Tehran: Amir Kabir, 1367/1988.

Ibn Athir, A. Ali. *Al-Kamil,* Vol. I. Tehran: Ilmi Publisher, n.d. (1960?).

Ibn Ishaq, Muhammad. *The Life of Muhammad (Sirat al-Nabi).* Calcutta: Oxford University Press, 1978.

Ibn Khaldun, Abd ar-Rahman. *Discours sur l'Histoire Universelle* (Al-Muqaddima), Vols. I, II, III. Paris: Sinbad, 1967–68.

Ibn, Tiqtaqa, Muhammad Ali b. Tabataba. *Tarikh Fakhri,* 3rd ed., Tehran: Entesharat Ilmi va Farhangi, 1367/1988.

Iranshar (UNESCO), Vols. I, II. Tehran: Tehran University Press, 1963, 1964.

Isfahani, Hamza b. Hassan. *Tarikh al-sini Muluk al-Ard Wal-Anbia.* Tehran: Amir Kabir Publisher, 1367/1988.

199

Bibliography

Ja'farian, Rasul. *Tarikh Siyasi Islam*. Qum: Moassesseh Dar Rahe Hagh, 1366/ 1987.

Jafri, S. Husain M. *The Origins and Early Development of Shi'a Islam*. London and New York: Longman, 1979.

Kashif al-Qita Najafi, M. H. *In Ast A'ieen Ma*. Qum: Hadaf Printing, 1347/ 1968.

Kersten, Holger. *Jesus Lived in India*. Dorset, England: Elements Books Ltd., 1986. (First published in West Germany by Droemer Knaur, Munich, 1983.)

Kister, M. J. "A Bag of Meat," *Bulletin of the School of Oriental and African Studies* 33 (1970): 267–275.

———. "Al Hira: Some Notes on Its Relations with Arabia," *Arabica* 15 (1968): 143–169.

Kohlberg, Etan. "From Imamiyya to Ithna Ashariyya," *Bulletin of the School of Oriental and African Studies* 39 (1976): 521–534.

Kuhn, Thomas. *The Structure of Scientific Revolution*, 2nd ed. Chicago: University of Chicago Press, 1970.

Lammens, Henri. *L'Islam, Croyances et Institutions*. Beyrut: Imp. Catholique, 1943.

Le Bon, Gustave. *Civilization Islamique (Tamadon, Islam va Arab)*. Tehran: Islamieh Books, n.d.

Lewis, Bernard. *L'Islam d'hier a Aujourd'hui*. Paris/Bruxelles: Elsevier Bordas, 1981.

———. *Islam in History*. New York: The Library Press, 1973.

———. *The Origins of Ismailism*. Cambridge: W. Heffer & Son, 1940.

Madelung, Wilferd. "Imamism and Mu'tazilite Theology," *Religious Schools and Sects in Medieval Islam*, VII. London: Vanovum reprints, 1985.

———. "Authority in Twelfer Shiism in the Absence of the Imam," *Religious Schools and Sects in Medieval Islam*, X. London: Vanovum reprints, 1985.

———. "Al Mahdi," *Encyclopedia of Islam*. Leiden, 1960, pp. 1231–1235.

Majlisi, Muhammad Baqir. *Bihar al-Anwar*, Vol. XIII. Tehran: Darul Kutub al-Islamieh, n.d.

———. *Jala ul Uyun*. Tehran: Entesharat Ilmieh Islamieh, n.d.

Bibliography

Mansuri, Zabihullah. *Maqz Mutefakere Jahane Shi'a—Imam Ja'far Sadig* (Centre des Etudes Islamiques à Strasbourg). Tehran: Entesharat Javidan, 1355/1976.

Margoliouth, D. S. *Mohammed.* London: Blackie & Son., 1939.

Mas'udi, Abul Hasan Ali b. Husayn. *Muruj ul-Dhahab*, Vols. I, II. Tehran: Bongah Tarjmeh va Nashre Ketab, 1960/1981.

Minqari, Nasr b. Muzahim al. *Wa'qat Siffin* (Paykar Saffin). Entesharat va Amozesh Enghelab Islami, 1366/1987.

Mir Ahmadi, Maryam. *Din va Madhab dar Asre Safavi.* Tehran: Amir Kabir, 1363/1984.

Momen, Moojan. *An Introduction to Shi'i Islam.* New Haven, Conn.: Yale University Press, 1985.

Moosa, Matti. *Extremist Shiites.* Syracuse, N.Y.: Syracuse University Press, 1988.

Morony, Michael. *Iraq after the Muslim Conquest.* Princeton, N.J.: Princeton University Press, 1984.

————. *The History of al-Tabari* (translation), Vol. XVIII. Albany: State University of New York Press, 1987.

————. "Religious Communities in Late Sasanian and Early Muslim Iraq," *Journal of the Economic and Social History of the Orient* XVII, Part II (1974): 113–135.

Moscati, Sabatino. "Per una storia dell antica Si'a," *Rivista degli Studi Orientali* XXX (1955): 251–267.

Mostaufi, Hamdollah. *Tarikh Guzideh.* Tehran: Amir Kabir, 1364/1985.

————. *Nodhat ul Quloub.* Tehran, 1336/1957.

Motahari, Mortaza. "Payambar Umi," *Muhammad Khatam Payambaran.* Tehran, 1348/1969.

Mufid, Sheikh. *Kitab ul Jamal* (Nabard Jamal). Tehran: Nashre Nay, 1367/1988.

Muir, William. *The Life of Mohammed from Original Sources.* London: Smith, Elder & Co., 1894.

Nawbakhti, Abu Muhammad al-Hasan b. Musa. *Firaq al-Shi'a.* Tehran: Khajeh Publisher, 1353/1974.

Nicholson, Reynold A. *Tafsir Masnavi Ma'navi* (researched and edited by Ovanes Ovanesian). Tehran: Nashre Nay, 1366/1987.

Bibliography

Nicholson, Thomas D. "Jupiter Stands Out," *Natural History*, Nov. 1985, pp. 98–102.

———. "Mars Is the One," *Natural History*, Jan. 1986, pp. 85–89.

———. "Games Planet Play," *Natural History*, Feb. 1986, pp. 80–84.

Nishaburi, Abu Ja'far. *Rawdat al-wa'izin*. Tehran: Nashre Nay, 1366/1987.

Nizam al-Mulk. *Siyasat Nama* (The Book of Government or Rules for Kings). London: Routledge & Keagan Paul, 1978.

O'Leary, De Lacy. *Arabia Before Muhammed*. New York: E. P. Dutton & Co., 1927.

Oppenheimer, Michael and Leonie Harmson. "The Comet Syndrome," *Natural History*, Dec. 1980, pp. 56–58.

Petersen, Erling Ladewig. *Ali and Mu'awiya in Early Arabic Tradition*. Copenhagen: Scandinavian University Books, 1964.

Petrushevsky, I. P. *Islam in Iran*. London: Athlone, 1985.

Pickthall, Mohammad Marmaduke. *The Meaning of Glorious Koran*. New York: New American Library, 1953.

Qazvini Razi, Abdul Jalil. *Naqz*. Tehran: Zar Publisher, 1358/1979.

Rahman, Fazlur. *Islam*, 2nd ed. Chicago: University of Chicago Press, 1979.

Rodinson, Maxime. *Mahomet*. Paris: Editions du Seuil, 1960.

———. *Islam and Capitalism*. Austin: University of Texas Press, 1981.

———. *Europe and the Mystique of Islam*. Seattle: University of Washington Press, 1987.

Sachedina, Abdol Aziz. *Islamic Messianism*. Albany: State University of New York Press, 1981.

Sadiq, Issa. *History of Education in Iran*, 7th ed. Tehran: Ziba Print, 1354/1975.

Sagan, Carl, and Ann Druyan. *Comet*, New York: Random House, 1985.

Said, Edward. *Orientalism*. New York: Vintage Books, 1979.

Scarcia, Gianroberto. "Intorno alle Controversie tra Akhbari e Usuli presso gli Imamiti di Persia," *Rivista degli Studi Orientali* XXXIII (1956): 211–250.

Serjeant, R. B. "The Constitution of Medina," *Islamic Quarterly* 8 (1964): pp. 3–16.

Shahrastani, Muhammad b. Abdulkarim b. Ahmed. *Al Milal wal-Nihal*, 2nd ed., Vols. I, II. Tehran: Offset Co., 1358/1979.

Stephenson, Richard and Kevin K. C. Yau. "Far Eastern Observations of Halley's Comet: 240 B.C. to A.D. 1368," *Journal of the British Interplanetary Society* 28 (1985): pp. 195–216.

Tabari, Muhammad b. Jarir. *Tarikh*, I–XVI. Tehran: Rushdieh, 1362/1983–1364/1985.

Tabatabai, Allamah. *Shi'ite Islam*. Albany: State University of New York Press, 1975.

Tucker, William. "Bayan b. Sam'an and the Bayaniyya: Shi'ite Extremists of Umayyad Iraq," *The Muslim World* LXV (1975): 241–253.

Van Ess, Josef and Hans Kung. *Christianity and the World Religions*. New York: Doubleday, 1986.

Vaziri, Mostafa. "Dogma Islamico e Problemi di Storiografia," *SYNESIS* VII (2/1990), pp. 29–33.

Von Grunebaum, Gustave. *Medieval Islam*, 2nd ed. Chicago: University of Chicago Press, 1954.

Waqidi, Muhammad b. Umar. *Al Moqazi*, Vols. I–III. Tehran: Center for University Printing, 1361/1982–1366/1987.

Watt, Montgomery. *Muhammad: Prophet and Statesman*. London: Oxford University Press, 1964.

———. *What Is Islam?*, 2nd ed. London: Longman, 1979.

———. *Truth in the Religions*. Edinburgh: Edinburgh University Press, 1963.

———. *The Formative Period of Islamic Thought*. Edinburgh: Edinburgh University Press, 1973.

———. "God's Caliph: Quranic Interpretations and Umayyad's Claim," *Iran and Islam*, ed. C. E. Bosworth. Edinburgh: Edinburgh University Press, 1971, pp. 565–574.

Wellhausen, Julius. *The Arab Kingdom and Its Fall*. Calcutta: University of Calcutta, 1927.

Bibliography

———. *Religio-Political Factions in Early Islam*. Amsterdam: North Holland Publishing Co., 1975.

Ya'qubi, Ahmad b. Ali (Ibn Wa'ez). *Tarikh*, 5th ed., Vols., I, II. Tehran: Entesharat Ilmi va Farhangi, 1366/1987.

Index

Index

Ali b. Hisham, 129
Ali b. Husayn. *See* Zayn al-Abidin
Alids, 114, 143. *See also* Shi'at Ali
al-Jamal, battle of, 83–84
al-Kazim, Abbas b. Musa, 129
al-Mahdi, 159
al-Ma'mun, 68, 127, 128–131
al-Mansur, Caliph, 135, 153
al-Milal wal Nihal (Shahrastani), 15, 118, 149, 163
al-Minqari, Nasr ibn Muzahim, 86
al-Miqdad, 69
al-Muqanna, 153
al-Muslim, 72, 73, 164
al-Nafs al-Zakiya, 117, 120, 134
al-Nawbakhti, Husayn b. Ruh, 165
al-Qa'im, 159
al-Qaim, al-Muntazar, 151
al-Qazwini, Sayyid Muhammad Kazim, 91
al-Qummi, 131–132
al-Samarri, Ali b. Muhammad, 165, 166
al-Taifa, 179
Amari, Muhammad b. Uthman, 165
Amari, Uthman b. Said, 165
Amini, Allamah, 71–73, 75
Amr ibn al-As, 87, 89
Anahid, Ardvisur, 111
Ansi, Aswad b. Ka'b, 65
Aqaba, 25
Arabs and Arabia, 3–6, 14, 15, 74
Ashraf, 84, 102
as'Shaqshaqiyya, 78
Athar al-Baqiya (Biruni), 152
Ayadi, Quss b. Saedehe, 14
Ayyashi, 172
Azwaj, 75
az-Zuhri, 98

Badr, battle of, 33–34
Baghdadi, 163

Banu Hashim clan, 6, 16, 23, 81–82
Banu Ijl, 145
Banu Qaynuqua tribe, 34
Banu Umayya, 81–82, 99
Baqir b. Mahan, 121
Baqiriya, 120, 150, 185
Basra, 172
Bayan ibn Sam'an, 115
Bayaniyya sect, 148
Bihar al-Anwar (Majlisi), 171
Bilal, Muhammad b. Ali b., 166
Biruni, Abu Rayhan, 9, 152
Blood revenge, 84, 107
Boyce, Mary, 110–111
Bravmann, M. M., 146–147
Browne, Edward G., 153
Bulliet, Richard, 123
Buyids, 76, 168, 170

Caetani, Leone, 26, 64
Caliphs, 79–94
Christians and Christianity, 22, 142, 145
Constitution of Medina, 29–30, 32
Conversion, Muslim-style, 44
Cook, Michael, 50
Corbin, Henry, 125–126, 158, 171
Crone, Patricia, 50, 51

Darmesteter, James, 142, 144, 146
Deputyship, issue of, 166
Dihgans, 122
Dihsalars, 122
Dinawari, 97
Donner, Fred, 65, 88

Elxai, 9
Encyclopedia of Islam, 143

Fadak, 42, 68
Fakhteh, 99
Faqih, 170, 180–181
Fard, Wallace D., 144

Index

Ithna Ashari (Twelver) Shi'ism,
114; development of, 59, 60;
doctrine of redeemer in, 141; and
faqih, 170; and ghayba, 196; imamate of, 127–128; Mahdi tradition of, 155–156; on messianic
promise, 182–183; as nonpolitical, 134; notion of return in,
186; religious orientation of, 185;
subsects of, 185; title of, 131–
132

Ja'far, 161–162
Ja'far al-Sadiq, 116, 117, 118, 120,
121, 124–127, 134, 150, 172,
180
Ja'far b. Abu Talib, 18
Jafri, Seyed Husain, 64, 77, 84, 99,
108, 114
Jahiliya, 182
Jama al-Tawarikh (Fazlollah), 152
Janahiyya, 115
Jews and Judaism, 32, 48, 145
Jili, Mehdi b. Thar Billah Husayni,
175
Jizya, 44, 122

Ka'ba, 27, 63
Kalam, 177–179
Kamal al-Din (Ibn Babuya), 157–
158, 172
Karbala, 105–110
Karkhi, Ahmad b. Hilal, 166
Kashf al-Ghuma (Kamal al-Din),
157
Kashif al-Quita Najafi, Husayn, 72
Kaysaniya, 103, 115, 121–123,
151, 185. See also Abbasids
Khadija, 6, 13, 24
Khandaq, battle of, 37
Kharaj, 98, 122
Kharijism, 172
Khatam al-awsiya, 178

Khawarij, Sistani, 87–89, 91–93,
124, 153
Khaybar, 42
Khazraj, 61
Khums, 30, 155, 167
Khurasan, 121, 122–123
Khurramdin, 153
Khuruj, 118
Khuzistan, unknown man from, 152
Kitab al-Akhbar al-Tiwal (Dinawari),
97
Kitab al-Maqalat wa'l Firaq (al-
Qummi), 132
Kitab Fihrist (Montakhib al-Din),
175
Kitab Firaq al Shi'a (Nawbakhti),
62, 130
Kitab Kamal al-Din (Mutawakkil),
175
Koran: ambiguity in, 70; changes
in, 48–49; contradictions in,
182; Muhammad's use of, 32–33;
purported alteration of, 71; re-
futes claims, 17; suras in, 13;
uniqueness of, 15; verses of, 49–
50
Kufa and Kufans, 77–78, 92–93,
96, 109–110, 112, 115–116
Kulayni, 111, 132, 159, 163, 166

Lakhmid kingdom, 82
Lammens, Henri, 134, 159

Mahdi, 90, 141–183; and faith,
176; first use of, 143; foreign ele-
ments in, 146; recognition of,
175; return of, 173
Mahomet, 10
Majlisi, Muhammad, 151, 166,
171–172, 175
Malik, 117
Mamtoriya, 128
Mani, 9
Manicheans, 145, 148, 152

Index

Nahrawan, battle at, 88
Naib al-Imam, 170
Naqi, as Imam, 156
Narjis, 136
Nass, 116, 125, 126
Nawbakhti, Abu Muhammad al-
Husan b. Musa, 62, 67, 97, 98,
118, 119, 121, 136, 153, 157,
161, 165
Nawusiya, 127, 150, 185
Nestorians, 93
Nishaburi, Abu Ja'far, 52
Nishaburi, Hakim, 73, 105, 118,
136–137
Nizam al-Mulk, 152
Numani, 166, 167, 175

Occultation, 160–162; major, 167–
171, 176–177; minor, 165–166;
and return, 149–150

Persia and Persians, 92–93, 110–
112, 144–145, 152, 182
Petrushevsky, I. P., 122
Polygamy, 40–41
Pro-Alids, 123, 129
Prophecy, Muhammad's gift of, 8–
9

Qadisiya, battle of, 92
Qarmat, Ahmad, 152
Qasim, 126
Qat'iya, 128
Qibla, 33
Qum, school of, 76
Quraysh and Qurayshites, 5, 61; at
Khandaq, 37; and Muhammad,
15–18, 20–23, 26, 29; peace
pact of, 41; political partnership
of, 43; and return, 172; rivalry
between clans of, 93; succession
through, 75
Qurayshites, authority of, 62

Rahman, Abdul, 123
Raj'a (return), 115, 146, 168–177,
179
Rawandi Shi'ites, 135
Rawdat al-Wa'izin (Nishaburi), 10,
52, 105
Religious sectarianism, Islamic, 88–
89
Return. *See* Raj'a
Reza, 111, 128–131, 156
Reza Khan, 76
Rodinson, Maxime, 10
Rumi, 53–54, 56
Ruqiya, 18, 74

Saba'iya, 135
Sachedina, Abdol Aziz, 148–149
Sa'd b. Ubada, 61
Saduq (Ibn Babuya), 157
Safavids, 76, 124, 176
Sahih, 72, 72n, 164
Sa'id b. Hamdani, 105
Sajah, 65, 66
Salman Farsi, 37, 69
Samarra, 174
Sanbad, 153
Saoshyant, 181
Sauda, 24
Sayyid Ja'far Shahidi, 110
Sayyid Razi, 60
Shahrastani, Muhammad b. Abdul-
karim b. Ahmed, 14, 15, 73,
115, 118, 135, 149, 152, 156,
157, 163
Shahrbanu, 110–112
Shari'a, 37
Shi'at Ali: defined, 60; develop-
ment of, 88–89; and Ghadir
Khum *hadith*, 69–73; Imams in,
139–140; as political, 84–85;
seeks leaders, 116; and succession
debate, 59–94
Shimr b. Dhil-Jawshan, 106, 173
Shi'ites and Shi'ism: categories of,

210

Index